BELLOTTO

The Königstein Views Reunited

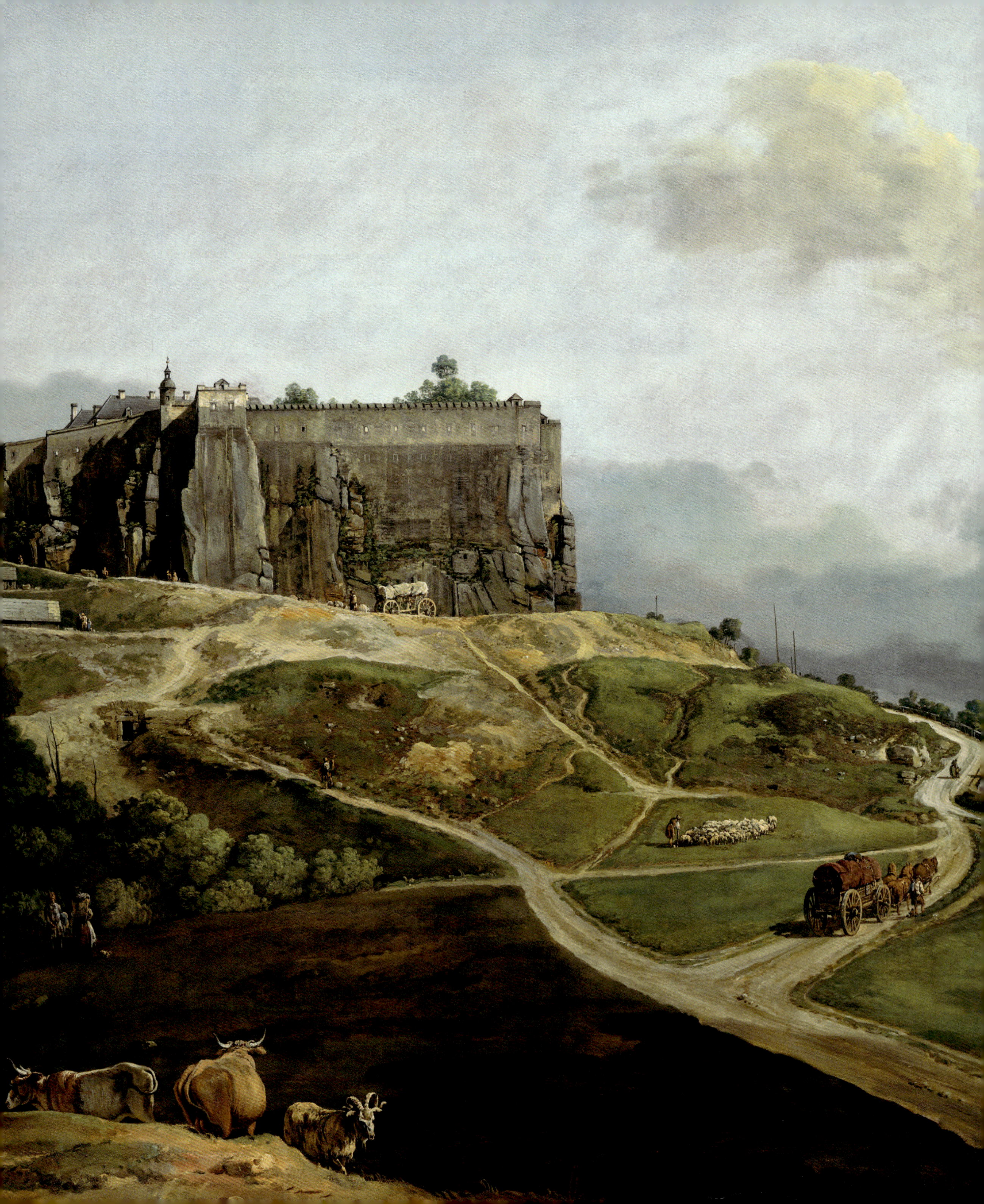

LETIZIA TREVES
with contributions by Lucy Chiswell, Stephen Lloyd and Hannah Williamson

BELLOTTO

The Königstein Views Reunited

NATIONAL GALLERY COMPANY, LONDON
DISTRIBUTED BY YALE UNIVERSITY PRESS

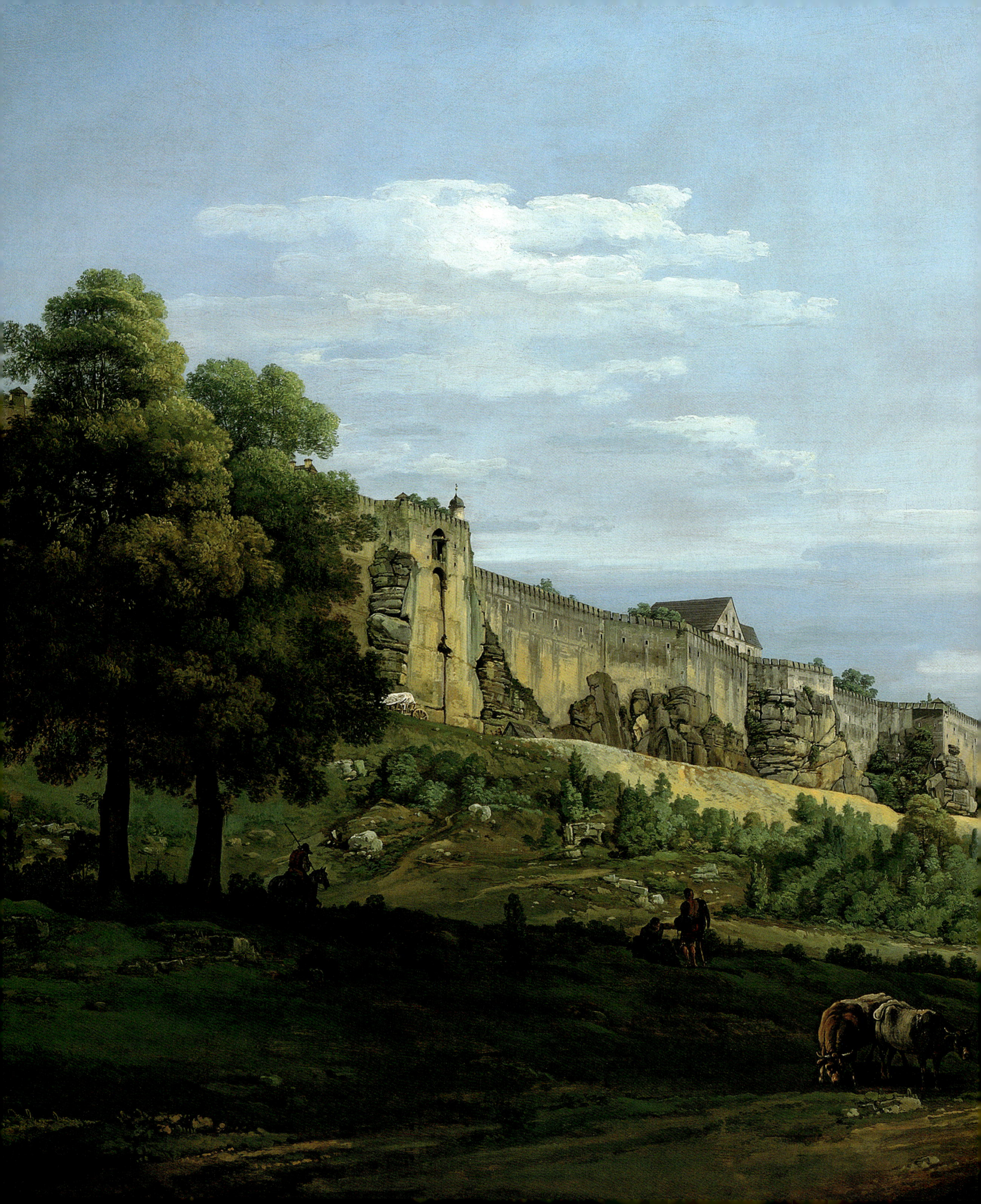

CONTENTS

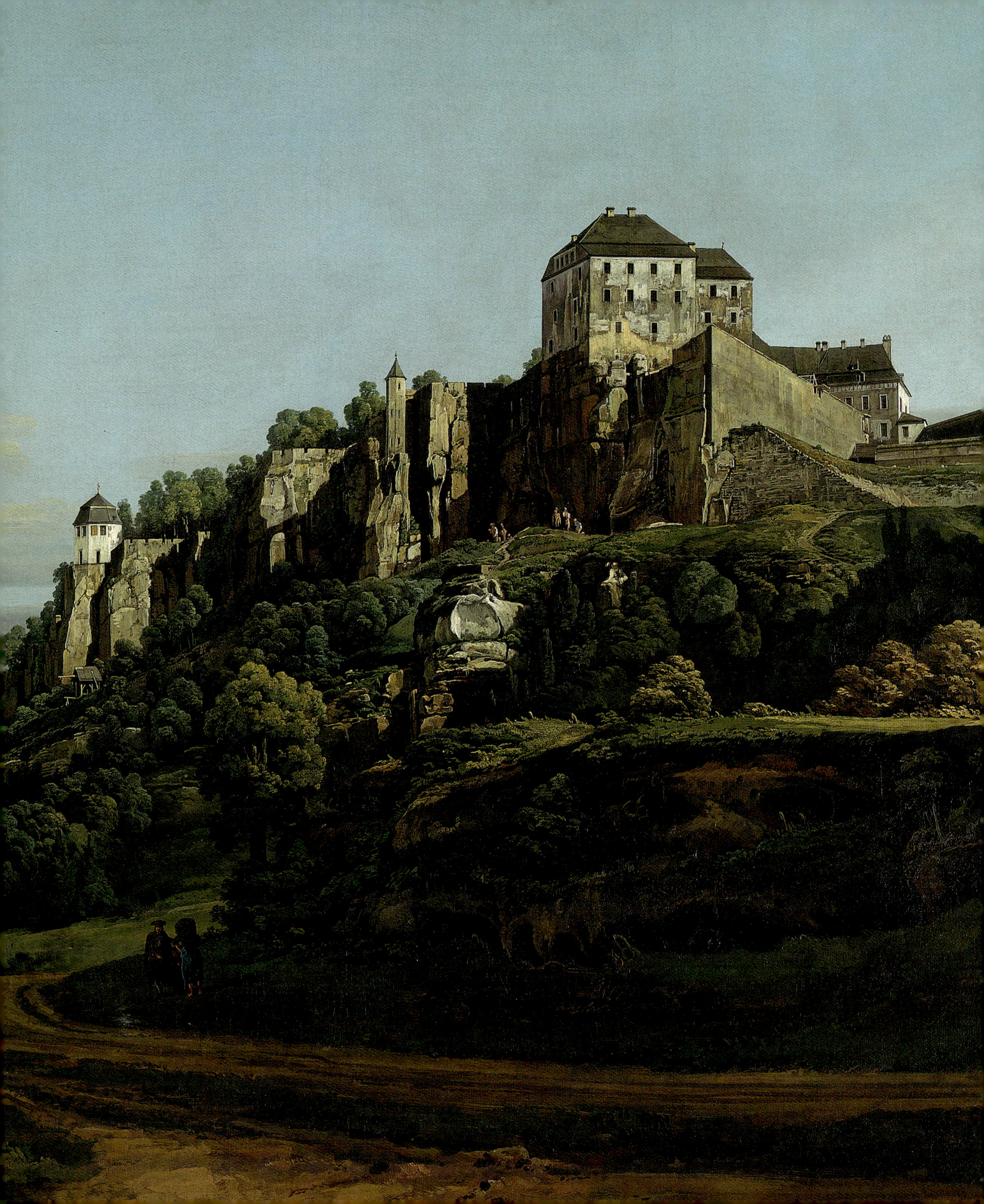

DIRECTORS' FOREWORD

Gabriele Finaldi and Alistair Hudson

Canaletto is the painter par excellence of the set piece views of Venice, its bridges and canals, its regattas and festivals. Supremely well represented in Britain, where he spent nearly 10 years in the 1740s, Canaletto's works can be found in museums and private collections across the country. His nephew, Bernardo Bellotto, known as 'Il Canalettino' (and in Eastern Europe as 'Canaletto'), who is as important and arguably even more influential, is not so widely celebrated in this country and is much less well represented in public collections. Bellotto's career took him in a different direction from that of his uncle: from the canals of Venice, he travelled to the courts of Saxony, Austria and Poland, and that is where his paintings are mostly to be found.

Manchester Art Gallery and the National Gallery, however, own three of Bellotto's most spectacular and large-scale views. They form part of a set of five paintings he made of the fortress of Königstein, the 'king's stone', a rocky outcrop that rises dramatically above the Elbe Valley some 25 miles south-east of Dresden. Quite how these five canvases arrived in England, already in Bellotto's lifetime, remains unclear, but this exhibition brings the group together – as the artist must surely have intended – for the first time in more than 250 years. We pay tribute to the councillors of Manchester and to Sir Timothy Clifford, then Director of the Manchester City Art Gallery, who brought the first two into public ownership in 1982 and 1983 (cats 5 and 4, respectively). The National Gallery acquired *The Fortress of Königstein from the North* in 2017, when it was about to be exported abroad (cat. 1). The collector who had bought it kindly agreed to let the Gallery purchase it for the nation, and the benefactors who enabled the acquisition are listed on p. 86. In this exhibition the three paintings are joined by the view generously lent by the Earl and Countess of Derby (cat. 3) and, in London, by the remaining canvas of the series belonging to the National Gallery of Art in Washington (cat. 2).

We wish to acknowledge the excellent work of Letizia Treves, the James and Sarah Sassoon Curator of Later Italian, Spanish and French Seventeenth-Century Paintings at the National Gallery, who originally conceived the exhibition. We are grateful to her and to the various teams in our two institutions, and also wish to extend our thanks to the authors who have contributed their insights on Bellotto in this book. The exhibition in London forms part of the H J Hyams Exhibition Programme in Room 1, which is generously supported by the Capricorn Foundation. In Manchester the paintings are presented in a single gallery in the former Athenaeum building. Our thanks also go to the staff and students of the Unit X course at Manchester School of Art, who have developed the interpretation of the exhibition as part of a commitment to embed education in all aspects of the Gallery's work. Additional thanks go to Louise Adkins and Chester Tenneson at Manchester Metropolitan University.

Art Fund helped with the purchase of the three paintings in our two museums; it has supported the recent travelling display of the National Gallery picture in four UK venues and has contributed to the costs of this exhibition in both our cities. We are conscious of the great debt we owe to Art Fund, not just in this particular instance, but for many decades of generosity.

THE CITY AS A WORK OF ART

Letizia Treves

In mid-July 1760, in the prime of his life and at the pinnacle of his career, the 38-year-old painter Bernardo Bellotto (1722–1780) suffered irreparable damages that left him and his family homeless and desperate, causing him to 'lose all hope'.[1] The onset of the Seven Years' War (1756–63), the ensuing Prussian occupation of Dresden and the devastating impact of a week-long bombardment of the city brought about a dramatic reversal in Bellotto's fortunes: from his position as the highest-paid artist at the Saxon court, he now faced a life of hardship, without home or employment, and almost all his worldly possessions destroyed.

The vicissitudes of Bellotto's life are perfectly epitomised by his two views of the Kreuzkirche, one of Dresden's most recognisable churches, painted about fifteen years apart.[2] The first dates from around 1751–2 (fig. 1). The imposing structure of the late Gothic-Renaissance church dominates the Altmarkt square, and the elegant townhouses flanking it on either side are evocative of Dresden's prosperity and baroque splendour. The scene is dotted with people going about their daily business, from the simply dressed women in the foreground, pausing to rest on their errands, to the fashionable figures promenading. The sharply foreshortened buildings on the left, leading our eye eastwards up the Kreuzstrasse, display Bellotto's keen interest in perspective. This, together with the astonishingly detailed rendition of the Kreuzkirche's stone- and brickwork, with particular attention given to the facade's weathering by the elements, implies topographical accuracy and authenticity. Bellotto gives us a clear vantage point in the corner of the square, in the shade of a building outside our field of vision which also casts a shadow across the immediate foreground of the picture – a framing device frequently used by Bellotto in his compositions. We are made to believe that we are physically present, at a specific moment in time: the clock on the church tower strikes two as figures emerge from the portal, filing out after mass into the midday sun. And yet, despite the view's apparent precision, there is a certain degree of artistic licence: by arranging his composition in an almost square format and introducing more space around the Kreuzkirche, Bellotto has achieved the desired

Fig. 1 Bernardo Bellotto, *The Kreuzkirche in Dresden*, about 1751–2. Oil on canvas, 196 x 186 cm. Gemäldegalerie Alte Meister, Staatliche Kunstsammlungen Dresden

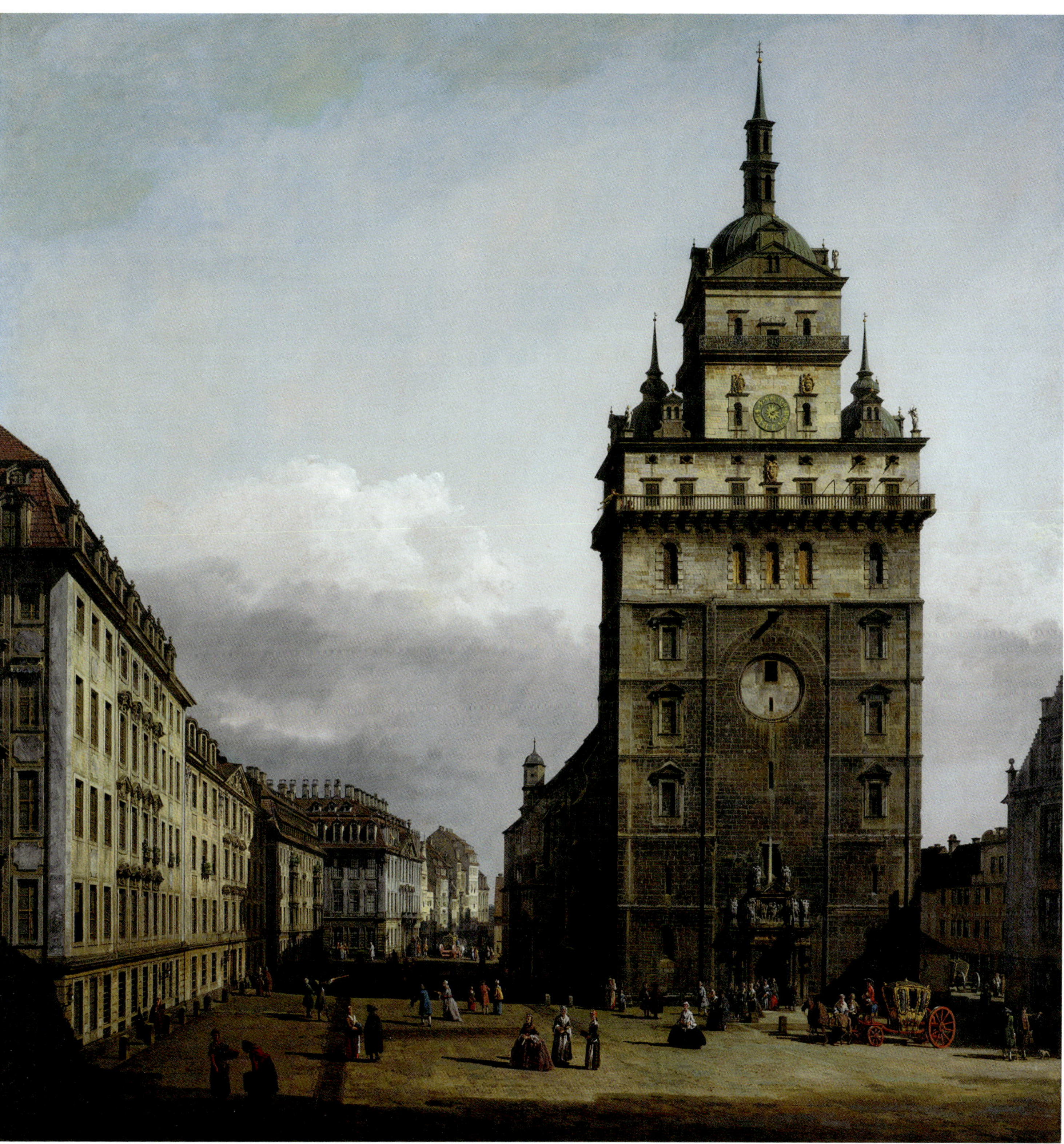

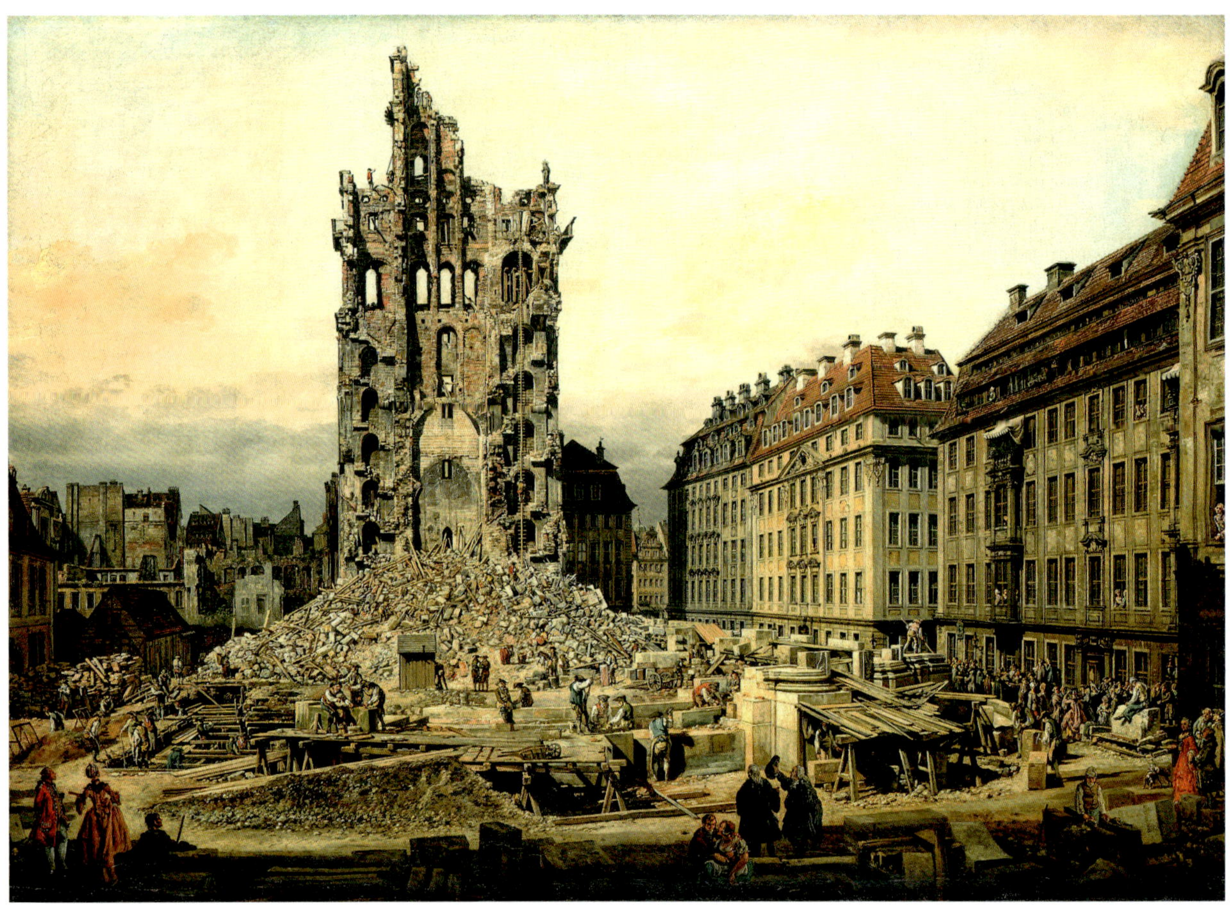

Fig. 2 Bernardo Bellotto, *The Ruins of the Kreuzkirche in Dresden*, 1765. Oil on canvas, 80 x 110 cm. Gemäldegalerie Alte Meister, Staatliche Kunstsammlungen Dresden

effect of enhancing the prospect of the church and giving solidity and monumentality to his chosen landmark. It was precisely this ability to skilfully compose views of a city's sites, while successfully capturing the character and atmosphere of a place, that led to Bellotto's appointment as official 'view painter' at the Saxon court in 1748.

How different is the smaller but more expansive view of the same square, seen from the opposite side, painted by Bellotto in 1765 (fig. 2). Five years have passed since Dresden was blasted by the army of Frederick the Great (1712–1786), King of Prussia, but the Kreuzkirche still lies in ruins – only a section of its 90-metre tower remains standing. Workmen scatter across the heaped rubble of bricks and stone fragments, as a crowd of onlookers gathers nearby. Following the partial collapse of the Kreuzkirche's tower on 22 June 1765, men set to work dismantling the tower's remaining wall brick by brick. Once again Bellotto transports us to a real place and, positioned as we are just east of where the church's nave would have been, we become eyewitnesses to this historical event.[3] An exceptionally tall ladder runs the height of the dilapidated structure and workmen perch precariously on the upper register of the ruined tower. The seemingly intact facades of the surrounding townhouses remind us of the city's former grandeur. Just as the Kreuzkirche lay in ruins, so too Bellotto's own life was in tatters: the once prosperous artist had lost his home and belongings, including an extensive library, his collection of paintings, hundreds of engravings and drawings, and countless other assets. With the sudden death of Frederick Augustus II (1696–1763), Elector of Saxony and King of Poland (as Augustus III), in 1763, Bellotto found himself without formal employment. The following year, when he took up a limited-tenure teaching post at the recently founded Dresden Academy of Fine Arts, he was obliged to accept an annual salary of 600 thalers: a third of the generous stipend he had received from the elector when he was first appointed court painter.

This moment undoubtedly marks a low point for Bellotto but, like the city of Dresden, he would rise from the ashes. In 1767, just two years after he painted the second of these pictures, he travelled to Warsaw and entered the service of one of the greatest art patrons of the age, Stanisław II August Poniatowski (1732–1798), King of Poland.[4] Bellotto was once again able to live comfortably and enjoy the social standing to which he had grown accustomed in Dresden, Vienna and Munich at the Saxon and Bavarian courts. By the time Bellotto's career ended, when he was aged 58, he had practised his art internationally over a 40-year period marked by global conflict and political upheaval. Notwithstanding his reputation in his own lifetime among the leading European rulers of his age, Bellotto was overlooked in the ensuing centuries in favour of his more famous uncle, the great Venetian view painter Giovanni Antonio Canal (1697–1768) – better known today as 'Canaletto' (the pseudonym by which Bellotto was widely known in the eighteenth century) – under whom he trained. Bellotto's extraordinary journey from Canaletto's Venice to the courts of northern Europe was driven by his desire for professional independence, stability and widespread recognition.

VENETIAN BEGINNINGS

Bernardo Bellotto was born in Venice on 20 May 1722, third child of Lorenzo Antonio Bellotto and Fiorenza Domenica Canal, the eldest of Canaletto's three sisters. Bellotto did not pursue an administrative career like his father, presumably because Lorenzo abandoned his wife and children early on.[5] Bellotto must have demonstrated considerable artistic talent and was apprenticed to his uncle: not an unusual practice at the time, particularly within the context of an extended family of painters. Bellotto's grandfather Bernardo Canal (1674–1744), after whom he was named, and his uncle Cristoforo were respected stage-set designers (*pittori da teatro*), as indeed was Canaletto himself in the earliest stages of his career.[6] By 1736 Bellotto was already an accomplished draughtsman and had probably been a pupil in Canaletto's studio for some time.[7] Two years later, when he was just 16, Bellotto became a member of the 'Fraglia dei pittori' (the Venetian painters' guild), presumably with his uncle's support. As Canaletto struggled to meet the growing demand for his work, it would have been advantageous to have his nephew's artistic talents officially recognised.[8] Bellotto, in turn, benefited greatly from being under his uncle's aegis, particularly in Venice where there was a burgeoning market for view paintings – a genre in which Canaletto truly excelled.

The Dutchman Gaspare Vanvitelli (1652/3–1736) was largely responsible for introducing view painting to Italy, and although it was Luca Carlevarijs (1663–1730) who established the genre in Venice at the turn of the century, the visual poetry Canaletto brought to his views was unparalleled by his predecessors and contemporaries.[9] It was from Canaletto that Bellotto learnt how to evoke light and shade, and to describe different surface textures of buildings and the effect of reflections or delicate ripples on water. Most importantly of all, Canaletto taught Bellotto how to draw – from large compositional drawings to detailed studies of individual buildings and people – and this remained a vital part of the artist's working method.[10] Bellotto grasped single- and multiple-point perspective and mastered the use of the camera obscura (pinhole camera), which both Canaletto and Bellotto employed extensively to compose their views.[11] They used such cameras first to capture the entire panorama before them, marking the exact positions of significant buildings in a perspectival drawing, and then again to record partial, detailed views, which could be convincingly assembled to create a larger whole.[12] Many eighteenth-century landscape and architectural painters utilised the camera obscura, but Canaletto and Bellotto were exceptional in 'correcting' the distortions of the projected image to ensure that their compositions aligned more closely with what the eye perceived: something for which the eighteenth-century art historian Antonio Maria Zanetti the Younger (1706–1778) particularly praised Canaletto.[13]

The scarce documentation and absence of signed works from this early period in Bellotto's apprenticeship have made it difficult to distinguish his hand from that of his master. This was the purpose, after all, of a successful artist's studio: to satisfy demand with assistance from the studio and for pupils to closely emulate their master's style. Since the landmark publication of the catalogues raisonnés of Canaletto and Bellotto's works – the former by W.G. Constable (1976) and the latter by Stefan Kozakiewicz (1972) – significant progress has been made in establishing Bellotto's early artistic development and defining his production within Canaletto's studio.[14] On the basis of the drawings, paintings and engravings that have come down to us, the two artists evidently worked together very closely. Many of their works are compositionally related, but the sequencing and interdependence of these works have been the cause of much debate.[15] A number of surviving examples seem to suggest the following practice: Bellotto would execute a linear pen-and-ink sketch of a particular site which Canaletto would replicate and then work up, vigorously blocking out shadows and with selected details frequently obliterated. This more 'developed' drawing would often form the basis upon which various painted compositions were produced within Canaletto's studio, some by the master himself, others (of varying quality) by assistants and, on occasion, by Bellotto.

One such painting is Bellotto's *Venice: Upper Reaches of the Grand Canal facing Santa Croce* (fig. 3), which, until relatively recently, was considered to be by an anonymous follower of Canaletto because of its correspondence with a drawing by Canaletto and a closely related engraving by Antonio Visentini (1688–1782).[16] It has been convincingly argued that the existence of a sketch by Bellotto of the same view (about 1738; Hessisches Landesmuseum, Darmstadt) points to Canaletto having had recourse to his pupil's drawing to develop his own composition – and numerous other instances of this exist.[17] The youthful Bellotto may not yet have fully mastered the quality and subtlety of Canaletto's technique in this painting, as is particularly evident in the schematically drawn water ripples and spindly figures, but he does apply the rigorous precision he has been taught – a ruled line, corresponding to the horizon line, cuts into the wet paint on the right.[18] Bellotto already demonstrates a great sensitivity to atmospheric effects and the changing weather, applying bold diagonal brushstrokes for the clouds upper centre and a streaky haze on the distant horizon painted wet-on-wet. The picture's richly textured surface, achieved through thickly applied paint, was to become a characteristic of Bellotto's mature work.

It seems logical that, while still apprenticed in Canaletto's studio, Bellotto would have encountered his uncle's clients. Indeed, like Canaletto, some of the earliest buyers of Bellotto's views were British aristocrats who had travelled to Venice on the Grand Tour.[19] Among these

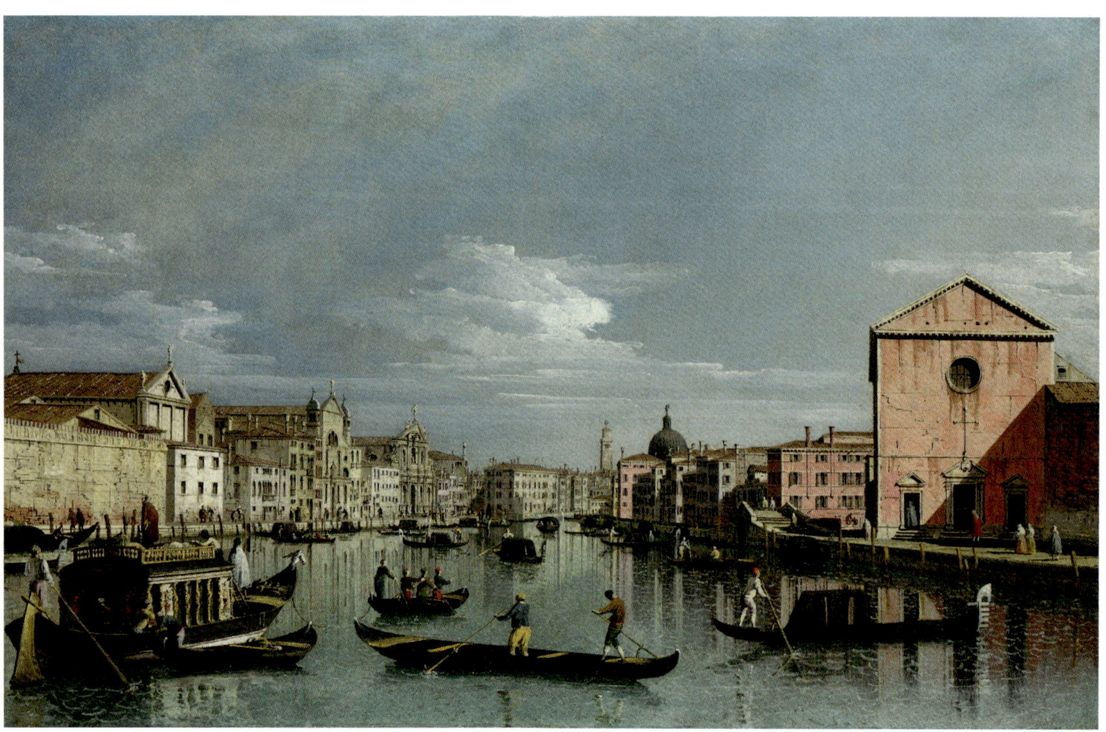

Fig. 3 Bernardo Bellotto, *Venice: Upper Reaches of the Grand Canal facing Santa Croce*, about 1738. Oil on canvas, 59.7 x 92.1 cm. The National Gallery, London

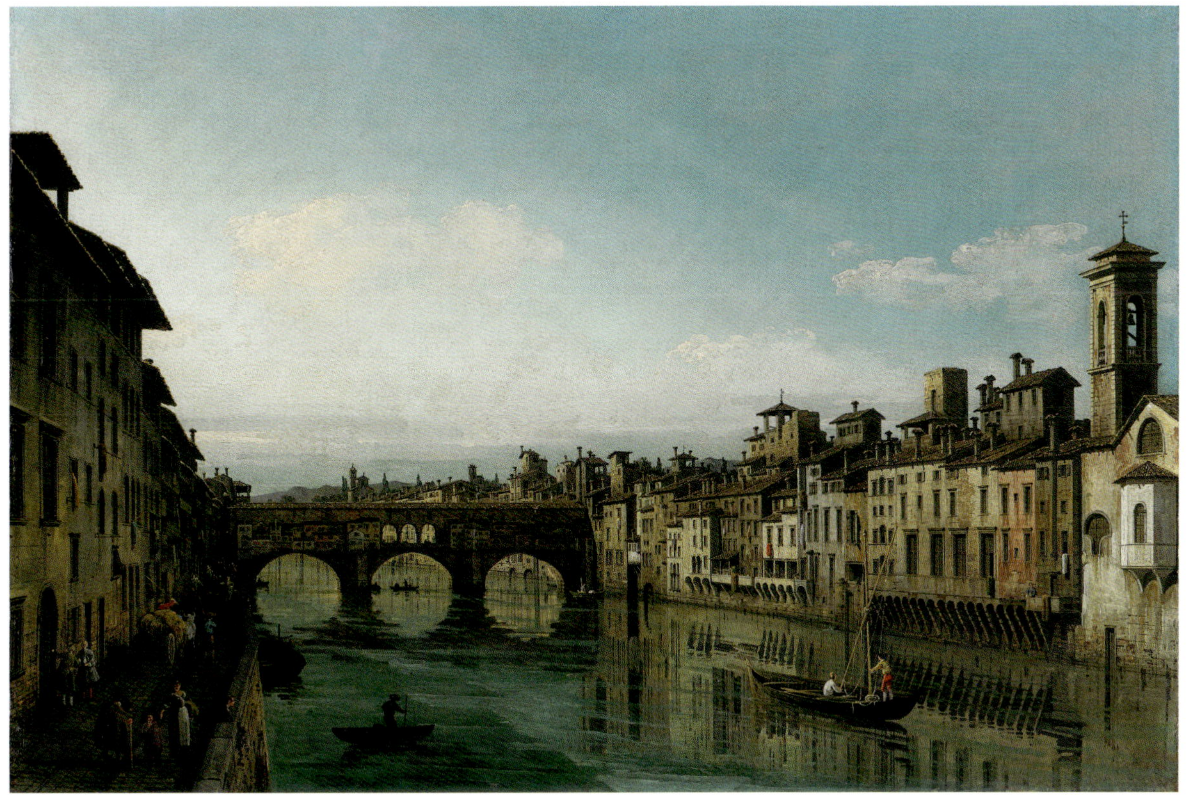

Fig. 4 Bernardo Bellotto, *The Arno with the Ponte Vecchio, Florence*, about 1742–3. Oil on canvas, 74.2 x 106.8 cm. The Fitzwilliam Museum, Cambridge

was Henry Howard (1694–1758), 4th Earl of Carlisle, who, following a trip to Venice in 1738–9, commissioned more than 40 Venetian views by different artists (including 15 by Bellotto) through his art agent Anton Maria Zanetti the Elder (1680–1767).[20] Zanetti seems to have assumed the role of intermediary for Bellotto at this time, rather as the Venice-based merchant and British consul Joseph Smith (about 1674–1770) became Canaletto's principal agent in Venice.[21] In June 1740 Zanetti wrote to Carlisle, inviting him to encourage friends to commission view paintings from Bellotto, describing him as 'the best there is, and who is as skilled as Canaletto'.[22] This was an opinion only partially endorsed by the art critic, agent and diplomat Francesco Algarotti (1712–1764). Impressed by the quality of the works Zanetti had sold, Algarotti was keen to uncover the identity of the artist whom he considered 'a painter who imitates extremely well the manner of Canaletto, perhaps does water much better than him, but is not quite as polished'.[23]

Bellotto's association with Zanetti was crucial in laying the foundations for the artist's future prospects, both within Venice and beyond. When Augustus III's son, Prince Frederick Christian (1722–1763), visited Venice in 1739–40, Bellotto painted a large view of the Grand Canal (Nationalmuseum, Stockholm) which, with Zanetti's position of influence with Augustus III, must have helped secure Bellotto's appointment as court painter in Dresden some years later.[24] It may also have been through Zanetti's agency that Joseph Wenzel (1696–1772), Prince of Liechtenstein, acquired four large views from Canaletto in the 1720s.[25] The same prince would commission a pair of pictures of his suburban palace in the Rossau, Vienna, from Bellotto many years later (1759–60; Liechtenstein Princely Collections, Vienna).[26] And it was certainly through Zanetti's active promotion of Bellotto's talents that in 1740 the 18-year-old painter was invited to Florence by Marchese Andrea Gerini (1691–1766), for whom he was to paint four magnificent prospects of the city (fig. 4).[27]

The views Bellotto painted of Florence mark a significant point of departure: Canaletto had never

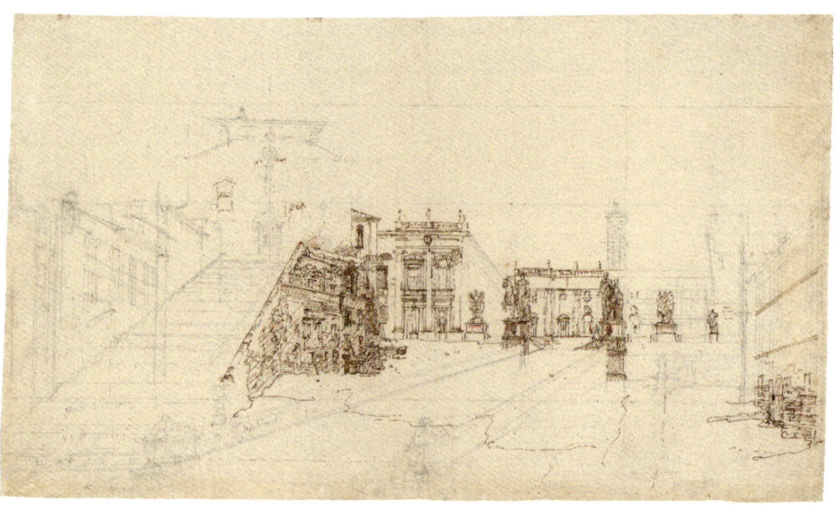

Fig. 5 Bernardo Bellotto, *The Campidoglio with Santa Maria in Aracoeli, Rome*, about 1742–3. Pencil with pen and dark brown ink, 31.3 x 53.3 cm. National Museum, Warsaw, Rys. Pol. 2040

painted the city and consequently Bellotto had to devise his own pictorial solutions.[28] Accuracy was important as these views had to appear convincing to clients who were permanent residents of Florence, unlike the Grand Tourists for whom his views of Venice served as 'souvenirs'. Bellotto was drawn to representing features that were familiar to him from Venice – squares framed by imposing architecture, waterways lined with palaces and scattered with boats, figures going about their daily business. He brilliantly describes the fabric and varying textures of the buildings – from stone and brickwork to crumbling plaster – but is equally attentive to evoking the Tuscan city's light and atmosphere. Many of the stratagems Bellotto adopted in his Florentine views would be reprised later in his career, such as views of the same site being frequently paired or shown at different times of day, enabling us to experience a place in varying conditions. In presenting the multiple aspects of a particular spot, the artist encourages us to inhabit his pictorial space: this dynamic viewing experience reaches its culmination in the five monumental views of the fortress of Königstein, where we are invited to follow in Bellotto's footsteps and circumvent the site.

In around 1741, shortly after his return to Venice, Bellotto undertook a number of study trips to mainland Veneto in the company of Canaletto, perhaps with the purpose of expanding both their repertoires. As he and his mentor travelled along the Brenta canal to Dolo and Padua, Bellotto recorded on paper the sites they visited: both he and Canaletto would have recourse to these drawings for years to come, adopting motifs for their paintings and etchings. And it was in the latter that Bellotto gradually surpassed his master: as a printmaker he was no mere imitator of Canaletto, but rather his 'formidable rival'.[29] Both artists recognised the importance of the print medium and its potential for disseminating their fame – and compositions – across Europe.[30] And it is at this early date in Venice, in eight small etchings of imaginary landscapes, that Bellotto first signs with the name by which he would become widely known: 'Canaletto' (meaning 'little Canal').[31]

With his wedding to Elisabetta Pizzorno (about 1724–1785) on 5 November 1741 and the birth of their first child Lorenzo the following year, it was time for Bellotto to move out of his uncle's shadow and establish his own professional reputation.[32] He embarked on another journey, this time to Rome (via Florence and Livorno), during which he drew prolifically and recorded motifs that he would make use of in his compositions for decades. Rome was a vital stop for any young artist, but instead of merely copying the city's ancient monuments as others did, Bellotto's drawings reveal a more sophisticated response to what he saw. His ability to choreograph highly original compositions, adopting unusual viewpoints and incorporating daring perspectives, is arguably his greatest innovation to view painting. In his *Piazza San Giovanni in Laterano* (1743–4; private collection) a perpendicular obelisk slices the composition audaciously in half – a motif Bellotto would repeat more than 30 years later.[33] In *The Tiber with San Giovanni dei Fiorentini, Rome* (1742–4; Toledo Museum of Art), the magnificent basilica of San Giovanni looms large over the Tiber, dwarfing the Castel Sant'Angelo beyond[34] – a compositional structure Bellotto adapted later for his *View of Dresden from the Right Bank of the Elbe* (1748; Gemäldegalerie, Dresden).[35] Figures promenade on a skewed 'stage' in the foreground and buildings with large windows frame both views on the left.

In August 1743, just over a year after his return to Venice, the 21-year-old Bellotto took part in the Venetian painters' annual exhibition held outside the Scuola Grande di San Rocco, as shown in Canaletto's painting of about 1735 in the National Gallery, London. Of the two views Bellotto exhibited there, one was an ambitiously composed Roman view of Santa Maria d'Aracoeli and the Campidoglio (about 1743; Egremont Collection, Petworth

House, National Trust), in which he displayed his rigorous drawing technique and mastery of perspective with sharp recessions and multiple vanishing points.[36] The scene's preparatory drawing (fig. 5) reveals Bellotto's powers of observation: carefully ruled lines mark out the scene's perspective, buildings and statuary are partially worked up in ink, and there are copious notes concerning colours, the fall of light and intensity of tones ('più chiaro', meaning lighter).[37] The city of Rome had widened Bellotto's sights and his repertory, and he was eager to show it.

NEW HORIZONS

Further excursions in Italy followed in 1744–6, taking Bellotto to Lombardy (where he painted Milan, Vaprio and Gazzada), Turin and Verona. Driven by a desire to search for subject matter outside his native Venice, he also wished to serve an expanding client base.

A pair of views of Turin, painted for Charles Emmanuel III (1701–1773), King of Sardinia and Duke of Savoy, constituted Bellotto's first royal commission and in *The Old Bridge over the River Po in Turin* (fig. 6) he took care to include the elegantly dressed figure of an artist drawing – surely a reference to himself, and the elevated position artists enjoyed at court.[38] In the Turin views Bellotto worked on an altogether different scale (each canvas measures approximately 130 x 170 cm), adapting the cityscape to a new format: a sweeping panorama leads your eye from the minutely detailed description of a brick tower or dilapidated bridge in the foreground to a hazy mountain range in the distance. Bellotto's use of light and colour to portray the reflections on still water and suggest moving currents is remarkably sophisticated:

Fig. 6 Bernardo Bellotto, *The Old Bridge over the River Po in Turin*, 1745. Oil on canvas, 127 x 171 cm. Galleria Sabauda, Turin

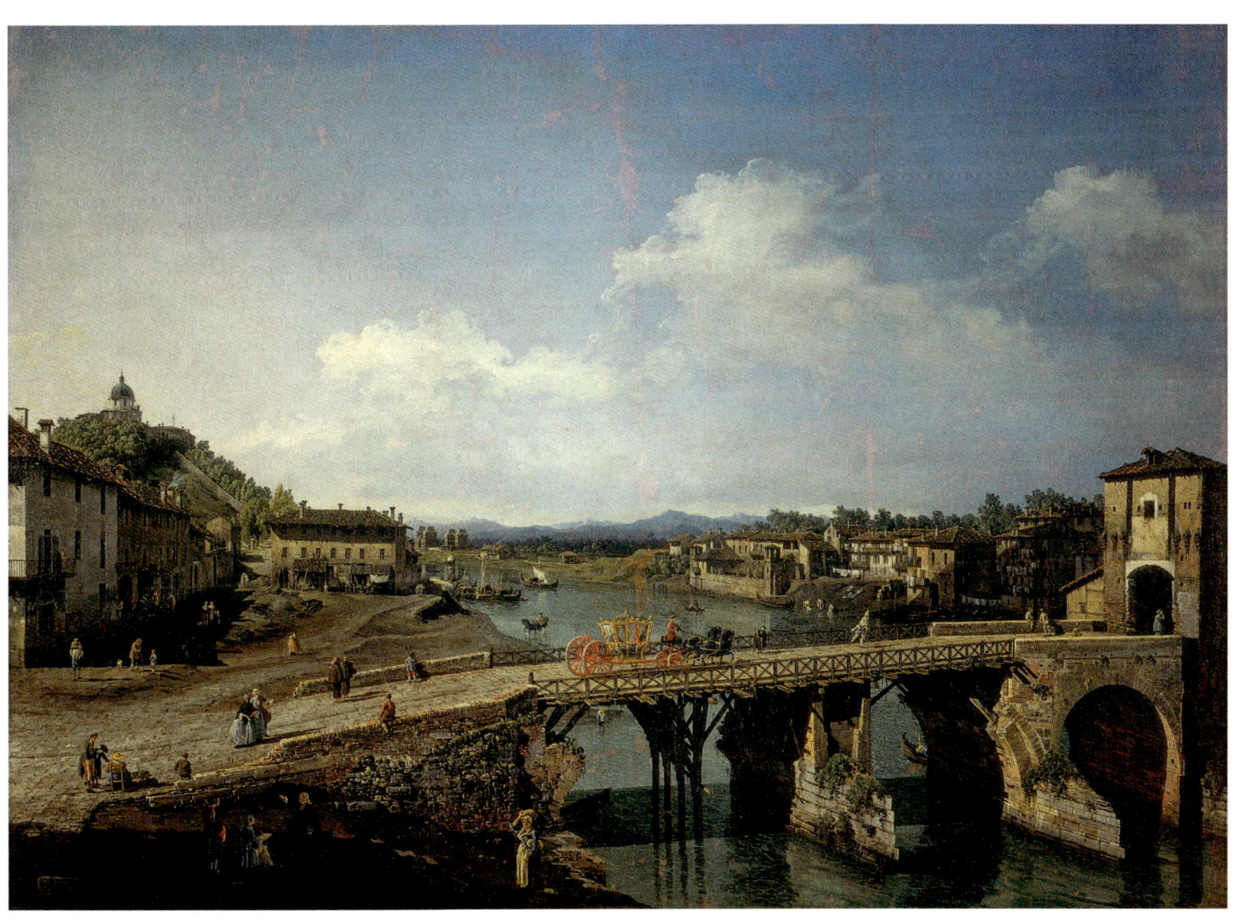

as Algarotti had remarked, Bellotto proves himself to be more accomplished than Canaletto in rendering these water effects. His two views of Verona looking up- and downstream the river Adige, painted around the same time, are intensely poetic and even larger in format, measuring approximately 130 x 230 cm (figs 21, 22).[39] This grand scale suited these expansive vistas and was favoured by Bellotto, particularly in Dresden where he produced dozens of views for the elector.

The mid-1740s mark a turning point for Bellotto. In May 1746 Canaletto left Venice for England, where he sought to satisfy the considerable demand for his pictures and adopted an increasingly stylised manner of painting.[40] By then the 24-year-old Bellotto had fulfilled his first royal commission and, like his uncle, was preparing to leave Italy. In spring 1747 he made his way to Dresden, hoping to find permanent employment there. Within a year of his arrival, he had entered the service of the elector, becoming the highest-paid artist at the Saxon court, and embarked on the most productive decade of his career.[41]

PAINTER AT THE ROYAL COURTS IN DRESDEN, VIENNA AND MUNICH

The city of Dresden – together with the idyllic village of Pirna and fortress of Königstein on the outskirts of the city – provided Bellotto with a whole new range of urban and rural panoramas. The painter varied his subject matter, as Canaletto had done previously in Venice, and turned equal attention to Dresden's familiar landmarks and the city's lesser-known spots. Imposing church buildings (the Frauenkirche, Kreuzkirche and Hofkirche) break through skylines and rise above squares and marketplaces; the city's royal complex (the Zwinger) is laid out for us to appreciate, though we are also given a 'backstreet' view from the adjacent moat; and Dresden's magnificent waterfronts are captured from either bank of the river Elbe, populated with fishermen, cattle-drivers and people hanging their washing out to dry. Bellotto's city is rooted in history, but such anecdotal details paint the picture of a budding metropolis.

For the elector Bellotto produced a series of views comprising 30 different prospects: 14 of Dresden (organised as 7 pairs), 11 of Pirna and 5 of Königstein.[42] These dramatic vistas served a clear political purpose: they were visual statements of Dresden's magnificence

Fig. 7 Bernardo Bellotto, *The Neumarkt from the Jüdenhof, Dresden*, about 1748–9. Oil on canvas, 136 x 236 cm. Gemäldegalerie Alte Meister, Staatliche Kunstsammlungen Dresden

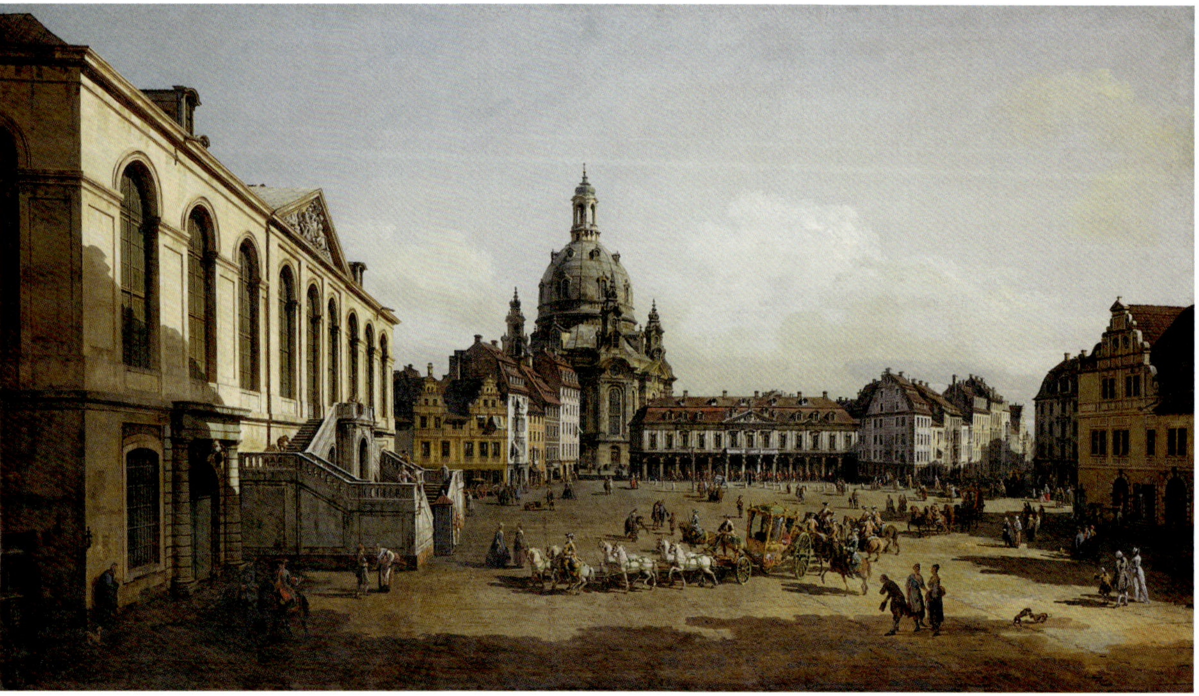

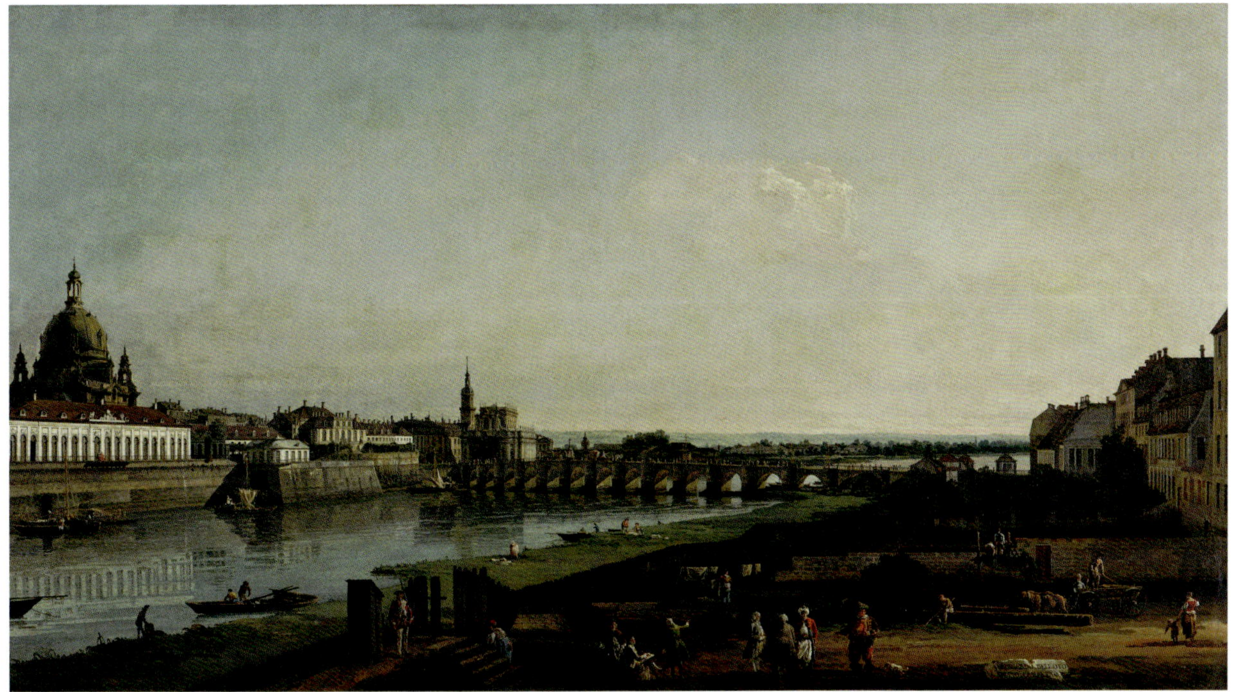

Fig. 8 Bernardo Bellotto, *Dresden from the Right Bank of the Elbe above Augustus Bridge*, 1747. Oil on canvas, 132 x 236 cm. Gemäldegalerie Alte Meister, Staatliche Kunstsammlungen Dresden

in the 'Augustan age' and proclaimed the city's status as one of the principal capitals of Europe. In *The Neumarkt from the Jüdenhof, Dresden* (fig. 7) Augustus III is present, seated in a tilting horse-drawn carriage.[43] A man bows respectfully as the king crosses the Neumarkt and heads towards the royal picture gallery, the royal guard lining up neatly on the other side of the square. Bellotto's views of Dresden were highly politicised – through them Augustus III hoped to immortalise the city and his power. The artist even produced a second series, in which many of the compositions from the royal cycle are repeated, for the prime minister, Count Heinrich von Brühl (1700–1763).[44] Bellotto knew to flatter his prospective high-ranking clients. In *Dresden from the Right Bank of the Elbe above Augustus Bridge* (fig. 8) he gives prominence to the Brühl Terrace – the count's palace and picture gallery, radiant in the sunshine, dominate the left bank.[45] Moreover Bellotto used the series, and this view in particular, as a vehicle for self-promotion: he appears in the form of an artist drawing in the foreground and signs the painting conspicuously on a stone fragment, to which he added the title 'Peiñ: RIe:' (Royal Painter) to the second state of the related engraving.[46] Bellotto depicts himself seated between the established court painters Johann Alexander Thiele (1685–1752) and Christian Wilhelm Ernst Dietrich (1712–1774), with other court figures conversing nearby – the royal physician, an opera singer, Turkish chamberlain and court jester.[47] Painted a year before his official appointment, Bellotto shows himself already deeply ensconced in court life. We know he was well versed in the art of diplomacy from the contents of his library in his Dresden apartment, and the fact that he displayed portraits of the king and queen in his dining room (a privilege normally reserved for senior court officials and ambassadors) implies a particularly close relationship with his royal patron.[48] In addition, Augustus III and Brühl, and their respective wives, together with Augustus's sons, all stood as godparents to four of Bellotto's five daughters who were born in Dresden.[49]

It is no surprise that Bellotto shows himself here, as in other paintings, in the act of drawing 'on location'. This had always been vital to Bellotto's working practice: among the hundreds of sheets lost when his Dresden apartment was destroyed by the Prussian army in 1760

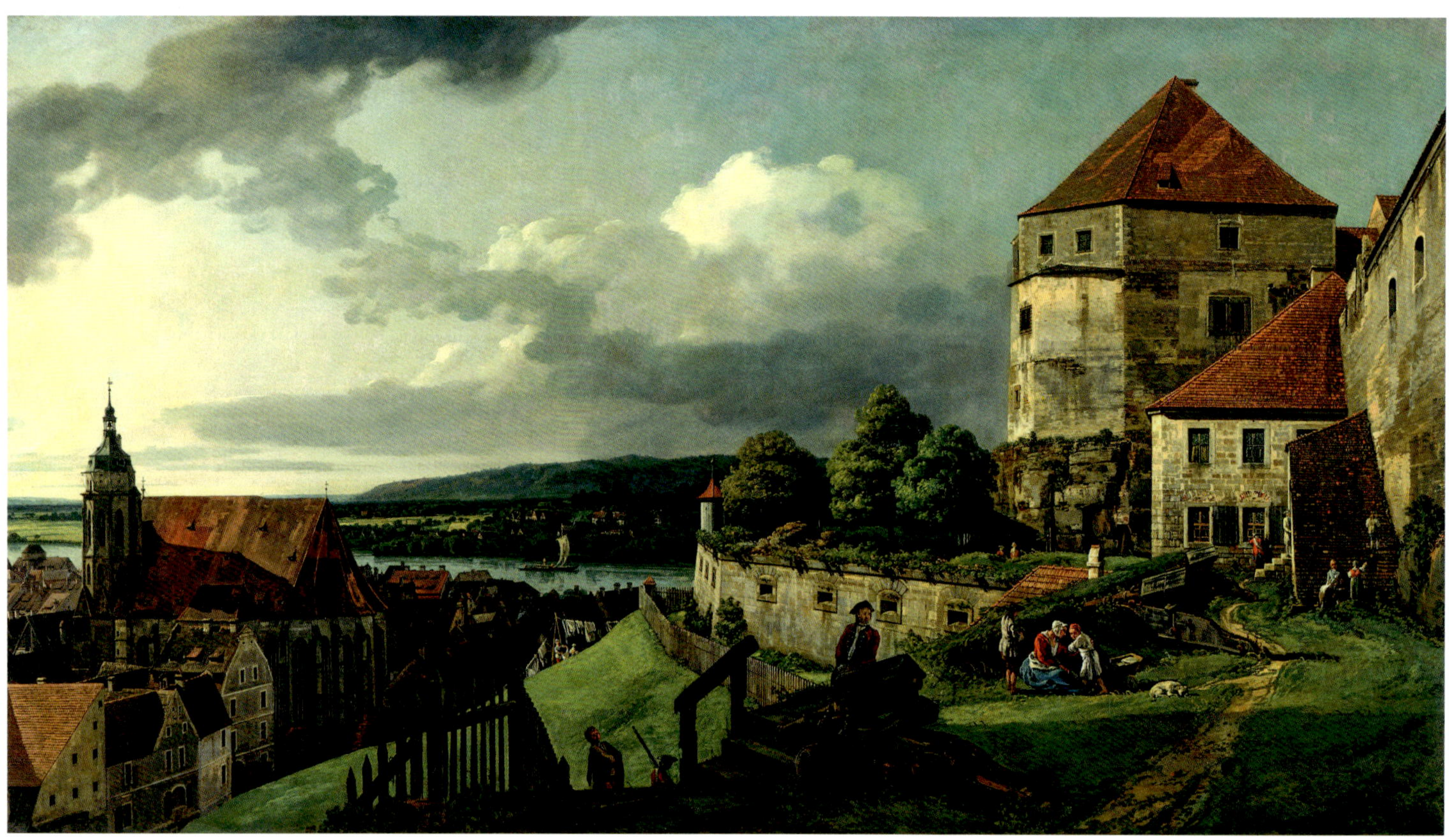

Fig. 9 Bernardo Bellotto, *Sonnenstein Fortress above Pirna*, about 1754–6. Oil on canvas, 133 x 234 cm. Gemäldegalerie Alte Meister, Staatliche Kunstsammlungen Dresden

were numerous drawings of figures and sites taken from life.[50] Further evidence of Bellotto drawing in situ is provided by two decrees issued on the painter's behalf to a Pirna official on 26 April 1753 and 30 March 1756, requesting assistance and privileged access for Bellotto as he headed to Pirna and Königstein 'charged with carrying out drawings of the situations of the surroundings of Pirna and further afield'.[51] Although these drawings have not come down to us, the paintings he produced of these two sites – with their breathtaking viewpoints and daring perspectives – would simply not have been possible without multiple preparatory drawings and the aid of a camera obscura. The sheets must have consisted of broad panoramic studies as well as detailed sketches, copiously annotated with the colours, materials and textures of the buildings. How else could Bellotto have captured so realistically the weathered stone and crumbling plasterwork of the austere fortress of Königstein perched atop the rocky crag, its jagged silhouette contrasting with the lush green landscape of the surrounding area? Bellotto was not the only one who saw the dramatic possibilities of the commanding structures of the fortresses of Sonnenstein (located above Pirna) and Königstein: Joseph Mallord William Turner (1775–1851) would sketch the exact same view as Bellotto's *Sonnenstein Fortress above Pirna* (fig. 9) in his Dresden and Saxon Switzerland sketchbook some 80 years later (Turner Bequest, Tate Britain, London).[52]

Bellotto had always intended his views of Pirna and Königstein to form part of the king's 'Dresden series' but, with the outbreak of the Seven Years' War, the five views of Königstein were never delivered (see pp. 30, 42–3). As the Prussian army occupied Saxony, Augustus III left Dresden for Warsaw, first barricading himself for several months in the fortress of Königstein with his younger sons and Brühl. Their hasty departure from Dresden marked the end of what had been a remarkably industrious decade for Bellotto: he had produced 30 paintings for the king, 21 views for the prime minister and 22 reduced replicas for himself, completing (on average) a large-scale view every 12–16 weeks.[53] In the service of Augustus III, Bellotto's generous remuneration had enabled him to live in relative luxury. His Dresden apartment, which included several reception rooms, was fitted out with sumptuous furniture and upholstery, Venetian mirrors, fine wallpaper and fabrics. He owned a vast collection of drawings and engravings, some sculptures, and two Meissen porcelain sets which had been presented to him by Brühl. In a picture cabinet Bellotto displayed his collection of 59 paintings (22 of which were by his own hand) and he even had a printing workshop at home ('Camera per la stamperia'). His extensive library and belongings – which included a harpsichord, globes, telescope and a compass – called attention to the culture, intellect and sophistication of an artist at the peak of his career.

With the Prussian invasion and Augustus III's departure, Bellotto was obliged to leave Dresden and seek employment elsewhere. In 1758 Bellotto obtained a passport to travel to Bayreuth, from where he journeyed on to Vienna, in the company of his 16-year-old son Lorenzo. He may have been encouraged to do so by Giuseppe Galli Bibiena (1696–1757), an architect and stage-set designer who had been employed in Dresden at the same time as Bellotto and had previously worked in Vienna, the dynastic capital of the Habsburg Empire.[54] Shortly after his arrival in Vienna, Bellotto received private commissions from the Prince of Liechtenstein and Wenzel Anton (1711–1794), Prince of Kaunitz, chancellor to Empress Maria Theresa (1717–1780). It was thanks to moving in such aristocratic circles that Bellotto soon entered the service of the empress herself, painting for her a series of 13 views of Vienna. The paintings were almost certainly intended to be displayed in a single space and the cycle comprised six views of the city of Vienna (conceived in pairs) and seven larger panoramic views of the Schönbrunn and Hof imperial palaces and gardens.[55] In the two-year period Bellotto resided in Vienna he worked at a furious pace, sometimes spending no more than six weeks on a single painting and fulfilling other commissions at court.[56] The speed with which these views were painted – and perhaps a certain degree of participation by Bellotto's son Lorenzo – might account for their being less carefully or finely executed than his views of Dresden.[57] But, like the series produced for Augustus III, Maria Theresa's paintings served to illustrate Vienna's imperial magnificence and were consequently heavily politicised.[58] In *Schönbrunn Palace from the Courtyard Side* (1759–60; Kunsthistorisches Museum, Vienna) an inscription identifies the scene as the moment when Maria Theresa (on the balcony wearing a blue dress) is about to be informed of her victory at the Battle of Kunersdorf, where the Prussian army was defeated by the allied Russian and Austrian forces.[59] And it may have been for political reasons that, following the Prussian bombardments in Dresden, Bellotto did not immediately return to his wife and daughters but instead journeyed on to Munich. He did so with Maria Theresa's authorisation for, in a letter addressed to her cousin Maria Antonia (1724–1780), Princess of Bavaria, the empress refers to Bellotto's good conduct at court and the several 'very beautiful works' he produced there ('il s'est conduit ici tres bien et nous at [sic] fournit plusieurs pieces de ces ouvrages tres belle').[60]

Maria Antonia had been staying in Munich with her husband Frederick Christian, son of Augustus III and heir to the Saxon electorate, since the Prussian siege of Dresden. She presumably encouraged Bellotto to come to Munich; after all, in his official capacity as painter to the Saxon court and with Augustus III away in Warsaw, he would have wished to serve the Electoral Prince of Saxony.[61] It seems that the three large paintings Bellotto produced during the few months he resided in Munich were always intended to stay there, pointing to Maria Antonia being the probable instigator of the commission.[62] The views were conceived as part of the rococo redesign of the Second Antechamber of the electoral apartments in the Residenz (where they still hang today).[63] The panoramic prospect of Munich from the east is flanked on either side by pendant views of the Nymphenburg Palace, Maria Antonia's birthplace and the Bavarian summer residence.[64] To achieve the elevated viewpoint in the latter paintings, Bellotto had to stand high up on a scaffold erected especially for him.[65] Located within the royal couple's living quarters, the Second Antechamber was where the king and queen enjoyed dining in the evenings, but the room had a dual function: it also served as a vestibule to the adjacent Audience Chamber. Consequently Bellotto's three paintings parading Munich's splendour would have been seen by every visiting dignitary and high-ranking official; and the political allegiance between the Bavarian and Saxon electorates, as signified by the Houses of Wettin and Wittelsbach, was apparent in

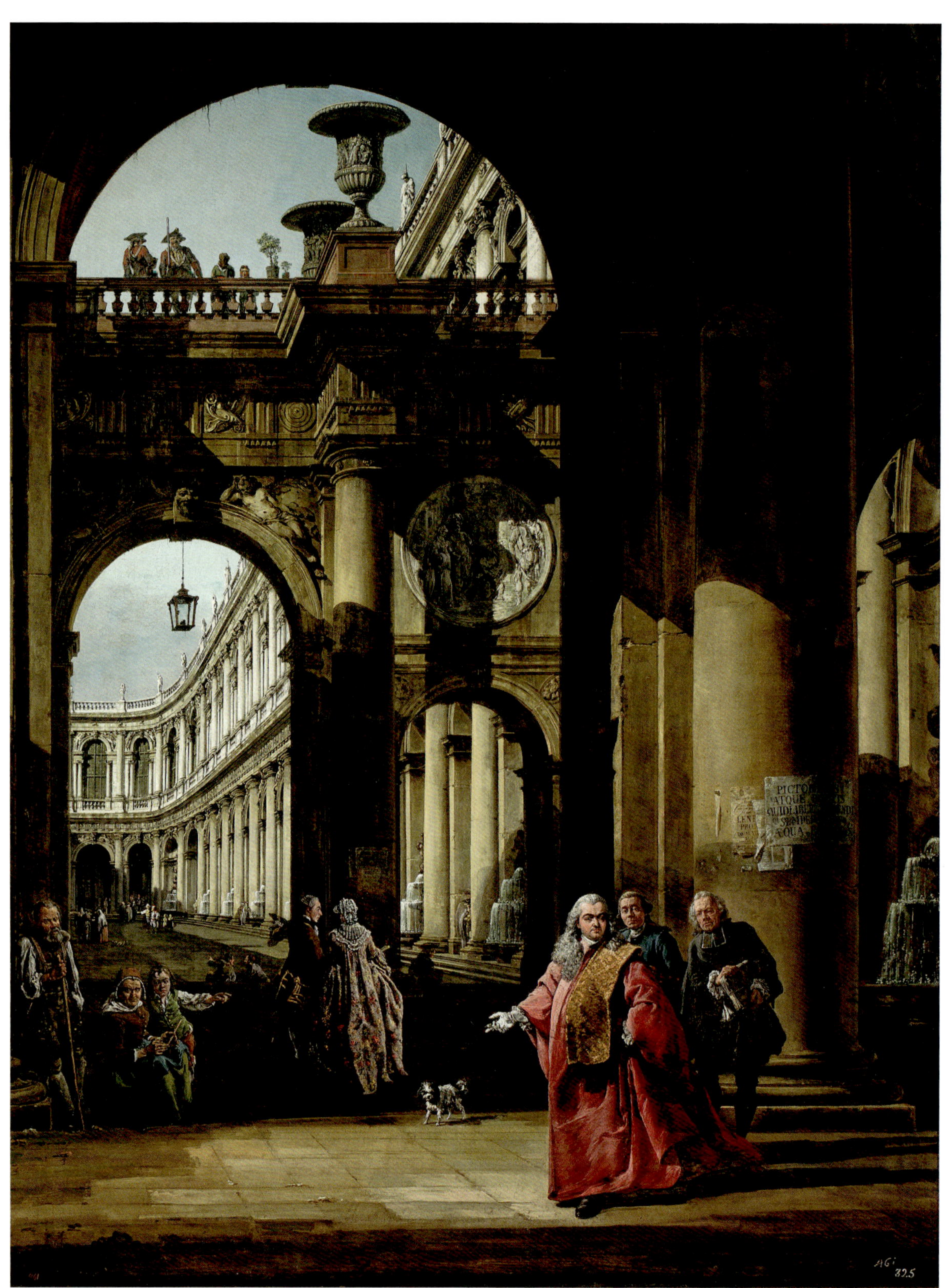

the combined coats of arms emblazoned on the paintings' gilt frames.[66]

On returning to Dresden towards the end of 1761 and discovering that his house had been completely devastated, Bellotto found himself in serious financial difficulty. In addition to losses amounting to 50,000 thalers, he had run up significant debts before the war broke out.[67] Bellotto's situation became even more precarious when, a couple of years later, his two most enthusiastic patrons died in quick succession. Augustus III, who had returned to Dresden ill and considerably weakened after signing a peace treaty between Prussia and Austria in February 1763, died on 5 October. Brühl passed away just three weeks later. Bellotto's melancholic views of the ruined Kreuzkirche (fig. 2) and destroyed suburb of Pirna'sche Vorstadt (1763–6; Musée des Beaux-Arts, Troyes),[68] which date from around this time, resonate with what must have been his mood. But he soon turned away from such subjects, as if deliberately reacting against the depressing effect of the scenes around him. In response to the contemporary revival of interest in classical antiquity, Bellotto turned to painting idealised views featuring architectural motifs that he had drawn in Venice and Rome many years previously. The foundation of Dresden's Academy of Fine Arts in 1764 coincided with the publication of *Geschichte der Kunst des Altertums* (*History of Ancient Art*) by the influential German scholar Johann Joachim Winckelmann (1717–1768), who, along with the Saxon painter Anton Raphael Mengs (1728–1779), championed the neoclassical movement in the arts. The renewed emphasis on the didactic function of art – which lay at the heart of neoclassical ideals – was clearly at odds with Bellotto's output to date, and so he was forced to reposition himself as a painter of classical architectural fantasies. Bellotto demonstrated considerable business acumen in this, even though his chosen path cannot have been easy. He was actively disliked by the academy's new director Christian Ludwig von Hagedorn (1712–1780), who deliberately overlooked Bellotto and appointed exclusively Saxons as professors.[69] It was only after the intervention of Prince Franz Xavier (1730–1806) and Maria Antonia, joint regents following the death of Frederick Christian, that Bellotto was admitted to the Academy.[70] He was granted a three-year teaching post as 'associate member for perspective' and, even though his annual salary of 600 thalers was equivalent to that of a full professor, it was a fraction of what he had earned as court artist.[71]

Bellotto's Academy reception piece, a view of Dresden from the Neustädter bridgehead (1765; Staatliche Kunsthalle Karlsruhe), advertised the painter's talents in producing topographically accurate views, and its rigorously drawn perspective served as a reminder of the discipline Bellotto had been appointed to teach.[72] At the Academy's first exhibition, on 5 March 1765, Bellotto submitted four paintings: a pair of allegories showing the Temples of Venus and Love (now lost) and two pendant architectural capricci, one with a Venetian nobleman (probably a self portrait) and the other with Christ driving the Traders from the Temple.[73] In spite of being known primarily as an architectural painter and having been hired by the Academy as a master in perspective, through his deliberate choice of varied subject matter (two allegories, one religious scene and a portrait) Bellotto was determined to demonstrate the full breadth and range of his art.

The *Architectural Capriccio with a Self Portrait in the Costume of a Venetian Nobleman*, known in three (almost identical) versions, is a particularly ambitious work (fig. 10).[74] Bellotto displays his command of perspective and underlines his Venetian origins: the architecture is a hybrid of recognisable buildings in Venice including the Marciana Library, Procuratie Nuove and a corner of Piazza San Marco reimagined as curved.[75] The man in the foreground, dressed in the red robes of a Venetian procurator and wearing a heavily embroidered sash on his left shoulder, has been identified as Bellotto himself (though not all scholars agree).[76] This theory is supported by the fact that the composition was repeated and the Warsaw variant – the only one to be signed – is described in an inventory of 1795, just 15 years after Bellotto's death, as 'Architectural fantasy, where the author has painted himself in the clothes of a Venetian nobleman'.[77] Behind him, fly-posted to a column, is a quotation from the Roman poet Horace (65–8 BC), proclaiming that painters can dare to do anything they please: 'Pictoribus atque poetis/Quidlibet audendi semper fuit aequa potestas' ('Painters and poets have always shared an equal right to dare to do whatever they wanted').[78] With this in mind, it seems likely that Bellotto chose to represent himself as a Venetian nobleman and that the painting should be read as an affirmation of what is possible. Rather than being a plea for artistic

Fig. 10 Bernardo Bellotto, *Architectural Capriccio with a Self Portrait in the Costume of a Venetian Nobleman*, about 1765. Oil on canvas, 153 x 114 cm. Royal Castle, Warsaw

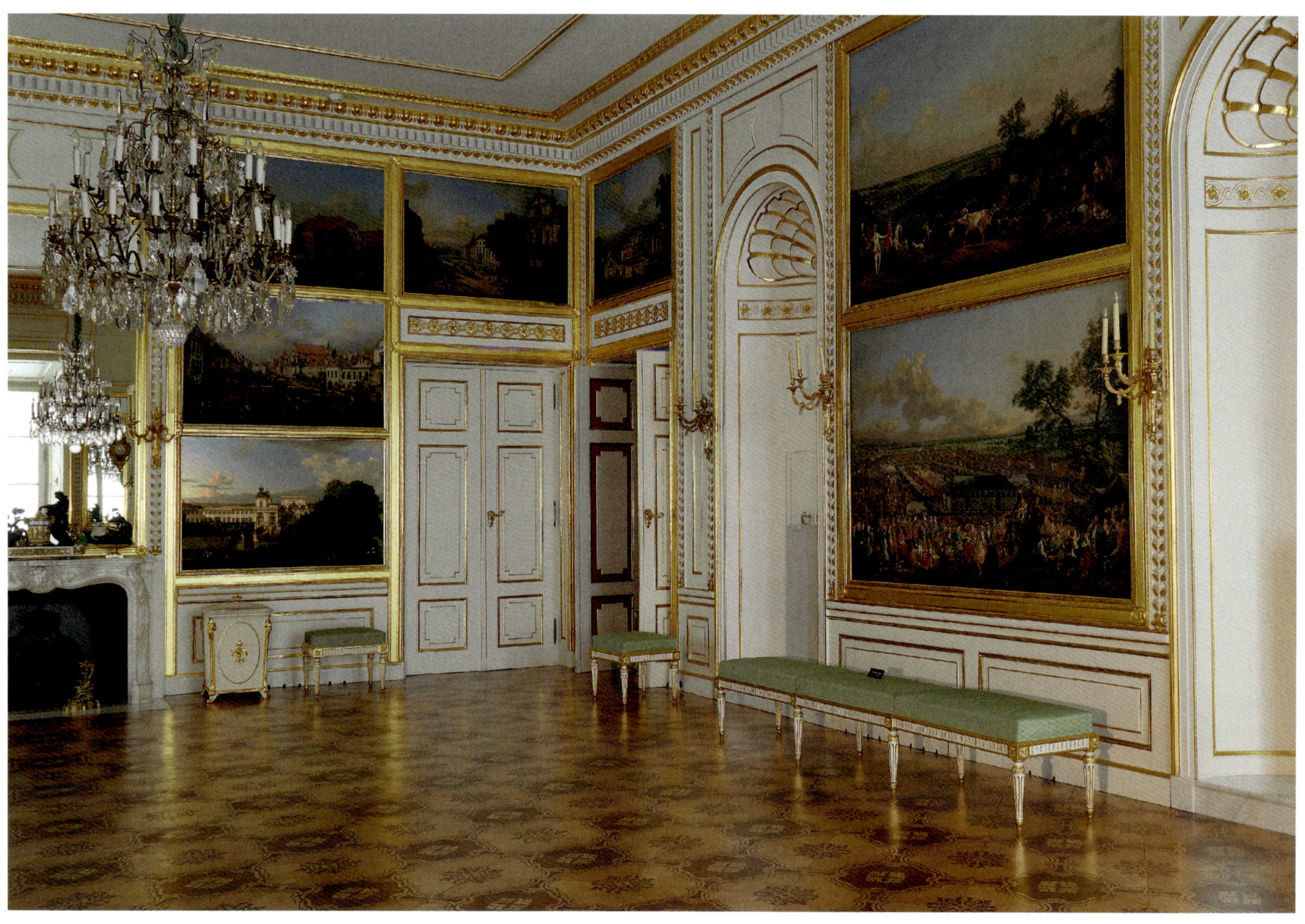

Fig. 11 Interior of the Canaletto Room with *The Election of Stanisław II August Poniatowski as King of Poland* (fig. 12) on the north wall. Royal Castle, Warsaw

freedom, this picture is an assertion of it, particularly when viewed in the context of the other three works that accompanied it in the Academy's exhibition. Perhaps Bellotto's self-promotion was too much for Hagedorn and his presence at the Academy became intolerable. In December 1766, less than halfway through his three-year tenure, Bellotto requested a leave of absence to go to St Petersburg, where the new Empress of Russia, Catherine the Great (1729–1796) – known for her enthusiastic patronage of foreign artists – resided. He left Dresden shortly thereafter, never to return.

PRESTIGE REGAINED

On his way to St Petersburg, Bellotto stopped over in Warsaw. It was here that the artist would regain his standing as court painter and live out the remaining 13 years of his career.[79] Perhaps introduced by the court painter Marcello Bacciarelli (1731–1818), who had also been employed by Augustus III in Dresden, Bellotto immediately entered the service of Stanisław II August Poniatowski, King of Poland. An avid collector and patron of the arts, Poniatowski had already amassed an impressive collection, to which he intended to add hundreds more paintings,[80] and two major projects were already underway when Bellotto arrived in Warsaw. The first was the refurbishment of the king's official residence,

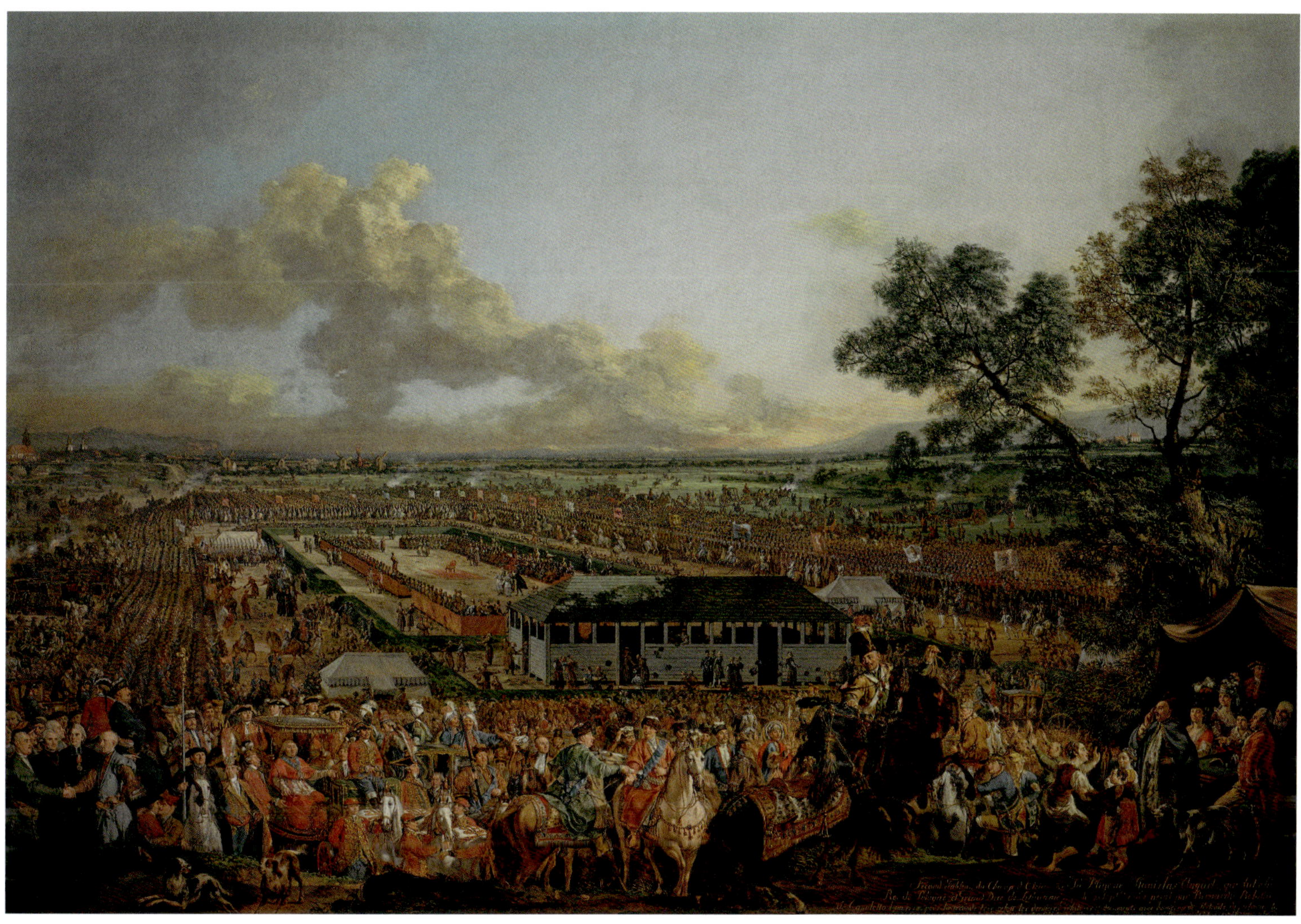

Fig. 12 Bernardo Bellotto, *The Election of Stanisław II August Poniatowski as King of Poland*, 1778. Oil on canvas, 177 x 250 cm. Royal Castle, Warsaw

the Royal Castle, and the other was the reconstruction of his private property, Ujazdów Castle, located just outside the city. Once Bellotto had obtained an extension to his leave of absence, he assumed the post of court painter and summoned his wife and daughters to Warsaw.[81] With an annual salary of 400 ducats and additional benefits, including a generous pension, the 46-year-old Bellotto had managed to reclaim his former status.[82]

He immediately set to work on a cycle of paintings intended for a large room on the ground floor of Ujazdów Castle. The series was to include views of historic sites, palaces, squares and churches in Warsaw and Rome, in a bid to present the city of Warsaw as the 'new Rome'. The scheme was close to Poniatowski's heart and he took special interest in Bellotto's progress: in 1767 the king is recorded as having visited the artist daily.[83] Bellotto's 16 views of Rome were based on engravings by Giovanni Battista Piranesi (1720–1778) and (judging from those that survive) they were of variable quality, suggesting that they were painted at speed and with the assistance of his son Lorenzo – indeed some canvases are jointly signed 'Canaletti Fecerunt'.[84] The derivative nature of these Roman views did not play to Bellotto's strengths for he was at his best producing grand-scale topographical views of his own invention, in which he could inject his sensitivity for light and atmosphere. The project was never completed: financial constraints compelled the king to abandon the refurbishment of Ujazdów in 1770 and concentrate his efforts on the Royal Castle instead. With the death of Lorenzo in the same year, Bellotto lost both his son and principal assistant. Bellotto's canvases were transferred to the Royal Castle in 1777 and new paintings of Warsaw gradually replaced the Roman views. The completed cycle of 22 views of Warsaw and its environs, including Wilańow Palace, was finally arranged in the antechamber outside the Throne Room where high-ranking dignitaries, visiting ambassadors and senators were received. This room, known as the 'Canaletto Room', appears today much as it did in the eighteenth century, thanks to its careful reconstruction from detailed historic inventories (fig. 11).[85] The views, stacked high and hung in rows, were evidently conceived as pendants and Bellotto was obliged to crop some of the canvases that were relocated from Ujazdów so they would fit into the room's purposely designed wooden panelling. Given the importance of the space in which these views were hung, the cycle served a clear political function – as had those in Dresden, Vienna and Munich – and Bellotto seems to have conceived some of the views with their ultimate destinations in mind.

Positioned at eye level, in the centre of the south wall, is his *View of Warsaw from the Suburb of Praga* (1770; Royal Castle, Warsaw), a sweeping vista that incorporates a panoramic view of the city and a self portrait of the artist.[86] Bellotto reappears in profile in the corresponding canvas on the opposite wall, as a witness to the historic event of King Stanisław II August's election, even though this had occurred in 1764, more than two years before Bellotto's arrival in Warsaw (fig. 12, and detail above).[87] Through its staged composition and a foreground thronged with awkward figure groups, Bellotto focuses our attention on the setting and political significance of the event depicted. The effect of the rising sun in a vast sky is poetic: the picture marks the dawn of a new age, with the king affirming his power as legitimate ruler and Bellotto asserting his position at court. Its location beside the door leading to the Throne Room was 'the ideal place for political propaganda and self-staging' – every visiting dignitary would have encountered it there.[88]

In 1780, just two years after this picture was painted, Bellotto died suddenly from a stroke. An unfinished painting found in the studio at the time of his death was presented to Poniatowski by the artist's family.[89] Bellotto was buried in the Capuchin church in Warsaw, whose

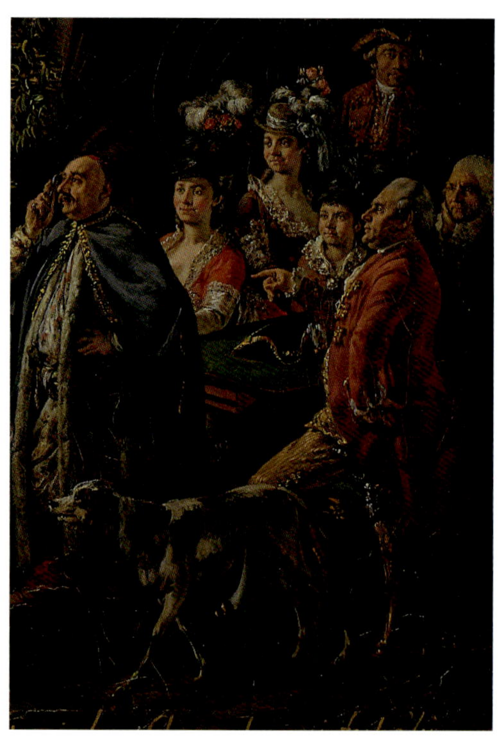

pediment and cross emerge from behind trees in his view of Miodowa Street (1777; Royal Castle, Warsaw).[90] Bellotto's wife Elisabetta died five years later and their daughter Theresia Francisca moved with her husband to Vilnius in Lithuania, taking hundreds of her father's drawings with them (these are now divided between Darmstadt, Hessisches Landesmuseum and Warsaw, National Museum).

During the course of his 40-year career Bellotto painted some 300 pictures, about a third of which were of and for cities where they still hang today. Bellotto served five different rulers, glorifying the great capitals of Europe in view paintings that were not only highly original but also met the social and political demands of his patrons. In presenting the city itself as a work of art, Bellotto can rightfully be called the first great 'European' view painter.

1 During the Prussian bombardment of Dresden on 14–20 July 1760, the apartment Bellotto rented on Salzgasse, and all his belongings within it, were destroyed. On leaving Dresden for Vienna in 1758, Bellotto had compiled a detailed list of his possessions as they were crated and entrusted to neighbours for safekeeping. This list was to form the core of Bellotto's 'Catalogo dei Danni' (Catalogue of Damages), which, written in his own hand, documented his losses – valued by him at 50,000 thaler (a figure almost 30 times his annual salary as court painter). The 'Catalogo', which is in the Wroblewski Library of the Lithuanian Academy of Sciences, Vilnius, was first discovered and published by Manikowska 2012, 2014; see also Marinelli 2016–17, and Kowalczyk in Milan 2016–17, cat. 83, pp. 232–7. On making the discovery that almost nothing remained of his possessions, Bellotto recorded his own desperate state of mind in an appendix to the 'Catalogo', dated February 1762: 'mi fa perdere Ogni Speranza, Stante alla mie Età di lasciare privi li mie Eredi di tal Capitale' ('it makes me lose all hope, at the age in which I find myself, to leave my heirs without any capital').

2 Kozakiewicz 1972, vol. 2, nos 181, 297. The Kreuzkirche (literally 'Church of the Cross') is named after a relic of the True Cross which was housed there until the original church's destruction by fire in 1491.

3 Peter Björn Kerber refers to such 'reportorial views' as having 'purposefully shaped the viewer's recollection and thereby determined the perception, memory and historical record of many of eighteenth-century Europe's formative events' (Kerber 2017–18a, p. 17).

4 Rottermund 2001, p. 33, citing bibliography for Poniatowski's artistic patronage on p. 39, n. 5.

5 Kowalczyk 1995, pp. 71–2. Bellotto's younger brother Pietro (1725–about 1804/5) was also a painter and from November 1741 to July 1742 Bellotto received payment for Pietro's board and training, indicating that he had taken him on as a pupil in Venice. Prior to this date Pietro was presumably apprenticed to Canaletto (Beddington 2010–11, p. 127).

6 Kowalczyk 2016–17, p. 15.

7 A reliable indication of this is Bellotto's skilfully penned drawing of the Venetian canal of Santa Chiara (Hessisches Landesmuseum, Darmstadt; Kozakiewicz 1972, vol. 2, no. 20), which can be dated with certainty to before June 1736 (see Kowalczyk 1995, p. 70, fig. 2).

8 In a letter to the Duke of Richmond, dated 28 November 1727, the art agent and theatre impresario Owen McSwiny (1676–1754), one of Canaletto's earliest patrons, remarked that 'He has more work than he can doe, in any reasonable time, and well' (Finberg 1920–1, p. 23).

9 Beddington 2010–11, p. 16.

10 Hundreds of drawings are listed in Bellotto's 'Catalogo dei Danni' as having been destroyed in 1760 (see n. 1 above). Only about 140 drawings by Bellotto have survived and, of the large group left in the possession of Bellotto's heirs and later sold by them, approximately 50 ended up in Darmstadt, Hessisches Landesmuseum, and 60 in Warsaw, National Museum.

11 The camera obscura consisted of a wooden box with a small hole in one side, through which an image was projected upside down onto a sheet of paper. Such cameras had been in use since the Renaissance but became more readily available to artists in the eighteenth century, when devices became portable and more sophisticated: one, resembling a large book once it collapsed, belonged to Joshua Reynolds (1723–1792) and is now in the Science Museum, London; another, inscribed 'A. CANAL' (suggesting it may have belonged to Canaletto), is in the Museo Correr, Venice (see Kowalczyk in Milan 2016–17, cat. 11, pp. 72–3). On Bellotto's use of the camera see Weber 2001, pp. 19–20, and Schütz 2005, pp. 51–8.

12 From the drawings that survive from this early phase in Canaletto's workshop, Bellotto seems to have been charged with producing drawings that combine disparate studies of buildings by his master (see Kowalczyk 2008, pp. 14–16).

13 In his treatise *Della pittura veneziana*, Zanetti wrote that Canaletto taught by example to show others how to use the camera correctly, recognising and correcting its defects in his work ('Insegnò il Canal con l'esempio il vero uso della camera ottica; e a conoscere i difetti che recar suole a una pittura, quando l'artefice interamente si fida della prospettiva che in essa camera vede'; Zanetti 1771, vol. 5, p. 463).

14 Notable contributions regarding this early period of Bellotto's development have been made by Bożena Anna Kowalczyk (see, for example, Kowalczyk 1995, 1998, 1999, 2001, 2016–17) and Charles Beddington (Beddington 2004).

15 On the complex relationship between Canaletto and Bellotto's drawings in the early phase of the latter's career see Clayton 2005, p. 182, who also discusses Canaletto's 'two-stage pen drawings', and Kowalczyk 2008, pp. 14–16.

16 Levey 1986, pp. 47–8. For a history of the painting and its attribution to Bellotto see Kowalczyk 1998, pp. 85, 88–9, and Kowalczyk in Venice and Houston 2001, cat. 1, pp. 42–4.

17 Kozakiewicz 1972, vol. 2, no. 18. See Kowalczyk in Turin 2008, cats 9–21, pp. 72–93.

18 Kowalczyk 2001, p. 4, and Kowalczyk in Venice and Houston 2001, cat. 1, p. 42.

19 A documented exception is the German military commander Johann Matthias, Count von der Schulenburg (1661–1747), who purchased four views by Bellotto in 1740 (Kowalczyk 2001, pp. 4–5).

20 The series – comprising 5 large views by Canaletto, 18 by Michele Marieschi (1710–1743), 2 by Giambattista Cimaroli (1687–1771) and 15 by Bellotto – was sent to England, arriving at Castle Howard in Yorkshire by June 1740. Only three paintings by Bellotto remain at Castle Howard: a number of paintings from the series were destroyed by fire in 1940 and others have been sold (Beddington 2010–11, p. 45).

21 On Zanetti's role in Bellotto's career see Kowalczyk 2012. Smith served as British consul in Venice from 1744 to 1760.

22 Letter dated 3 June 1740: 'vous me ferez grande grace de m'en ordonner pour faire plaisir au Peintre qu'il les a fait, qui est le plus bon homme du monde, et qui en est aussy abil, que Cannalletto' (Kowalczyk 1995, pp. 74, 76, n. 43).

23 'un pittore che imita estremamente la maniera di Canaletto, fa' forse l'acqua molto meglio di lui, ma non à la finitezza sua' (Kowalczyk 1995, pp. 73, 75–6, n. 38).

24 *The Grand Canal from the Palazzo Foscari towards the Carità*, 1740. Oil on canvas, 101 x 162 cm, Nationalmuseum, Stockholm; Kowalczyk 2001, fig. 1. The Crown Prince Frederick Christian visited Venice from 21 December 1739 to 11 June 1740, during which time he sat to Rosalba Carriera (1673–1757) for a pastel portrait and a special regatta was held in his honour, as memorialised by Michele Marieschi. In Bellotto's painting in Stockholm the prince is probably to be identified with the elegantly dressed young man stepping out from the canopied doorway of Palazzo Foscari, where he is known to have resided (Kowalczyk 1999, pp. 199–201 and Kowalczyk in Turin 2008, cat. 4, p. 62).

25 Datable to about 1723, two of these are now in Ca' Rezzonico, Venice, and the other two in the Museo Nacional Thyssen-Bornemisza, Madrid (Beddington 2010–11, p. 22).

26 Kozakiewicz 1972, vol. 2, nos 271, 277. See Frank 2001, p. 28. Zanetti certainly knew the Prince of Liechtenstein personally and in 1751 gave him a volume of his own engravings (Kowalczyck 2012, p. 26).

27 Bellotto arrived in Florence between May and August 1740, departed sometime in the autumn of that year, and returned on his way to Rome two years later (Kowalczyk 2012). For Gerini he painted two pairs of pictures: the first dates from Bellotto's 1740 trip to Florence (Alfred Beit Foundation, Russborough House; Kozakiewicz 1972, vol. 2, nos 52, 56) and the other was probably executed slightly later, based on drawings from the earlier trip (about 1742–3; Fitzwilliam Museum, Cambridge; Kozakiewicz 1972, vol. 2, nos 54, 55). In 1740 Bellotto also painted a pair of Florentine views for a close friend of Gerini's, Marchese Vincenzo Riccardi (1704–1752), now in the Museum of Fine Arts, Budapest (Kozakiewicz 1972, vol. 2, nos 53, 57).

28 Bellotto no doubt encountered the Florentine painter Giuseppe Zocchi (about 1717–1767), whom Gerini employed from 1734 to 1740 and who was engaged in producing a series of 26 engraved views of Florence. The Venetian's spacious and perspectival views of the city seem to have influenced Zocchi, rather than the other way around (see Kowalczyk 2012, pp. 27–30).

29 While the print collector Pierre-Jean Mariette (1694–1774) considered Bellotto a 'worthy pupil of his uncle' ('digne élève de son oncle'), Alexandre de Vesme (1854–1923) described him as Canaletto's

'formidable rival' ('le rival redoutable'; Vesme 1906, p. 489).

30 On the role of Antonio Visentini's *Prospectus Magni Canalis Venetiarum*, first published in 1735, in boosting Canaletto's fame internationally see Beddington 2010–11, p. 24. Bellotto's extensive collection of prints (including those of his own creation) was obliterated when his Dresden apartment was destroyed during the Prussian bombardment of 1760. The loss of these prints and his printing plates – a key source of income for him – left him in despair: 'impedito il Proseguimento della mia Interpresa di Stampe fate di tutta Dresda e di Pirna, e mi fa perdere Ogni Speranza' ('prevented from continuing with my enterprise of prints of all of Dresden and of Pirna, it makes me lose all hope'), as noted in the Appendix to his 'Catalogo dei Danni' (see n. 1 above).

31 The eight etchings, printed from individual plates on a single large-format sheet, are signed in variations of 'Bernardo Bellotti detto Canaletto' (Kupferstichkabinett, Staatliche Kunstsammlungen, Dresden; see Gottdang in Munich 2014–15, cat. 32, pp. 214–15). On Bellotto's pseudonym and the use of diminutive nicknames in Venice, see Kowalczyk 2016–17, p. 37, n. 25.

32 Bellotto's next three children all died young and of his five daughters born between 1748 and 1757, only three survived to adulthood. In addition to providing for his family, Bellotto had the responsibility of his mother and younger brother Pietro since his father had abandoned them (Kowalczyk 1995, p. 77, doc. 9; Rottermund 2005a, p. 16).

33 A related drawing of *Piazza San Giovanni in Laterano* (1743, Royal Collection), believed to have been done by Bellotto in preparation for this painting, has the obelisk positioned just right of centre: although the drawing is classified as Canaletto's by the Royal Collection, an attribution to Bellotto was first proposed by Beddington and Chapman in Venice 2001, pp. 47 and 60, and has been taken up more recently by, for example, Kowalczyk in Milan 2016–17, cats 47 and 48, pp. 152–5. Bellotto's *The Entry of the Polish Ambassador Count Jerzy Ossoliński to Rome in 1633* (1779; National Museum, Wrocław) also has a centrally placed obelisk; Kozakiewicz 1972, vol. 2, no. 430.

34 The discrepancy in size between the two main buildings is enhanced in the painting, compared to the preparatory drawing in Darmstadt, Hessisches Landesmuseum, where the woman leaning out of the window is also omitted (see Kowalczyk in Munich 2014–15, cat. 23, pp. 196–7; Kozakiewicz 1972, vol. 2, nos 65, 66).

35 Kozakiewicz 1972, vol. 2, no. 146.

36 Kozakiewicz 1972, vol. 2, no. 77. The other painting Bellotto exhibited was a Venetian view of the 'Chiovere di San Giovanni Evangelista', now lost (see Bowron in Venice and Houston 2001, cat. 20, p. 100, n. 9, and Succi 2011, p. 34).

37 Kozakiewicz 1972, vol. 2, no. 78; Kowalczyk in Munich 2014–15, cat. 24, pp. 198–9.

38 Kozakiewicz 1972, vol. 2, nos 92, 93. Although this figure of an artist cannot be firmly identified with Bellotto on grounds of physical resemblance, it is widely assumed to be a self portrait. The corpulent figure conversing with him is said to be Filippo Juvarra (1678–1736), the architect largely responsible for the redesign of the city of Turin, even though he was long dead by the time this picture was painted (see Wagener 2014–15, p. 118).

39 Kozakiewicz 1972, vol. 2, nos 98, 101.

40 Canaletto may have set his sights on England due to the diminishing number of international visitors to Venice as a consequence of the War of the Austrian Succession, which had reached Italy in 1742. In June 1749 George Vertue (1684–1756) wrote in his notebooks that Canaletto 'dos [sic] not produce works so well done as those of Venice or other parts of Italy ... especially his figures in his works done here, are apparently much inferior to those done abroad ... his water & his skys at no time excellent or with natural freedom', leading to conjecture that he was not 'the veritable Cannelleti of Venice' (presumably due to the confusion arising from Bellotto adopting the same nickname) and that, at the very least, Canaletto had an unknown assistant (Vertue 1933–4, p. 149).

41 Bellotto's annual salary of 1,750 thalers was almost double that granted to established court painters Johann Alexander Thiele (1685–1752), who earned around 1,000 thalers, and Christian Wilhelm Ernst Dietrich (1712–1774), who earned as little as 400 thalers (see Thoma 2014–15, p. 70, n. 63; Henning 2011, p. 15). Bellotto was also awarded a gold snuffbox, set with diamonds, and 300 louis d'or (gold coins).

42 For Bellotto's first Dresden period, see Kozakiewicz 1972, vol. 1, pp. 79–108 and vol. 2, pp. 107–92.

43 Kozakiewicz 1972, vol. 2, no. 167.

44 Between 1747 and 1755 Bellotto painted 13 views of Dresden and 8 of Pirna for Brühl, for which he was never remunerated. Fifteen out of the twenty-one works were bought by Catherine the Great, Empress of Russia, in 1768 and these are now divided between the Hermitage, St Petersburg, and Pushkin Museum, Moscow (Kozakiewicz 1972, vol. 1, p. 102).

45 Kozakiewicz 1972, vol. 2, no. 140. Brühl's palace was listed as the main subject of this view in the 1754 inventory of the royal picture gallery (Weber in Venice and Houston 2001, cat. 39, p. 148; Thoma 2014–15, p. 60).

46 See Wagener in Munich 2014–15, cats 38 and 39, pp. 226–9.

47 For their identification see ibid., p. 228.

48 Manikowska 2012, pp. 33, 34.

49 His daughters were Maria Anna Henrica Isabella (baptised 1748), Maria Josepha Friedrica (baptised 1750); Antonia Friedrica (baptised 1751), Christiana Xaveria (baptised 1752) and Theresia Francisca Florentia (baptised 1757): see Venice and Houston 2001, pp. xii, 268–9. On the portraits of Augustus III and Maria Josepha in Bellotto's apartment and his extensive library containing texts on diplomacy, the European courts and famous rulers, see Manikowska 2012, pp. 32, 34.

50 Hundreds of drawings are listed in Bellotto's 'Catalogo dei Danni' (see n. 1 above): 400 loose sheets with figure drawings; an album with 638 drawings by various authors (including Bellotto himself); 513 sheets with 'Abozzi di Pittura' (presumably compositional drawings for his paintings); an album with 215 drawings of both real and imaginary places; and an album with 304 drawings of figures 'fatti dal Naturale' (that is, drawn from life). See Manikowska 2012, p. 34, n. 17; Kowalczyk 2016–17, p. 17; and Marinelli 2016–17, p. 46.

51 The decrees, certified by Brühl, were addressed to a local administrator named Crusius, who was commanded to render assistance and not 'in any way obstruct' Bellotto from working 'around the mountain fortress of Königstein' (Weber 2001, p. 16, citing Schmidt 2000, pp. 39–40); see Chiswell's essay in this volume (p. 34).

52 Kozakieweicz 1972, vol. 2, no. 220.

53 In the picture cabinet of his Dresden apartment, Bellotto had 22 views of Dresden, Pirna and Königstein, all by his hand, of the same dimensions and displayed in identical gilt frames. These views presumably replicated those that he had produced for Augustus III and Brühl, though on a smaller scale (see Manikowska 2012, p. 33). What function they may have served is unclear: were they produced as *modelli* (or presentation pieces), to be scaled up into the larger views, or did they serve as *ricordi* (visual records), to facilitate the making of painted replicas or engravings?

54 Galli Bibiena, who worked alongside Bellotto in Dresden from 1748 to 1754, had previously designed decorations for the Vienna opera (1742) and the interior of the theatre in Bayreuth (1747–8). See Frank 2001, p. 29, and Rottermund 2005a, p. 24.

55 For Bellotto's activity in Vienna, see Kozakiewicz 1972, vol. 1, pp. 113–202.

56 Thoma 2014–15, p. 54.

57 This is particularly true of the figures which, in some cases, appear rather clumsy.

58 Frank 2001, pp. 29–31.

59 Kozakiewicz 1972, vol. 2, no. 280. Kerber 2017–18a, p. 8.

60 Letter dated 4 January 1761 (Sächsisches Staatsarchiv, Hauptstaatsarchiv, Dresden; reproduced by Wagener in Munich 2014–15, p. 145, fig. 116). Her comment regarding Bellotto's conduct implies that he had a reputation for being difficult, something perhaps confirmed in a letter written by Bellotto's estranged father Lorenzo to Brühl on 16 November 1754, which refers to the fact that 'The whole city [of Dresden] knows the beastly mind of my son' ('Tutta la città conosci il cervello bestiale die esso mio figlio'; Kozakiewicz 1972, vol. 1, p. 83, citing Fritzsche 1936, p. 16).

61 Maria Antonia was clearly a supporter of Bellotto: a few years later she would underwrite his salary at the Academy of Fine Arts in Dresden (Wagener 2014–15, pp. 132, 142, n. 142).

62 Kozakiewicz 1972, vol. 2, nos 290, 292, 294.

63 Bellotto's paintings seem to have been 'made to measure' and set into the room's wooden panelling from the very beginning (see Quaeitzsch 2014–15).

64 The Nymphenburg Palace was also where an opera by Maria Antonia, a talented composer and musician, was performed the previous year (*Talestri, regina delle Amazzoni*, 1760).
65 See Thoma 2014–15, pp. 65–7, and Schumacher in Munich 2014–15, cats 51–3, pp. 250–9.
66 Schumacher in Munich 2014–15, under cat. 51, pp. 250 and 252, fig. 144.
67 The Appendix to his 'Catalogo dei Danni' is dated February 1762 (see n. 1 above). Kozakiewicz 1972, vol. 1, p. 135; Wagener 2014–15, p. 141, n. 132. On his return to Dresden, Bellotto sought (without success) an outstanding payment of 4,200 thalers from Brühl's heirs for his 21 views.
68 Kozakiewicz 1972, vol. 2, no. 301, where the painting is listed as lost.
69 Hagedorn openly disliked Bellotto and once wrote, 'He loses no opportunity of bringing up the subject of his dreary art and his enormous family' (Kozakiewicz 1972, vol. 1, p. 135, citing Stübel 1911, p. 479). Hagedorn's prejudice against Bellotto cannot have been helped by the fact that the latter could not speak German – his son Lorenzo acted as interpreter during classes – and in 1765 Hagedorn remarked upon Bellotto's poor command of the German language (Kozakiewicz 1972, vol. 1, p. 135; Wagener 2014–15, pp. 132, 142, n. 143).
70 Frederick Christian succeeded Augustus III as Elector of Saxony and King of Poland but his 74-day reign came to an end on 17 December 1763. His son and successor, Frederick Augustus I (1750–1827), was only 13 at the time, so Maria Antonia served as regent (with her younger son Franz Xavier) until 1768.
71 Bellotto's salary was paid out of the privy purse (see Wagener 2014–15, p. 132).
72 Kozakiewicz 1972, vol. 2, no. 296.
73 See the account of the first Dresden Academy exhibition cited by Kozakiewicz 1972, vol. 2, p. 265.
74 Of the three versions listed in Kozakiewicz (1972, vol. 2, nos 333, 334, 334a) – now in the Royal Castle, Warsaw, Terruzzi Collection, Bordighera, and Agnes Etherington Art Centre, Queen's University, Kingston (Ontario) – only the Warsaw painting is signed. For a detailed discussion and proposed chronology of the three versions, see Bowron 2011.
75 On the identification of the buildings and other motifs, such as the bas-relief and vases, see Bowron 2011, p. 3, and Kowalczyk in Milan 2016–17, cat. 82, pp. 228–31.
76 Both Bowron and Kowalczyk believe the man in red to be Bellotto himself (Bowron 2011, p. 10; Kowalczyk in Milan 2016–17, cat. 82, pp. 228, 230, noting the figure's similarity to that in a painting by Canaletto). The young man behind him is most likely Bellotto's servant Checo (Francesco) and the ecclesiastic carrying a bundle of papers (or drawings) has been variously identified (see Bowron 2011, p. 3, citing Kozakiewicz 1972, vol. 2, p. 264; Kowalczyk in Milan 2016–17, cat. 82, p. 230). Other scholars have questioned whether Bellotto would have been so arrogant as to represent himself as a Venetian procurator (Wagener 2014–15, pp. 132–3). The catalogue accompanying the 1765 Academy exhibition did not mention a self portrait in Bellotto's painting of 'idealised architecture with a large forecourt and many pleasant figures' but it did note that the artist had portrayed himself in the allegory showing the Temple of Love (Gottdang 2014–15, pp. 96–8). The sash denotes him as a knight of the Order of the Golden Stole, an honour normally bestowed by the senate on an ambassador returning to Venice – as, for example, in Nazario Nazari's *Portrait of Andrea Tron*, about 1750, in the National Gallery, London (see Kerber 2017–18b, p. 22, citing Grevembroch 1981, vol. 1, no. 42).
77 'Architecture de fantaisie, ou l'auteur s'est peint dans l'habit de noble Vénitien' (Gottdang 2014–15, pp. 96–8, citing Mańkowski 1932, no. 461). Presumably there was some commercial gain in replicating this composition, and this would only have made sense if the main protagonist was the artist himself. Bowron has suggested that Bellotto may have painted the Warsaw version last, to impress the Polish king to whom it was presented (Bowron 2011, p. 10).
78 Horace, *Ars Poetica*, lines 9–10. The quote also appears in a pen-and-ink drawing relating to this composition (about 1762–5; Hessisches Landesmuseum, Darmstadt; see Kozakiewicz 1972, vol. 2, no. 335, and Bowron 2011, p. 10), as well as much earlier, on a sheet of etchings dating from the early 1740s (Gottdang in Munich 2014–15, cat. 32, pp. 214–15).
79 For Bellotto's Warsaw period, see Kozakiewicz 1972, vol. 1, pp. 153–202, and vol. 2, pp. 297–391.
80 Many of the paintings acquired for Poniatowski by Noël Desenfans (1744–1807) and Francis Bourgeois (1753–1811) went on to form the core of the collection at Dulwich Picture Gallery, London. Poniatowski attempted three times to found an artists' academy in Warsaw (see Rottermund 2001, p. 33).
81 To secure an extension to his leave, Bellotto informed Hagedorn that he was engaged on painting frescoes. This was almost certainly a lie, fabricated to ensure that permission to stay in Warsaw would be granted, for frescoing cannot be easily interrupted while in progress (Kozakiewicz 1972, vol. 1, p. 156).
82 In addition to his salary, Bellotto received 150 ducats for keeping his household and 120 for carriage and horses (Rottermund 2001, p. 33).
83 Rizzi 1991, p. 20.
84 Four of the sixteen views of Rome are jointly signed (see Kozakiewicz 1972, vol. 1, pp. 186–7).
85 The castle was largely rebuilt following its destruction by bombing during the Second World War and Bellotto's paintings, which had been removed for safekeeping, were not rehung in their original locations until 1983 (Rottermund 2001, pp. 37, 39, n. 19; Rottermund 2005b).
86 Kozakiewicz 1972, vol. 2, no. 399. The man seated before the canvas, with his back turned, had traditionally been identified as Bellotto, but Rottermund has convincingly argued in favour of the artist's son Lorenzo, with Bellotto being the more corpulent figure gesticulating towards Warsaw beyond (Rottermund in Vienna 2005, cat. 33, pp. 169–70).
87 The first version of this composition, painted in 1776, was rejected by Poniatowski and is now in the National Museum, Poznań (Kozakiewicz 1972, vol. 2, no. 428), while the second, painted in 1778, is still in situ in the Royal Castle, Warsaw (Kozakiewicz 1972, vol. 2, no. 429; see Rottermund 2001, p. 36). Bellotto places himself prominently in the lower right corner, dressed in an elegant red embroidered coat and conspicuously revealing the hilt of a sword. He is flanked by his daughters, even though they only joined him in Warsaw in 1768, four years after the event depicted took place.
88 Wagener 2014–15, p. 136.
89 In the catalogue of the royal collection the painting was described as 'Tableau non achévé et le dernier de ce maitre, sur le devant 2 hermites' ('Unfinished painting, the last by the master, with two hermits on the front'; Kozakiewicz 1972, vol. 1, p. 165, vol. 2, no. 435).
90 Kozakiewicz 1972, vol. 2, no. 412.

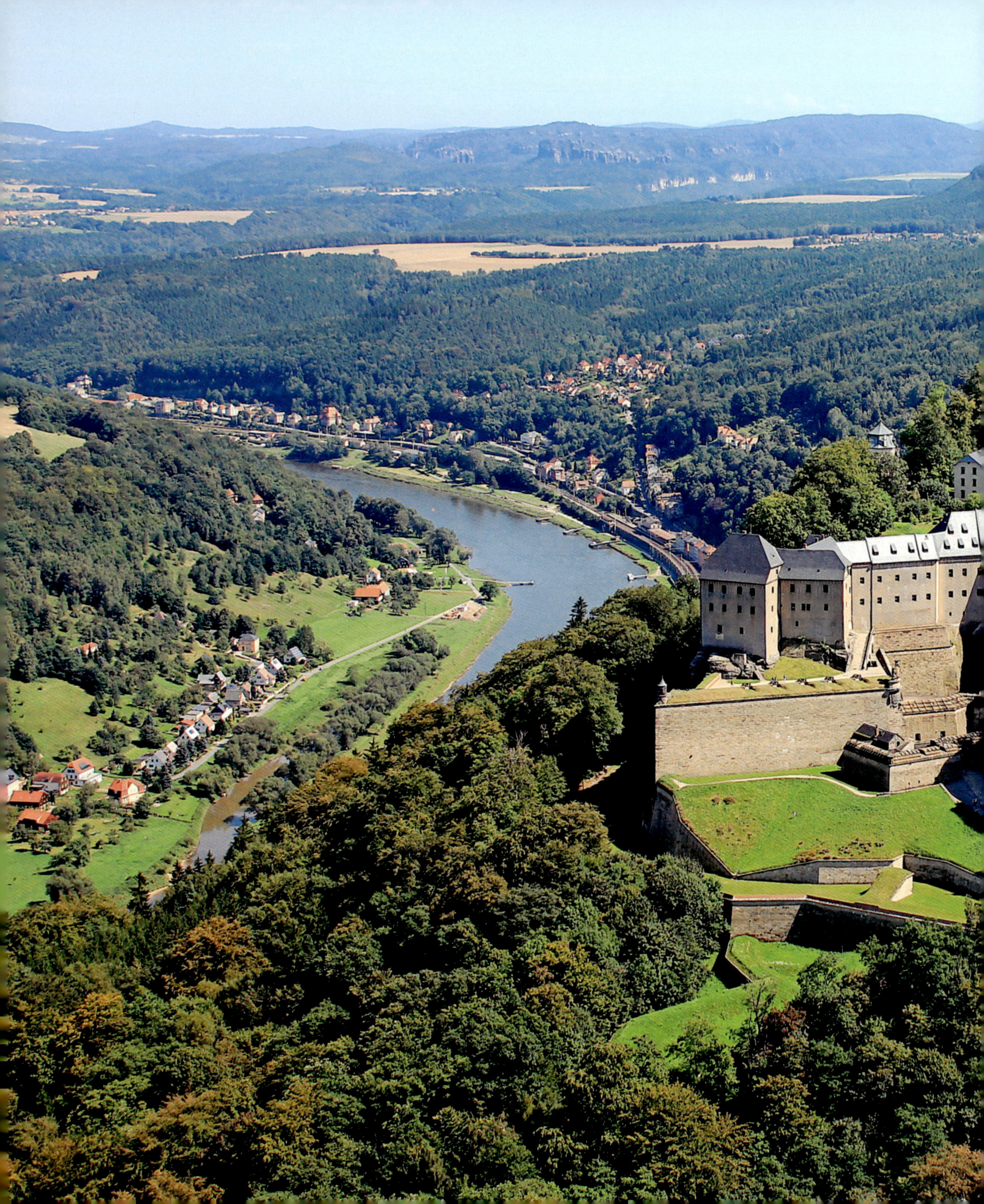

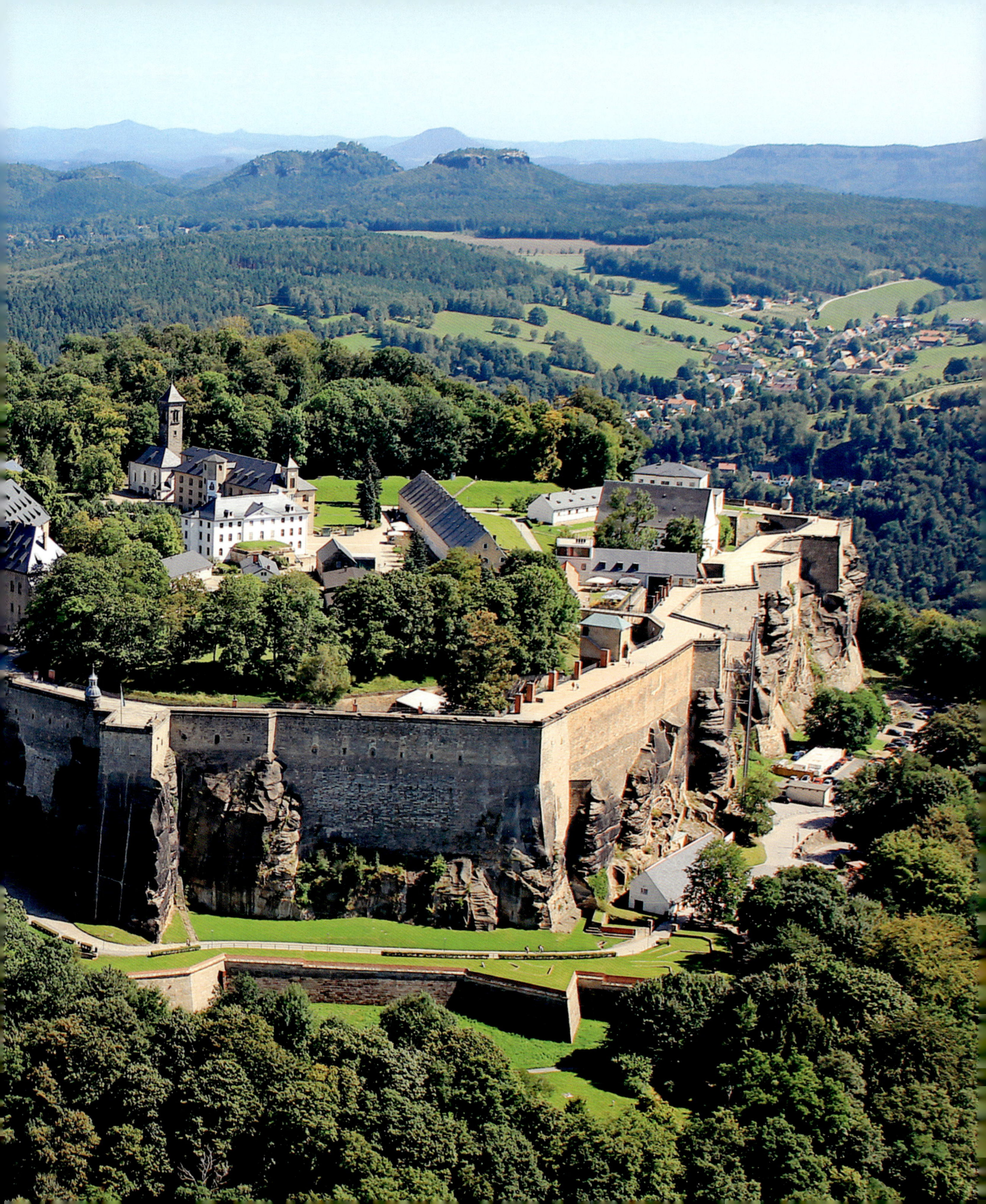

BERNARDO BELLOTTO AND THE FORTRESS OF KÖNIGSTEIN

Lucy Chiswell

When Stefan Kozakiewicz published his catalogue of the complete works of Bernardo Bellotto in 1972, *The Fortress of Königstein from the North-West* (cat. 2) had not yet come to light.[1] At the time of the painting's rediscovery in 1991, it was recognised as one of five views of the Saxon fortress that Bellotto produced between 1756 and 1758, towards the end of his first stay in Dresden.[2] Bellotto had arrived in the city a decade or so earlier and by 1748 he was officially employed as court painter to Frederick Augustus II, Elector of Saxony and King of Poland (as Augustus III). By the time these pictures were painted, Bellotto had already produced views of the city of Dresden and the nearby town of Pirna for his royal patron. Kozakiewicz was the first to propose that the Königstein views were also made for the king but, unlike the earlier paintings, they never reached the royal collection.[3]

On 29 August 1756, Frederick the Great of Prussia crossed the Saxon frontier with his army, imposing himself on Saxony and instigating the Third Silesian War between Prussia and Austria (together with its allies), in turn initiating the Seven Years' War across Europe. The Prussian advance on Dresden resulted in Augustus retreating to the fortress of Königstein on 3 September with his sons Franz Xavier and Charles (1733–1796) and the prime minister of Saxony, Count Heinrich von Brühl. On 17 October, the Saxon forces surrendered and Augustus III fled with his sons to Warsaw three days later, followed by Brühl. It is unclear whether Bellotto's paintings of Königstein were completed before the artist left Dresden in the winter of 1758, but the appearance of two of the views at a Christie's sale in London in the spring of 1778 suggests the paintings may have been sold independently and made their way to England during Bellotto's lifetime (see pp. 42–3).[4]

THE 'KING'S STONE'

Königstein, literally meaning 'king's stone', had served as an important military outpost for Saxon rulers since the beginning of the fifteenth century (fig. 14). Located

Fig. 13 Photograph of the fortress of Königstein today (previous spread)

Fig. 14 Plan of the fortress of Königstein with key, after 1743 (modified image). Pen, brush, ink and watercolour on paper, 46.5 x 63 cm. Saxon State Office for Conservation of Monuments, Dresden, ZKW 453

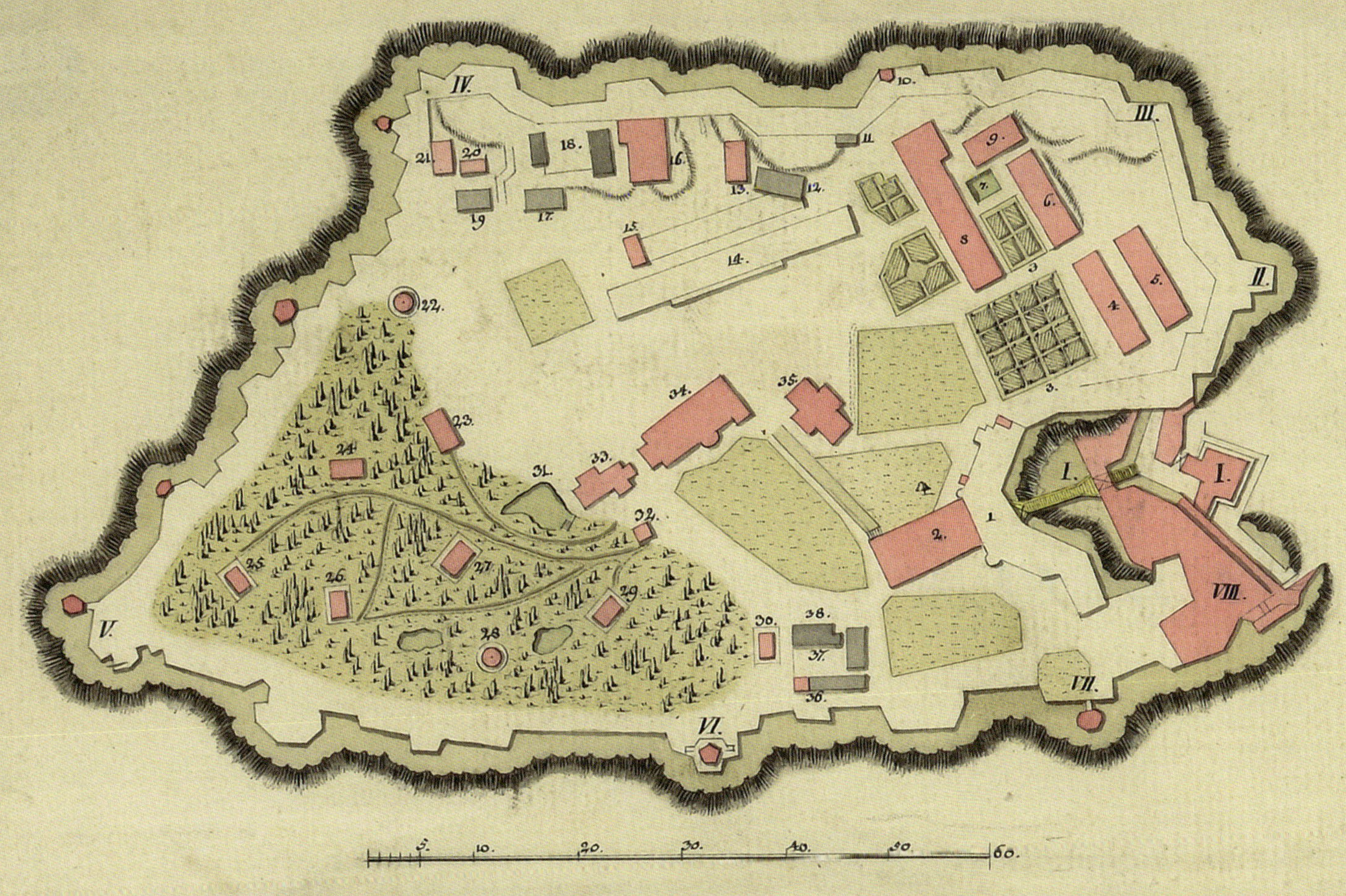

Explication derer Ziffern

I. Contre Garde nebst Sortie. II. Das Hornwerk. III. Hempels Eke, oder der Baer. IV. Zebels Eke. V. Königs Nase. VI. Die Friedrichs Burg. VII Das Rösßgen und VIII. Die Johann Georgen Burg.

1. Commendanten Hauß. 2. Der Helden Saal. 3. Commendanten Garten. 4. Vordere Casernen. 5. Hintere Casernen mit der Haupt Wacht. 6. Officiers Casernen. 7. Cisterne. 8. Mittel Caserne 9. Proviant Hauß. 10. Der Krannicht. 11. Neue Backerey. 12 Proviant Schuppen. 13. Fleischer Hauß. 14. Alte Caserne. 15. Vieh Stall. 16. Zeug Hauß. 17. Artillerie Schuppen. 18. Bau Gefangnen Behaltnis. 19. Wagen Schuppen. 20. Back Hauß. 21. Kleine Caserne. 22. Alter Pulver Thurm. 23. Neuer Pulver Thurm. 24. Neuer Pulver Thurm. 25. Alter Pulver Thurm. 26. Neuer Pulver Thurm 27. Neuer Pulver Thurm. 28. Alter Pulver Thurm 29. et 30. Neue Pulver Thürme. 31. Cisternen 32 Sprizen Hauß. 33 Die Kirche. 34. Brunnen Hauß. 35. Die Magdalenen Burg. 36. Das Wasch Hauß. 37. Der Zimmer Hoff. 38. Die Alte Kirche.

approximately 25 miles south-east of the city of Dresden, in the picturesque Elbe Valley, it provided both refuge and respite for rulers in flight of the Saxon capital. During its 800-year history, this colossal plateau of rock, 9.5 hectares in breadth and 361 metres above sea level, has served many functions: a medieval castle, a monastery, a military fortress, a royal retreat, a state prison, a safehouse for the royal art collection and archives, a prisoner-of-war camp, a military hospital and a youth detention centre.[5]

The earliest known reference to Königstein dates from 7 May 1241, when a decree was sealed by King Wenceslas I of Bohemia (1205–1253) '*in lapide regis*', or 'on the stone of the king'. A medieval castle probably already existed by this date, but the establishment of the Kaiserburg, the 'emperor's castle' (now the Georgenburg), probably resulted from the stay of Charles IV (1316–1378), Holy Roman Emperor and King of Bohemia, in 1359. The site remained part of the territories of the Kingdom of Bohemia until the early fifteenth century, when Königstein was seized by the House of Wettin, a noble Bohemian family.[6] The Wettin dynasty became Electors of Saxony in 1423 and the castle was conferred into their name after the Saxon-Bohemian borders were established in 1459. Following a brief spell as a small Celestine monastery under George the Bearded (1471–1539), Duke of Saxony and a committed Roman Catholic, Königstein was transformed from castle to fortress. This was prompted by the installation of a well between 1563 and 1569, under the instruction of Elector Augustus (1526–1586), which allowed it to function as an autonomous site. Though Augustus investigated the feasibility of fortifying Königstein, it was not until June 1588 that his son, Elector Christian I (1560–1591), ordered his master builder, Paul Buchner (1531–1607), to start working on plans for a fortress, with major works commencing in spring of the following year.

It was during these final decades of the sixteenth century and the early seventeenth century that the site underwent significant change. After this flurry of construction, Königstein became a protective fortress and a place of royal leisure pursuits and festivities. In the eighteenth century, Augustus II ('Augustus the Strong', 1670–1733) was keen to make his mark at Königstein as he had done in the city of Dresden: he improved the defensive works and gateway, constructed new barracks, and transformed the Friedrichsburg into a magnificent baroque pavilion. The year after the elector's death, a document records the intention of his son and heir, Augustus III, to use the fortress to store artistic treasures and archives to protect them against the threat of war. Just over 20 years later, at the start of the Seven Years' War, the royal picture galleries in Dresden were shut; with the city in danger, the entire royal collection was packed up in 1759 and dispatched to various locations, with the 'good and middle supply' of paintings sent to Königstein for safe keeping.[7] The same military threat had spurred Augustus III to improve the defensive capabilities of the fortress, notably by building the Flèche, an outwork on the north side from which arrows could be fired. This project was overseen by Count Rutowski (1702–1764), half-brother to Augustus III and commander-in-chief of the Saxon army. The scaffolding in Bellotto's two exterior views from the north shows that construction was clearly underway when he was making drawings of Königstein before the Prussian invasion of 1756.

The site went on to gain further significance during the Napoleonic Wars, when Saxony came under French occupation. In 1813 Königstein was visited and admired by Napoleon Bonaparte (1769–1821), and the surrounding area became an important part of his defence strategy against the Russian-Prussian alliance.[8] By the nineteenth century, a small, independent garrison city existed at Königstein, inhabited by permanently stationed officers, soldiers, civilian officials and their families, all of whom were under the jurisdiction of the commandant. During these years, the fortress also functioned as a state prison, a prisoner-of-war camp and a military hospital, and the threat of another Prussian invasion required its use as a store for the Saxon state treasury, archives and works of art once again. Technological advances in the second half of the century saw further attempts to modernise the fortress, but these were soon outdated, and during the First World War the military importance of Königstein diminished; it reverted to functioning primarily as a prison camp for French and Russian officers and soldiers. The fortress was eventually disarmed in the summer of 1920, and during the Second World War it served again as a prisoner-of-war camp and a depository for state treasures. On 29 May 1955 Königstein was declared a museum by the Ministry of Culture of the German Democratic Republic. Today it is an open-air military history museum and exhibition venue at the heart of the Saxon Switzerland National Park. This area of outstanding natural beauty – named 'Saxon Switzerland' after the dramatic outcrops of rock that punctuate the landscape – spans 93 square kilometres and was granted

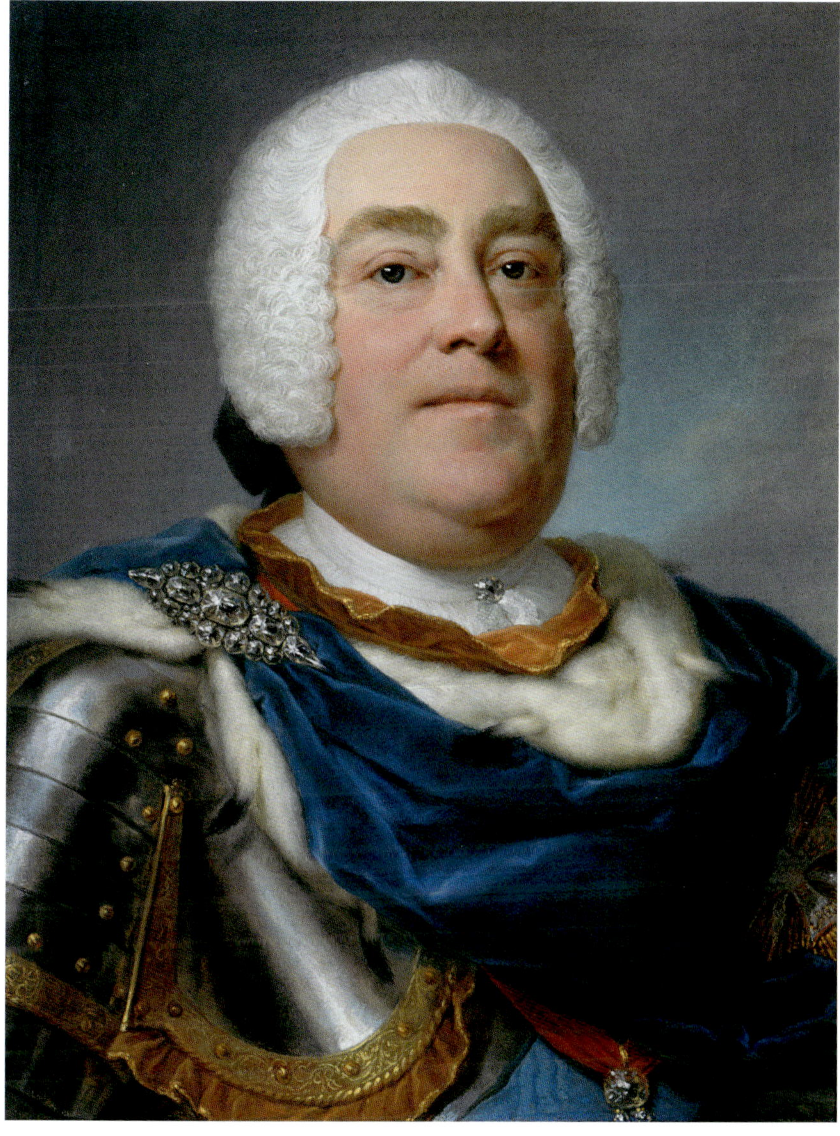

Fig. 15 Anton Raphael Mengs (1728–1779). *Frederick Augustus II (1696–1763), Elector of Saxony and King of Poland (as Augustus III)*, 1745. Pastel on paper, 55.5 x 42 cm. Gemäldegalerie Alte Meister, Staatliche Kunstsammlungen Dresden

national park status in 1990. Its 700 sandstone summits, forests and winding river valley make it one of Germany's most popular outdoor tourist destinations (fig. 13).

A ROYAL PATRON

Frederick Augustus II succeeded his father as Elector of Saxony in 1733, and in January 1734 he was crowned Augustus III, King of Poland and Grand Duke of Lithuania (fig. 15). Electors of Saxony had been collecting works of art since the second half of the sixteenth century, but it was not until the reigns of Augustus II and Augustus III that the royal collection achieved its full breadth and magnificence. The Electorate of Saxony was one of the richest territories in the Holy Roman Empire (a result of commerce and abundant natural resources) and an impressive art collection was a means by which it could assert itself on the world stage. Augustus II had been responsible for several major building projects in the city of Dresden, including Matthäus Daniel Pöppelmann's (1662–1736) Zwinger Palace (1710–32) and George Bähr's (1666–1738)

Protestant church, the Frauenkirche (1726–43), and he also assembled an outstanding collection of antiquities, porcelain and works of art.[9] Following his father's example, Augustus III funded architectural projects, supported the theatre, opera and ballet, and amassed a spectacular art collection. Augustus III purchased historic works and employed artists from all over Europe, favouring Venetian art in particular, owning paintings by the Renaissance masters Titian, Tintoretto, Veronese, Palma Vecchio and Jacopo Bassano, as well as works by contemporary Venetian artists Rosalba Carriera and Bellotto's celebrated uncle, Giovanni Antonio Canal, better known today as Canaletto.[10]

According to Pierre-Jean Mariette (1694–1774), the connoisseur, dealer and agent to Augustus III, Bellotto was only invited to Dresden because Canaletto was away in England at the time.[11] Yet by the 1740s Bellotto was in fact an accomplished painter in his own right, and already had independent ties to the royal court in Saxony. In 1739–40 he had been commissioned to paint a large canvas commemorating the visit to Venice of Augustus III's eldest son, Frederick Christian (see p. 13).[12] Bellotto's association with the art agent Anton Maria Zanetti the Elder and Count Francesco Algarotti, connoisseur, diplomat and acquaintance of Canaletto, both of whom had close ties with the Saxon court, may have prompted his invitation to Dresden. Algarotti, whose brother Bonomo had been a witness at Bellotto's wedding, visited Dresden in 1742 and encouraged the king to expand his collection of contemporary Venetian art, returning again in 1746, shortly before Bellotto's arrival. That same year, Pietro Maria Guarienti (about 1700–1753) was appointed gallery inspector of the Italian paintings in the royal collection. Guarienti, who was originally from Verona but spent 20 years living and working in Venice, had acted as godparent at the baptism of Bellotto's daughter, Francesca Elisabetta, on 5 December 1745.

Bellotto arrived in Dresden in the early summer of 1747, with his wife, young son Lorenzo (b. 1744) and servant Checo (Francesco). He started working for the king immediately. By 1748 he had been appointed court painter and was already working on 14 views of the city of Dresden for the king, a series he replicated on the same scale for Brühl.[13] Bellotto was paid 1,750 thalers, the highest salary ever to have been awarded to a painter working at court and significantly higher than the sums afforded to his fellow court painters Johann Alexander Thiele and Christian Wilhelm Ernst Dietrich. The challenge of depicting the city, its river and large bridge was not unprecedented for Bellotto, who had trained and worked in Venice and spent much of the 1740s painting views of Italian cities, including Rome, Florence, Verona and Turin. Five years later, by 26 April 1753, Bellotto was at work on 11 views of the town of Pirna, a small settlement not far from Dresden, strategically situated on the prosperous trade route of the river Elbe. The Dresden and Pirna paintings, together with two views of Verona and an architectural *capriccio*, amounting to 28 works in total, have remained part of Dresden's glorious artistic heritage in the collection of the Gemäldegalerie Alte Meister.[14]

FIVE SPECTACULAR VIEWS

The only known record of Bellotto's commission to paint the fortress of Königstein is a warrant dated 30 March 1756, authorised by Brühl and addressed to Crusius, a bailiff of the neighbouring town of Pirna, demanding that he and other officials assist Bellotto while he works on his drawings 'around the mountain fortress of Königstein' (fig. 16).[15] The preparatory drawings can therefore be dated to the spring and summer months before the Prussian invasion of Saxony on 29 August 1756. Though drawings of Königstein certainly existed, none are known to have survived.[16] Bellotto probably mapped out the composition with an initial sketch in situ, aided by a camera obscura, and also made separate, more detailed drawings of specific areas.[17] These drawings would then have been adjusted and combined in the studio, and the resulting design used as the final composition for the large-scale painting. Bellotto appears to have composed his paintings spatially, starting with the sky. He painted the staffage (the figures and animals that populate the scene) last, incorporating elements he may have drawn from life with those borrowed from engravings.[18]

It seems likely that Bellotto completed the five Königstein canvases before he left Dresden at the end of 1758.[19] Queen Maria Josepha (1699–1757) and several of her children had remained in Dresden after the Prussian invasion and a receipt issued by Bellotto for the first quarter of 1758 shows that he was still being paid by the state.[20] Bellotto's Königstein paintings are of almost identical size and format to the Dresden and Pirna views and were almost certainly intended to form part of the existing series, which was destined for the new picture

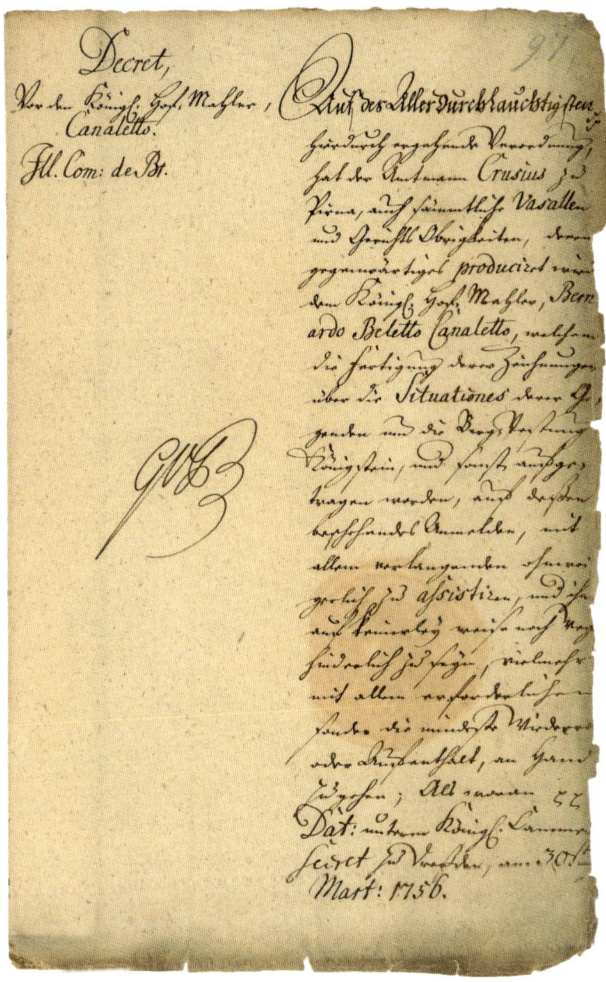

Fig. 16 Electoral decree giving Bellotto (here named 'Canaletto') privileged access to the fortress of Königstein, 30 March 1756. Saxon State Archives, Main State Archives, Dresden, 10024 Privy Council (Secret Archive), Loc. 8575/6, fol. 97

gallery in the former Stallgebäude (the Electors' Stables).[21] Unlike the Dresden and Pirna paintings, Bellotto did not replicate the views of Königstein for Brühl; he may not have been commissioned to do so (Brühl was absent from Dresden between 1756 and 1763), or perhaps personal circumstances prevented Bellotto from completing a second set.[22]

Before his departure from Dresden, Bellotto also completed etchings for all 14 of the Dresden views. He made five etchings of the Pirna views, which are undated, while the sixth can be dated to Bellotto's return to Dresden between 1761 and 1766. It was during his second stay in the city that Bellotto also produced etchings of the north-west and south-west views of Königstein (figs 19 and 20).[23] Since the early 1740s, when Canaletto started experimenting with etching, the medium had become an integral part of Bellotto's practice. Etchings allowed Bellotto to reproduce his views with exactitude, preserving them in perpetuity while also creating multiples for the open market. The retrospective inventory of his Dresden apartment laments that the destruction of his print studio and its contents during the Prussian bombardment is among the most significant of his losses. His unstable financial circumstances and the absence of his two main patrons perhaps encouraged him to start producing prints again when he returned to the city in 1761.

It is tempting to interpret Augustus's Königstein commission as responsive to the territorial unrest that was being experienced across Europe at this time. Was Bellotto's commemoration of this mighty fortress, recorded from five different viewpoints, intended to communicate the strength of Dresden's defence network? Bellotto's 11 views of the nearby town of Pirna were also dominated by the town's imposing medieval castle, Sonnenstein. While it may have been Augustus's intention to highlight the magnitude and strategic location of Königstein, Bellotto's views were a continuation of several earlier efforts by artists working at the Saxon court to memorialise the fortress for their royal patrons.

BELLOTTO'S KÖNIGSTEIN IN CONTEXT

By the time Bellotto arrived in Dresden, view painting was a firmly established genre, and had been since the middle of the sixteenth century. The architect and engineer Wilhelm Dilich (1571/2–1655) had been a notable contributor, leaving 130 drawings after his death depicting towns in the duchies of Saxony and Meissen. Among them was a schematic view of Königstein, drawn in 1626–9 from the banks of the river Elbe (fig. 17) and showing a detailed rendition of Königstein village at the base of the mountain. Seventeen of Dilich's views were used as models for a series of mural paintings at the royal palace in Dresden, but these had disappeared by the time Bellotto arrived in the capital, having been destroyed in a fire in 1701. Others went on to depict Königstein, as can be seen in the series of 12 engraved views published by Martin Engelbrecht

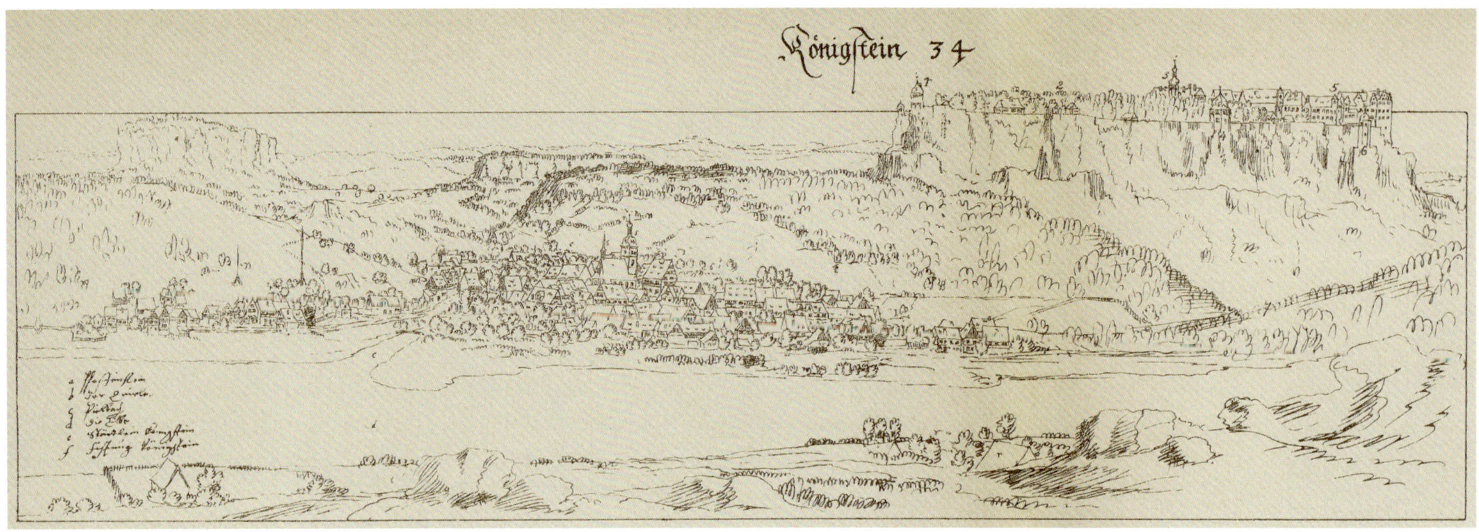

(1684–1756) which illustrate the main buildings inside the fortress (fig. 32).

Among the many native and foreign painters who worked in Dresden, the most significant for Bellotto was Johann Alexander Thiele, whose shoes it was assumed the young Venetian artist would fill. Originally from Erfurt, in what is now central Germany, Thiele was celebrated for his architectural and landscape views, the latter heavily inspired by Dutch Italianate painting of the previous century. He had been appointed *Prospektmaler* – a role at court dedicated to painting 'prospects' – by Augustus III in 1738, after having worked for Augustus II a decade or so earlier. In 1726 Thiele had produced six engraved views of the fortified landscape surrounding Dresden for Augustus II, including two views of Königstein. The composition of one of these engravings is loosely followed by Thiele in a painting of 1748 (fig. 18), completed when both he and Bellotto were in the service of Augustus III. Thiele's dramatic view, with its aerial perspective, elevates Königstein and its surroundings to an almost fantastical degree. The fortress and its neighbouring peak Lilienstein tower formidably over the river Elbe, which snakes its way through the wide, sweeping valley below. His exaggeration of scale and employment of warm pastel tones anticipate the glorification of nature by the German Romantics, rather than drawing on the naturalistic approach of many of the Dutch painters he so admired. Bellotto would of course have been aware of Thiele's painting, and his inclusion of Thiele's portrait in his first view of Dresden suggests the close working relationship between the two artists.[24]

Fig. 17 Wilhelm Dilich (1571/2–1655), *Königstein*, 1626–9 (reproduced as facsimile, 1907; original manuscript, with inv. Mscr.Dresd.J.291, vol. 3, damaged in 1945). From *Wilhelm Dilich: Pen-and-ink Drawings of Localities in Electoral Saxony and Meissen from 1626–1629*. Dresden: Meinhold, 1907, vol. 3, plate 34. Saxon State Library, State and University Library Dresden, RH 35217 D576-3

Though Bellotto's Königstein series sits within a long-standing tradition of view painting at the Saxon court, his innovative approach to the site was unprecedented. The five paintings comprise three exterior views, depicting the fortress from the north, north-west and south-west, and two prospects of the internal courtyards.[25] They show Bellotto's exceptional skill as a painter of both architecture and landscape, placing the magnificent stony fortress within its context of open plains and wooded valleys. The most striking development introduced by Bellotto was scale. Until this point, only his two views of Verona matched the Dresden canvases in size (most of which measure approximately 134 x 235 cm).[26] No artist had yet depicted the fortress as part of such grand, panoramic compositions, each of which interrogates different aspects of the site, both inside and out. The dramatic, expansive landscape surrounding Dresden must have had a significant impact on the Venetian painter who, until recently, had not ventured outside his native Italy. His training with Canaletto had taught him to paint using the theatrical effect of light and shadow, to meticulously record the cracks and dirt on building facades and to animate his scenes with groups of people. But Bellotto's Königstein views are a far cry from the glittering waters and layered *palazzi* of Venice. The exterior scenes show his inimitable skill as a view painter. Sharp perspective and dramatic chiaroscuro create the illusion of photographic clarity, but tufts of grass and clouds are described expressively with the flick of a brush. The fortress stands triumphant in earthy, pastoral compositions where green, grey and brown tones are only interrupted by vibrant darts of colour in the clothing of the countryfolk who populate the scene. Even the stark facades of his interior scenes are softened by grass and trees, and his *Courtyard with the Brunnenhaus* (cat. 5) is fronted by a small garden, planted with colourful roses and topiary. Unlike Thiele a decade earlier, Bellotto chooses to ground Königstein in nature, depicting the verdant environment, pale sky and sharp light with his characteristically cool tones.

It is no surprise that Bellotto looked to the great landscape painters of the seventeenth and eighteenth centuries for inspiration. Gregor J.M. Weber's enlightening studies have revealed how Bellotto repurposed animals and figures from pastoral scenes by Nicolaes Berchem (1620–1683) and Francesco Zuccarelli (1702–1788) for his Königstein paintings.[27] Certainly, the inventory of Bellotto's apartment confirms that he owned volumes containing 1,260 prints reproducing landscape paintings by Flemish and French masters, and more containing a thousand prints after German, Flemish and Dutch artists.[28] We can also assume that Bellotto was familiar

Fig. 18 Johann Alexander Thiele (1685–1752), *View of Königstein*, 1748. Oil on canvas, 105 x 150 cm. Staatliches Museum, Schwerin

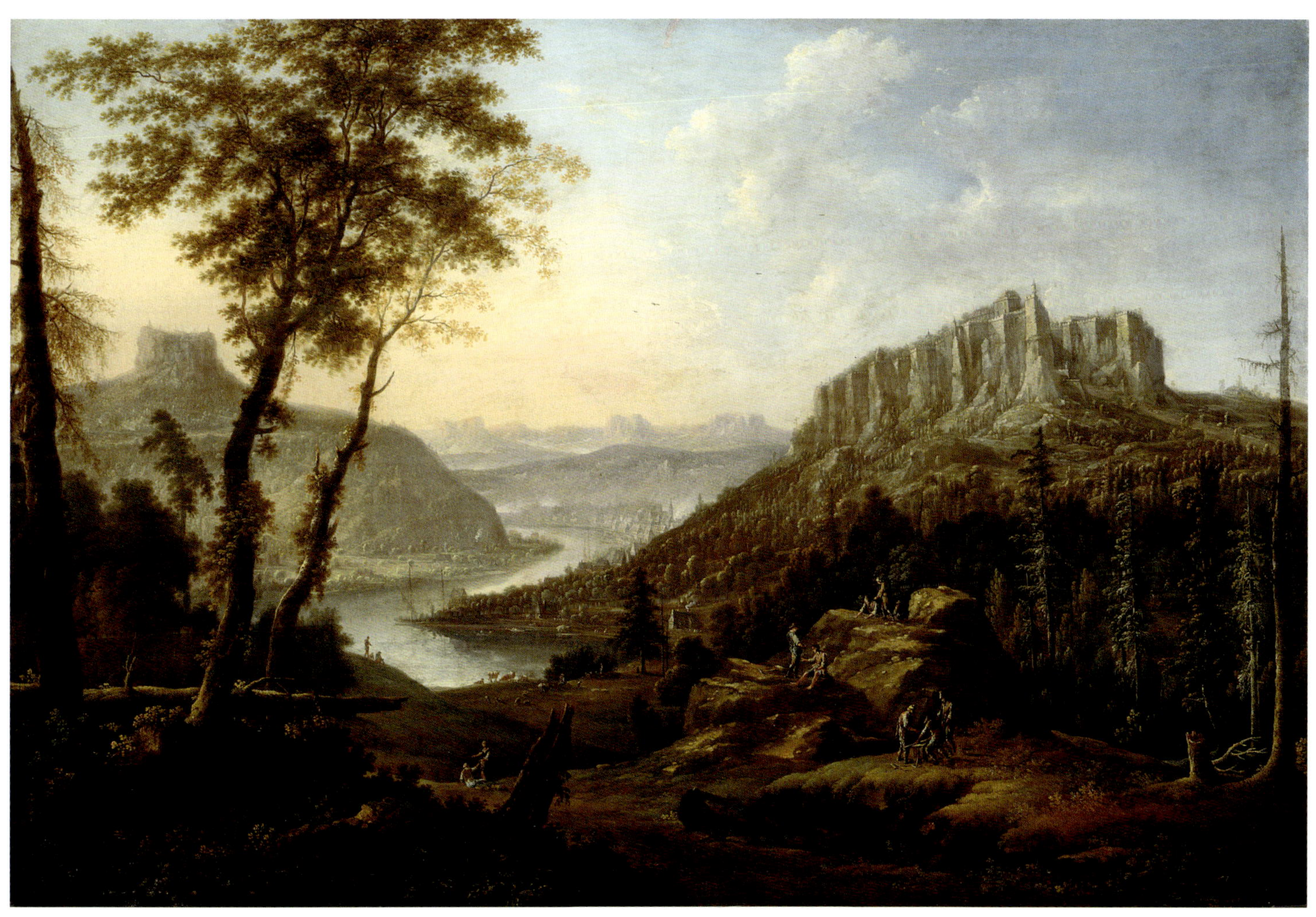

with the work of Jacob van Ruisdael (1628/9?–1682), whose textured skies, naturalistic landscapes and splintered branches permeate the Königstein views. While Bellotto may have known Ruisdael's paintings through copies or engravings, both Brühl and Augustus III had impressive examples of his work in their collections by the early 1750s. One such painting was a view of Castle Bentheim by Ruisdael, listed in the collection of Augustus III by 1754, in which Ruisdael exaggerates the scale of the castle by depicting it from a low viewpoint, integrating tiny figures into the landscape and counterbalancing it with a monumental sky (see also cat. 3).[29] As court artist, Bellotto would have had access to the paintings owned by his patrons; his preference for studying Dutch masters in such collections is affirmed by his etching after a painting by Jan van der Heyden (1637–1712) owned by Brühl.[30]

The topographical accuracy of Bellotto's views of Königstein are invaluable in demonstrating how little the site has changed since the middle of the eighteenth century. Despite never having reached the royal collection, Bellotto's spectacular paintings serve to commemorate the magnificence of the Königstein fortress and stand as a tribute to his royal patron and to the artistic tastes and traditions of the Saxon court.

1 Kozakiewicz catalogues a smaller replica in a private collection in Zürich and the etching of the north-west view, remarking that 'this is the only one of the Königstein views of which no large-format version is known'; Kozakiewicz 1972, vol. 2, nos 231, 232; also see Kozakiewicz 1972, vol. 1, p. 84.

2 The painting was sold by the executors of the late Countess Beauchamp at Sotheby's, London, 11 December 1991, lot 18 (see Sotheby's 1991 under Bibliography). It was bought by Bernheimer Fine Arts Ltd and Meissner Fine Art Ltd, London, from whom it was acquired by the National Gallery of Art, Washington, in 1993; see provenance on p. 56 in this volume. For the provenance of the other four views of Königstein, see pp. 50, 62, 68 and 74.

3 Kozakiewicz 1972, vol. 1, p. 100.

4 On 5 December 1758, Bellotto was issued with a pass to travel to Bayreuth. He is recorded in Vienna in January 1759; see Schmidt 2000, p. 41.

5 For a chronology of the history of Königstein, see Schmidt 2000, pp. 31–2; for a detailed history, see Taube 2000. For the function of Königstein around 1750, see A. Pawluschkow, 'Die Festung Königstein um 1750', in Schmidt 2000, pp. 33–7.

6 Bohemia was an historical kingdom to the south of Saxony and Lusatia that formed part of the Holy Roman Empire (and was later a province of the Habsburgs' Austrian Empire); it also shared borders with Austria, Bavaria, Silesia and Moravia. Today it is the largest region in the Czech Republic, bordering the region of Moravia to the east, Germany to the west, Poland to the north-east and Austria to the south.

7 Taube 2000, p. 58. Together with the paintings, the most precious pieces from the Green Vault – a secure hidden chamber in the royal palace used for the safe storage of money, state documents, jewels and decorative objects – were taken to Königstein. After the picture galleries closed on 7 September 1756, they remained under the protection of Queen Maria Josepha until her death, when the Crown Prince Frederick Christian took possession of the key. The picture gallery in Dresden was open again by March 1768, when Johann Wolfgang von Goethe wrote a letter to Ernst Wolfgang Behrisch, reporting on his visit; see Koja 2019, p. 118.

8 Napoleon visited Königstein on 20 June 1813 and decided to erect a fortified camp on the nearby Lilienstein. For more on the fortress in the nineteenth century, see Taube 2000, pp. 66–103.

9 For the collecting activities of Augustus II and the development of the Gemäldegalerie Alte Meister, see Koja 2019. Also see New York 1978.

10 Augustus III possessed 157 pastels by Rosalba Carriera, and her pupil, Felicità Sartori (about 1714–1760), was invited to Dresden in 1741. Other Italian painters at court included Stefano Torelli (1712–1784) and Giovanni Battista Casanova (1730–1795). Among the German artists at court were Anton Raphael Mengs, who was in Dresden from 1744 to 1746 (and again from 1749 to 1752) and appointed court painter in 1745; Christian Wilhelm Ernst Dietrich; and the latter's former master, Johann Alexander Thiele. In 1730 Thiele presented Dietrich to Augustus II, who made him court painter the following year, a position he retained under Augustus III, and he was appointed inspector of the painting collection in 1748. The French painter Louis de Silvestre (1675–1760), who had been invited to Dresden by Augustus II, left in 1748 and was replaced by Charles-François Hutin (1715–1776) the same year. See Kozakiewicz 1972, vol. 1, pp. 80–1, and Koja 2019.

11 Mariette 1851–3, p. 115.

12 See Treves' essay in this volume (p. 13).

13 Bellotto completed a total of 21 views for Brühl between 1747 and 1755: 13 views of Dresden and 8 of Pirna, thus 1 view of Dresden and 3 of Pirna fewer than Augustus III's cycle. For works completed during Bellotto's first Dresden period, see Kozakiewicz 1972, vol. 2, pp. 107–92.

14 Augustus III also owned replicas of Bellotto's two views of Verona (figs 21, 22) – either brought with him or replicated after his arrival in Dresden – and the *Capriccio with the Lock at Dolo*, painted in Dresden in 1748 (Kozakiewicz 1972, vol. 2, nos 99, 102, 107).

15 Weber 2001, p. 16, citing Schmidt 2000, pp. 39–40. Schmidt reproduces both sheets, transcribing them in full.

16 Any drawings of Königstein were most likely among the hundreds of sheets destroyed in the Prussian bombardment of Bellotto's apartment in 1760. There are two surviving drawings related to works from his Dresden period: the Old Kreuzkirche in Dresden and the marketplace at Pirna; Kozakiewicz 1972, vol. 2, nos 183 and 216. Bendfeldt suggests the former is likely to have been produced after the painting, perhaps as a study for the etching; Bendfeldt 2019, pp. 91–2.

17 For Bellotto's use of the camera obscura, see Liebsch 2019.

18 Detailed drawings found in infrared reflectograms follow the exact lines of the construction of the painting. No traditional underdrawing or marks left behind by a transfer process have yet been found in paintings from the early Dresden period, though Bellotto could have used a material such as chalk or gypsum, that may not be detectable under infrared light but which would have been visible to him on the light grey ground of the canvas. For the technical analysis carried out on seven of Bellotto's Dresden views, see Bendfeldt 2019.

19 Although we know little about Bellotto's activities during these two years in Dresden, 22 of his views – including those of Dresden, Pirna and 'four views of Königstein' (whose exact viewpoints are not specified) – and architectural *capricci* are recorded in his 'Catalogo dei Danni', which lists the contents of his apartment before his departure from Dresden in the winter of 1758; see Manikowska 2012, 2014, 2017; Marinelli 2016–17; and Kowalczyk in Milan 2016–17, cat. 83.

20 Stübel 1911, pp. 476–7, with n. 1 on p. 477.

21 Twenty-two of Bellotto's views are listed as being in store in an inventory drawn up between July and August 1754; *Inventarium von der Königlichen Bilder Galerie in Dresden*, compiled by Matthias Oesterreich (1716–1778), Dresden 1754, nos 528–49, cited in Weber 2001, p. 15. In 1765, a catalogue of the Dresden Gemäldegalerie mentions a single painting by Bellotto on display in the gallery, while others are described in general terms (see Weber 2001, p. 15, n. 3). It was not until 1834 that John Friedrich Matthäi (1777–1845), then gallery inspector at the Gemäldegalerie, presented them to the public for the first time, in the '*Galerie vaterländischer Prospekte*' ('Gallery of Views of the Fatherland'); the history and condition of the Dresden paintings is discussed in Bendfeldt 2019, pp. 85–8.

22 Either way, the writ drawn up by Bellotto in 1764, claiming 4,200 thalers from the count's heirs, lists 13 views of Dresden and 8 views of Pirna, with the absence of any mention of Königstein, confirming that this particular series did not form part of Brühl's collection.

23 Kozakiewicz 1972, vol. 2, nos 232 and 237; see also Kowalczyk in Milan 2016–17, cat. 83 and Wagener in Munich 2014–15, cat. 48. For the etchings of the Dresden, Pirna and Königstein views, see Kozakiewicz 1972, vol. 1, pp. 104–6.

24 In his first view of the city, *Dresden from the Right Bank of the Elbe above Augustus Bridge* (fig. 8), Bellotto includes himself sketching and talking to Thiele and artist Christian Wilhelm Ernst Dietrich.

25 The views from the north-west and south-west are described in their respective etchings as from the west and south. It seems that for the exterior views, Bellotto positioned himself roughly north, west and south of the site.

26 Only Bellotto's views of the Frauenkirche and Old Kreuzkirche are smaller in scale (193 x 186 cm and 196 x 186 cm respectively) and his Pirna view on the platform of Sonnenstein castle is larger (204 x 331 cm); Kozakiewicz 1972, vol. 2, nos 179, 181, 230.

27 Weber also discusses the impact of Gerrit Berckheyde (1638–1698); see Weber 2001, pp. 15–25. For the staffage, Bellotto used engravings after works by Berchem and Zuccarelli: see Weber 2005 and cats 1–3 in this volume.

28 See n. 19 above.

29 In the 1650s, Jacob van Ruisdael had visited Castle Bentheim in Westphalia. The drawings he made in situ were translated into 14 paintings of the castle after his return to the Netherlands. Ruisdael's *Bentheim Castle* is listed in the Dresden manuscript inventory of 1754, 2, no. 460, cited in Slive 2001, cat. 14. Ruisdael's *Pond in a Wood with a Blasted Beech Tree* was in the collection of Brühl, Dresden, by 1750; Slive 2001, cat. 416. Interestingly, Nicolaes Berchem accompanied Ruisdael to Castle Bentheim and made two paintings of his own, one of which is also in the Gemäldegalerie in Dresden.

30 Kozakiewicz 1972, vol. 2, no. 247.

BELLOTTO, BRITAIN AND THE KÖNIGSTEIN PAINTINGS

Stephen Lloyd

The reuniting in London of Bernardo Bellotto's series of five masterly views of the massive Königstein fortress in Saxony marks the first time they have been shown together since they were painted at Dresden in 1756–8. It is not just a moment to admire the artist's exceptional pictorial achievement as an eighteenth-century European landscapist of the first rank, but is also an opportunity to reflect on the fascinating role of British collectors and curators in the five paintings' acquisition, preservation and almost complete transfer to public ownership over the last 40 years.[1]

It is not known exactly when or how the five Königstein fortress paintings left the artist's studio in Dresden.[2] They do not appear to have ever been delivered to either of Bellotto's two main patrons, Frederick August II, Elector of Saxony and King of Poland, or his prime minister, the powerful but corrupt Count Heinrich von Brühl. After the elector's flight to Warsaw in 1756, followed seven years later by the ruler's death and that of Brühl, both in Dresden, it may be surmised that either Bellotto or agents for the occupied Saxon state sold the series of five Königstein pictures. Before the outbreak of the Seven Years' War in 1756, Bellotto – a master etcher – had made many impressive large etchings after his great series of painted views of Dresden. A decade later he executed a group of etchings after his landscapes of the Saxon town of Pirna on the river Elbe, alongside two fine prints of the nearby Königstein fortress after the paintings now at Washington and in the Derby Collection (cats 2, 3).[3] These large etchings were published in or around 1765 at Dresden, with French lettering, and offered for sale in Amsterdam, demonstrating the artist's international reach and ambition (figs 19, 20).

In London during the late eighteenth century, when Bellotto's paintings began to emerge on the art market and be purchased for British private collections, the artist was known as 'Canaletti'. Later in the nineteenth century he was also known as 'Il Canalettino', or 'the little Canaletto',

Fig. 19 Bernardo Bellotto, *Vue du Roc. et de la Forteresse de Koenigstein, du Coté du Midi [...]*, 1765. Etching, 42.2 x 64.1 cm. Kupferstichkabinett, Staatliche Kunstsammlungen, Dresden

Fig. 20 Bernardo Bellotto, *Vue du Roc. et Forteresse de Koenigstein du coté de l'Occident [...]*, about 1765. Etching, 42 x 62.8 cm. British Museum, London

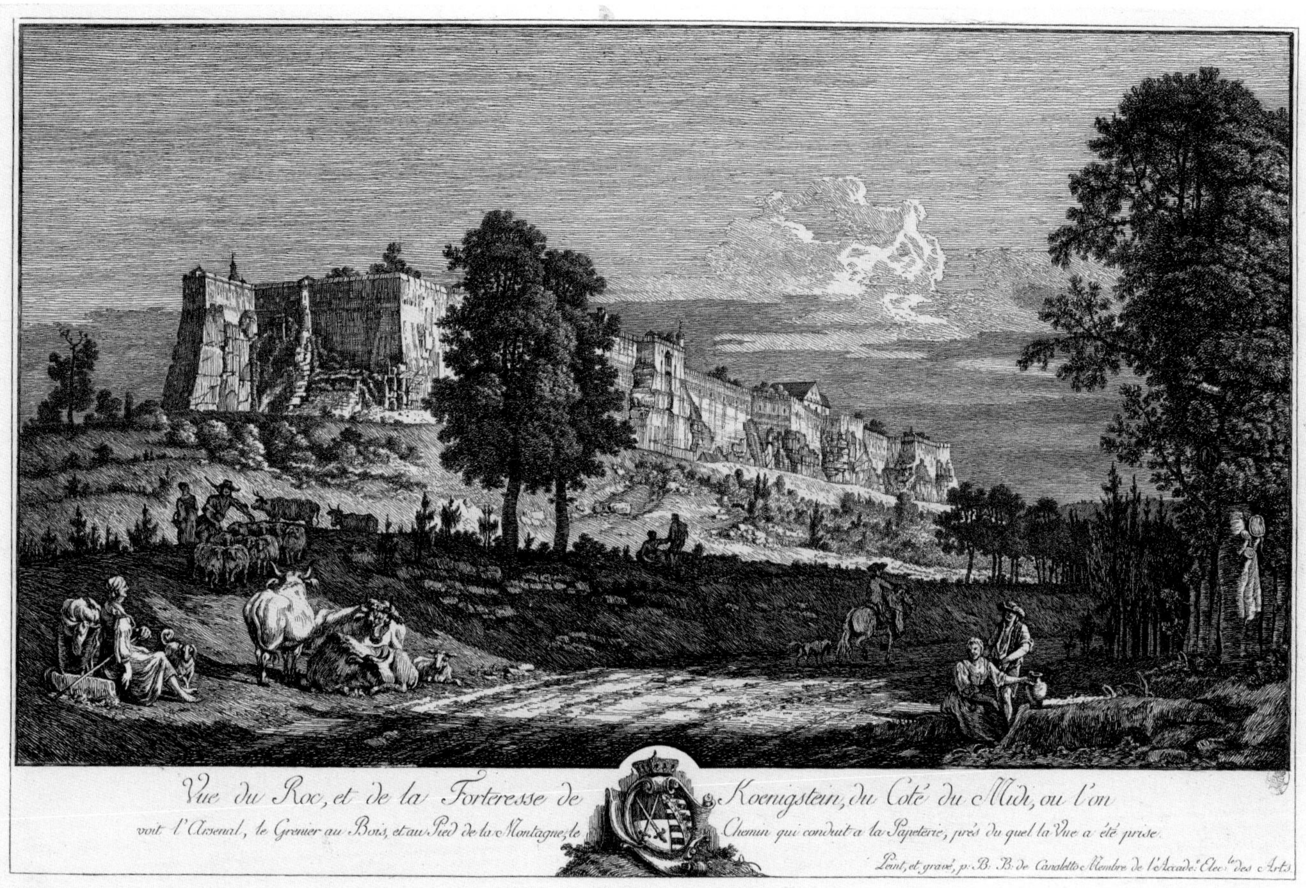
Vue du Roc, et de la Forteresse de Koenigstein, du Coté du Midi, ou l'on
voit l'Arsenal, le Grenier au Bois, et au Pied de la Montagne, le Chemin qui conduit a la Papeterie, prés du quel la Vue a été prise.
Peint, et gravé, p: B: B: de Canaletto Membre de l'Accade: Elec: le des Arts.

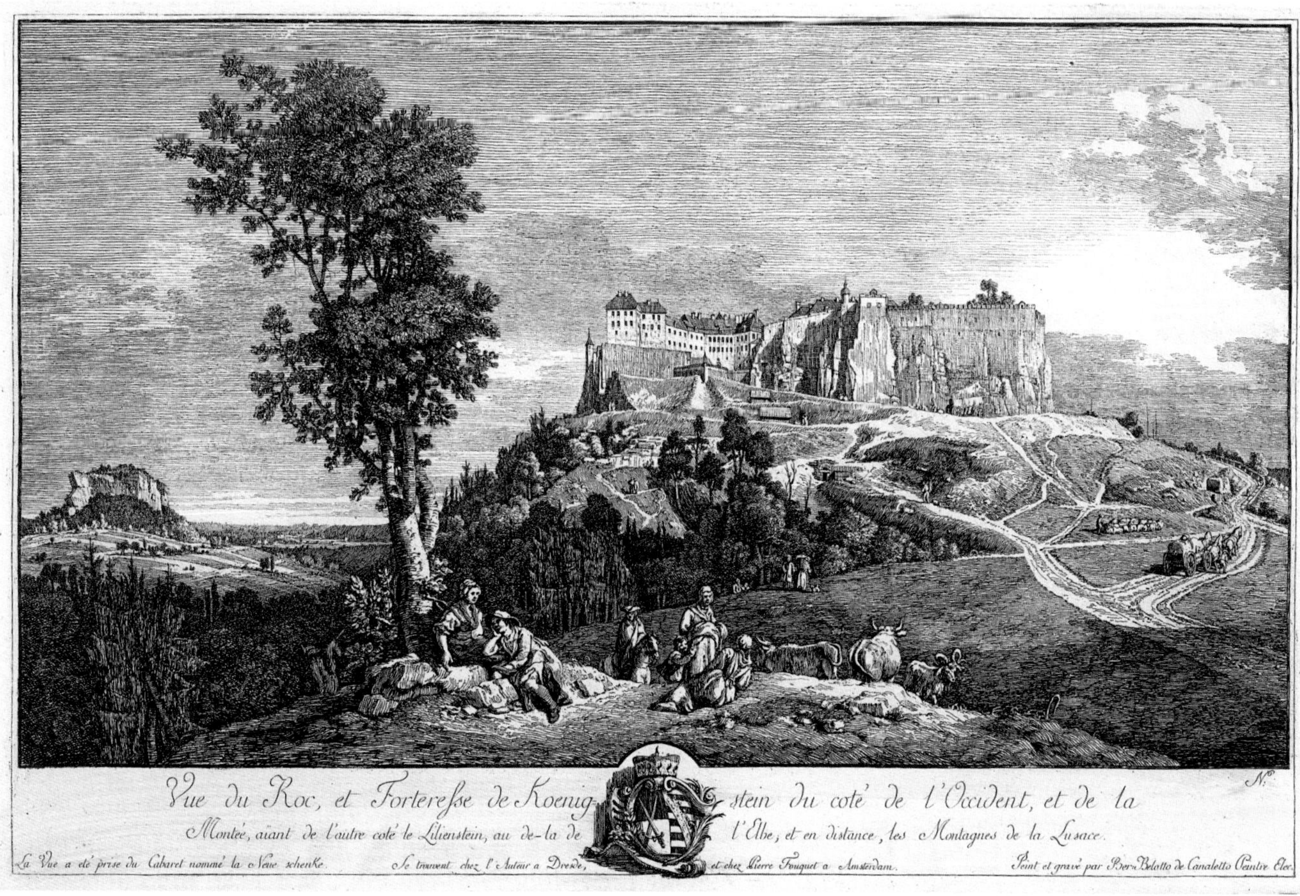
Vue du Roc, et Forteresse de Koenig-stein du coté de l'Occident, et de la
Montée, aïant de l'autre coté le Lilienstein, au de-la de l'Elbe, et en distance, les Montagnes de la Lusace.
La Vue a eté prise du Cabaret nommé la Neue schenke.
Se trouvent chez l'Auteur a Dresde, et chez Pierre Fouquet a Amsterdam.
Peint et gravé par Ber: Belotto de Canaletto Peintre Elec.
N:

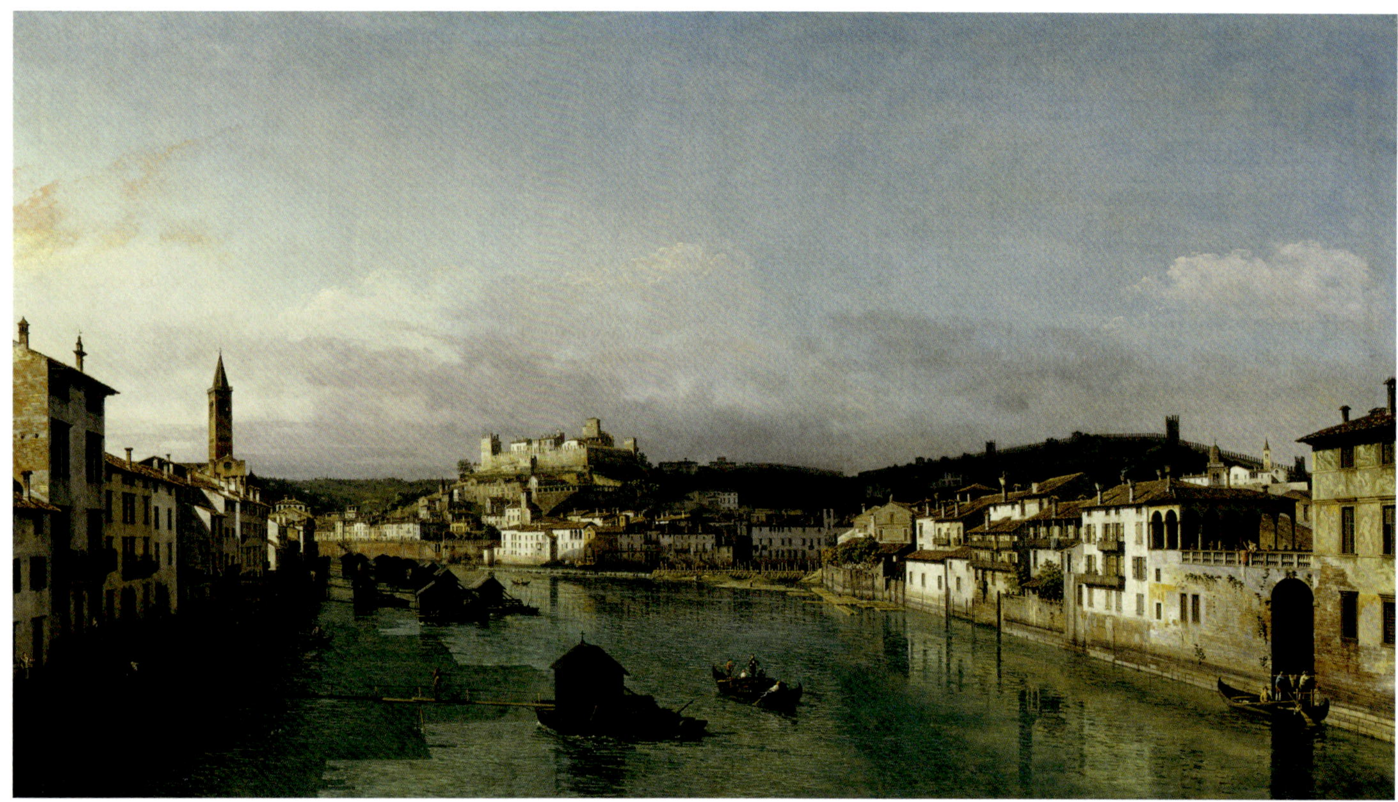

Fig. 21 Bernardo Bellotto, *View of Verona with the River Adige from the Ponte Nuovo*, about 1745–7. Oil on canvas, 132.5 x 231 cm. Powis Castle, National Trust

to distinguish him from his better-known uncle Canaletto.[4] From 1770, and during the following three decades, a very select group of Bellotto's most important larger paintings, including the Königstein series, were offered for sale by the London auction houses. One possible route for facilitating the transfer of the Königstein paintings from Dresden to London may have been through the prime minister's nephew. In 1764 Hans Moritz von Brühl (1736–1809) was appointed ambassador extraordinary to the Court of St James, where he was known as John Maurice, Count of Bruhl.[5]

The first masterpiece to arrive in Britain, created at the end of his earlier Italian period in 1745–7, was one of a pair of expansive and detailed views of the river Adige in Verona, looking upstream towards the Visconti fortress of Castel San Pietro (fig. 21).[6] This painting was acquired almost certainly at auction in London during the early 1770s by the rapacious Robert, 1st Baron Clive of Plassey (1725–1774), often known today as 'Clive of India', as part of a rapidly amassed collection of old masters, formed in the last three years of his life before he committed suicide. This Bellotto view of Verona was first recorded in an inventory compiled between 1771 and 1774, where it was listed as hanging at Clive's London house, 45 Berkeley Square. In 1775 it was valued at 147 guineas. By 1798 the painting had been moved to Powis Castle near Welshpool in mid-Wales, the residence of Clive's son and his daughter-in-law, where it has remained to this day.[7]

The second large painting from the Verona pair is an equally arresting view looking at the bridge over the river Adige known as the Ponte delle Navi (fig. 22).[8] The first recorded owner of this picture in Britain was the politician, man of letters, art collector and connoisseur George Agar-Ellis, 1st Baron Dover (1797–1833).[9] Despite passing through three auctions in London, this picture has always remained in Britain. Since 1973, until recently, it has been on long-term loan from a private collection to the National Galleries of Scotland, Edinburgh.

Bellotto's views of the Königstein fortress were created 10 years after the two Verona masterpieces,

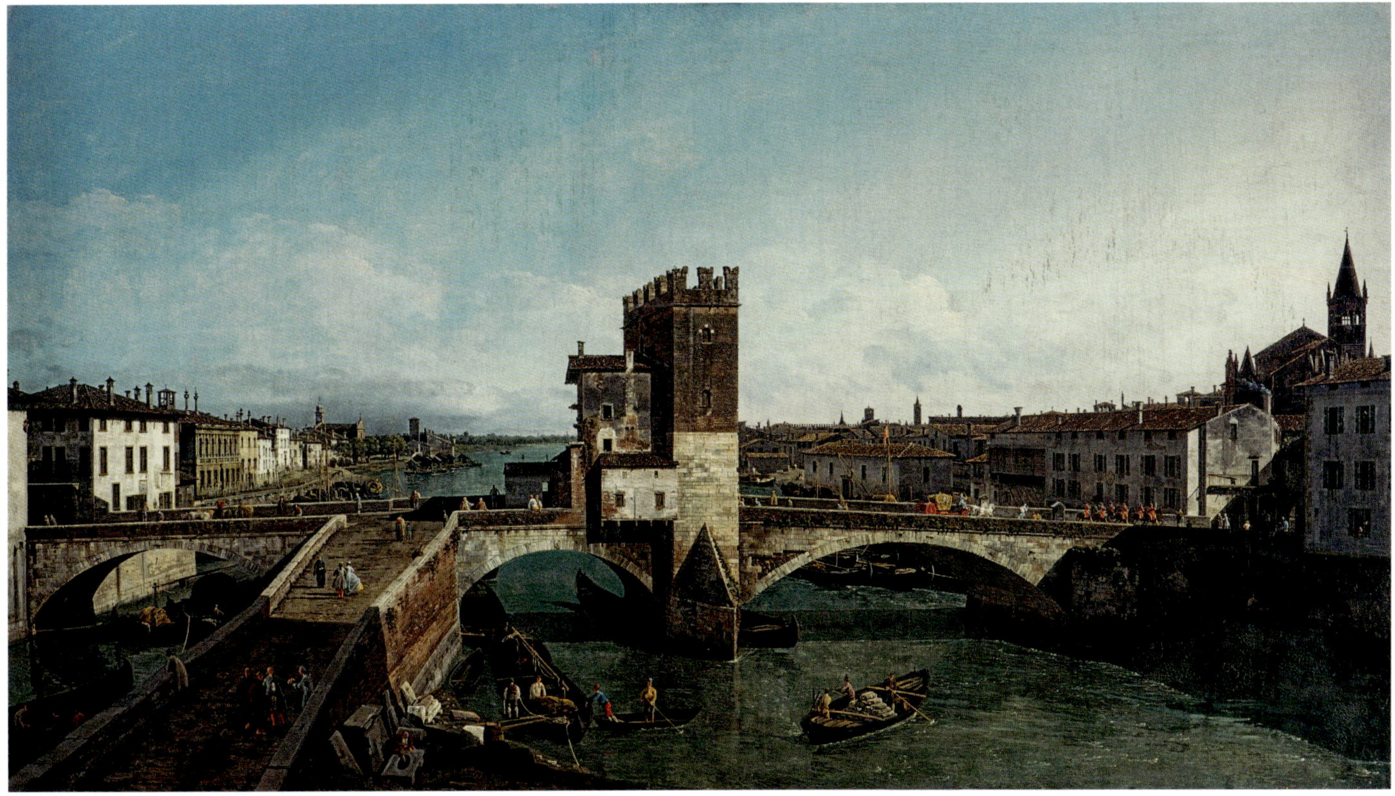

Fig. 22 Bernardo Bellotto, *View of Verona with the Ponte delle Navi*, about 1745. Oil on canvas, 132 x 233.7 cm. Private collection

at the end of his first long stay in Dresden. The first paintings from the Königstein group to be recorded in Britain were the two courtyard scenes now in Manchester (cats 4, 5).[10] At a Christie's auction held in London on 7 March 1778 of 'A Capital Collection of Italian, French, Flemish and Dutch Pictures', lot 79 was described as by 'Canaletti' and showing 'A View of the fortress at *Koningstein* [sic] in Saxony painted for the King of Poland', while lot 80 was listed as 'Ditto, ditto, its companion'. The pair of paintings, which had been consigned by 'Ly Bwn', were bought for £79 16s (or 76 guineas) each by 'Tempest'. It has been suggested that the vendor was almost certainly Lady Margaret Brown, née Cecil (1698–1782), widow of the politician Sir Robert Brown, Bt (d. 1760), who earlier in his life had been a rich merchant living in Venice and a collector of contemporary Italian pictures.[11] The purchaser of the painting, 'Tempest', was likely to have been John Tempest (1739–1794) of Wynyard in County Durham, a landowner and Member of Parliament for the city of Durham. As his son had predeceased him in a riding accident, John Tempest's estate was eventually inherited by his niece Frances Anne Vane-Tempest (1800–1865), who married Charles Stewart, later 3rd Marquess of Londonderry (1778–1854). The two Bellotto paintings of the Königstein courtyard buildings became part of the Londonderry collection, and were displayed at Wynyard Park, a large neoclassical mansion built by the 3rd marquess in the 1820s, until they were sold by the 9th marquess to Manchester City Art Gallery in 1982 and 1983, in a stunning double acquisition by the enlightened city councillors.[12]

Bellotto's remaining three views from his Königstein series, all showing the exterior of the fortress, were purchased in the early 1790s by Henry Temple, 2nd Viscount Palmerston (1739–1802). He was a Whig politician, a Member of Parliament for 40 years and a junior minister, but his real passion was for society, travel and the arts. At Broadlands, his country house and estate in Hampshire, he commissioned Lancelot 'Capability' Brown to improve the park between 1767 and 1788.

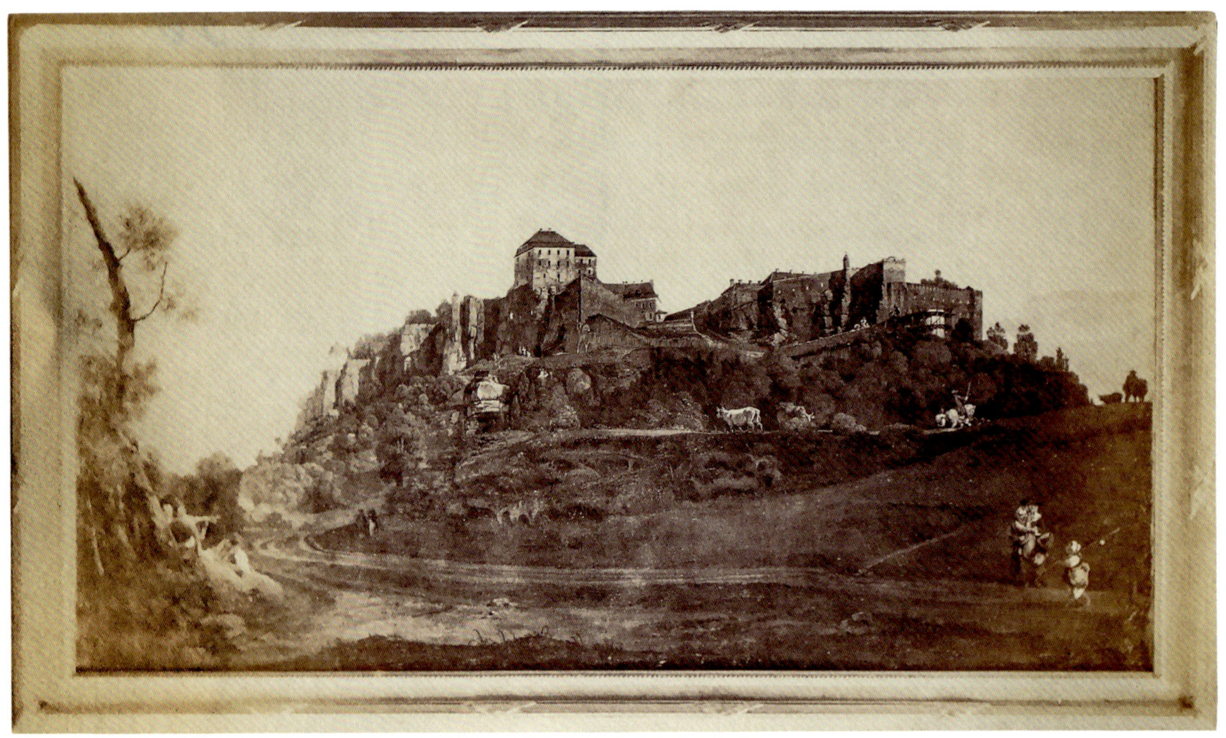

Fig. 23 Photograph of *The Fortress of Königstein from the North* (cat. 1) in its frame, about 1865. From George Scharf, *A Descriptive and Historical Catalogue of the Collection of Pictures at Knowsley Hall*, privately printed, London 1875. Albumen print, 7.5 x 11.8 cm. The Derby Collection, Knowsley Hall

Brown, together with his son-in-law Henry Holland, rebuilt the house to display Henry Temple's collection of classical sculptures which he had bought on his various grand tours to Italy. The 2nd viscount also avidly collected old master paintings both in London and on his European travels. The pictures were then displayed at his town house in Hanover Square, which was remodelled by Henry Holland during the mid-1790s.[13] In the Palmerston archives are two references to Bellotto's paintings.[14] The first listing is in an undated manuscript (but with the paper watermarked 1796), a 'Cataloge [sic] of Pictures Belonging to Lord Palmerston in Hanover Square', where in the Dressing Room is recorded a 'View of Keenigsteen [sic]' by 'Cannaletti', valued at £250, which may refer to all three of the paintings.[15] A few years later, in another undated mansucript (but with the paper watermarked 1804), featuring a list of 'Pictures in Stanhope S[tree]t. and Han[ove]r. Sq[ua]re', there is an entry for 'Cannaletti Keeningstein [sic], £105', which must refer to a valuation of one work from the trio of Bellotto's compositions.[16] All three paintings were probably reframed around the 1790s. Their elegant neoclassical gilt-wood frames feature a pearl motif on the inner sight edge, with the flat and then the tied ribbons over reeded top edges.[17] Remarkably, the three paintings in Washington, London and the Derby Collection still retain these refined late eighteenth-century Palmerston frames to this day (figs 23, 24).

The three Bellottos had left the Palmerston collection in or before 1850, having been sold by Henry Temple's son Henry John, 3rd Viscount Palmerston (1784–1865), better known as the prime minister Lord Palmerston. Two groups of old master pictures from his father's collection were sold at auction in London by the 3rd viscount, firstly at Christie's on 10 June 1844, and then at Foster's on 5 November 1850. [18] Only one of the Bellotto paintings from the Palmerston collection was sold, at the second of these two auctions, being *The Fortress of Königstein from the North-West* (cat. 2), when it was probably purchased by Henry, 4th Earl Beauchamp (1784–1863). However, according to the Lygon family, it had been given by the 3rd Viscount Palmerston to William, 1st Earl Beauchamp (1747–1816), to settle an

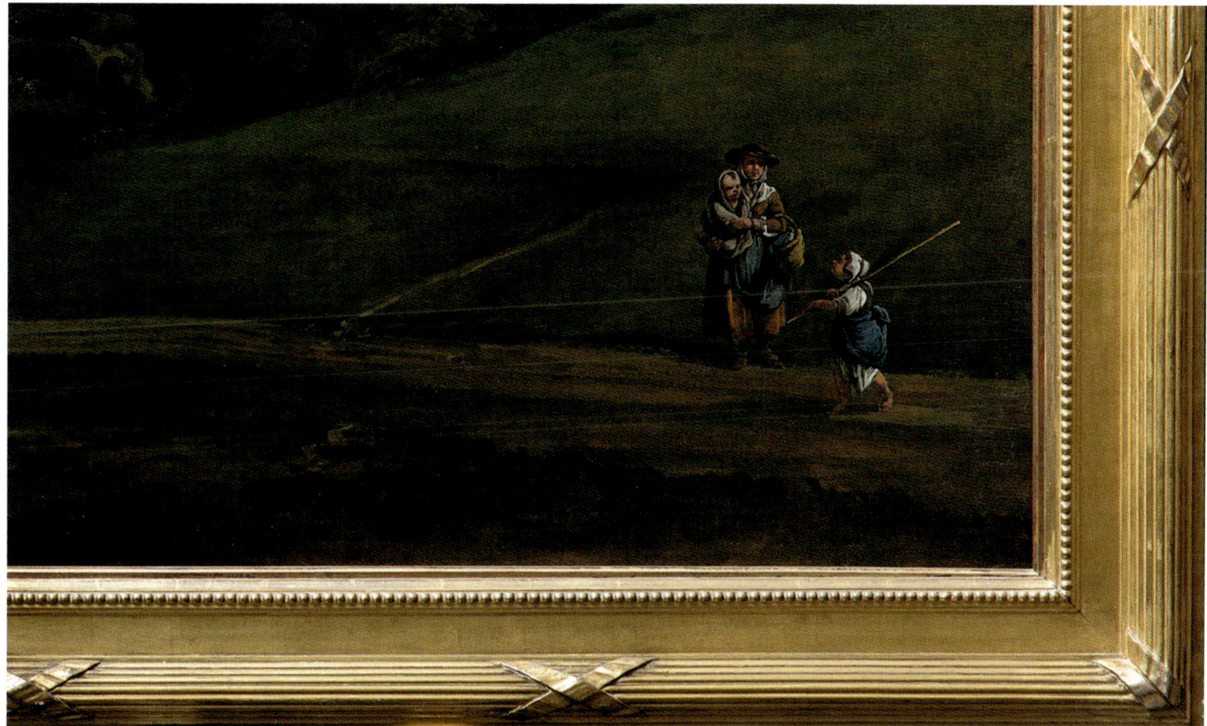

Fig. 24 Frame detail of *The Fortress of Königstein from the North* (cat. 1)

unspecified debt.[19] This picture certainly remained in the Beauchamp family collection of historical portraits, miniatures and old masters at Madresfield Court in Worcestershire, where it hung on the Staircase Hall. The painting was almost completely unknown to art historians and Bellotto scholars until it was sold at Sotheby's, London, on 11 December 1991, lot 18.[20] Surprisingly, it was granted an export licence from the United Kingdom and was acquired by the National Gallery of Art, Washington, in 1993.[21]

It is not known when the 3rd Viscount Palmerston sold the remaining two of his three Bellotto paintings (cats 1, 3) to Edward Smith Stanley, 13th Earl of Derby (1775–1851). Lord Derby was a committed natural historian who was also a collector of exotic animals as well as art, books and watercolours. He displayed most of his inherited old master pictures and family portraits at Knowsley Hall near Liverpool, but with some important paintings shown at Derby House, his town house designed by Robert Adam in Grosvenor Square, London, where his eldest son Lord Stanley lived.[22]

The acquisition of the two Bellottos by the 13th earl was most likely to have been made between 1846 and 1850. The 1846 manuscript catalogue of the pictures at Knowsley Hall does not include the two fortress views. Illustrated with drawings of the picture hangs on the walls, the manuscript was printed privately four years later. The 1850 catalogue includes the first reference in print to the Bellottos in the Derby Collection, with the two pendant paintings being listed as hanging on either side of the door on the east side of the Mahogany Bedroom as numbers 7 and 8, 'Fortress of Koniqstein Canaletti'.[23] However, inserted into the privately printed 1850 catalogue is a loose note written in Lord Derby's hand stating: 'Konigstein Castle 2 Canaletti (Palmerston) £200'.[24] This indicates that the two Bellotto paintings were purchased privately between 1846 and 1850 by the 13th Earl of Derby from the 3rd Viscount Palmerston. They were initially displayed at Derby House, before being transferred to Knowsley Hall before 1850.

Lord Derby died a year later and was succeeded by his eldest son Lord Stanley, also known as Edward Geoffrey Stanley, who became the 14th earl and served three times as prime minister. He supervised a complete rehang of the paintings at Knowsley Hall and Grosvenor

Square. From the 1860 manuscript catalogue of the pictures at Knowsley, it can be seen that he had now hung the two Bellottos in the First Drawing Room, where they were stated explictly to have come from Grosvenor Square. These pictures were described as numbers 40 and 56, 'Fortress of Königstein Bellotti B detto Il Canalettino'.[25]

The two paintings were still displayed in the First Drawing Room at Knowsley between 1864 and 1875, when Sir George Scharf (1820–1895), the eminent art historian and first director of the National Portrait Gallery in London, visited the house to prepare his full and detailed catalogue of the pictures in the Hall. Scharf made outline sketches in pencil of the two Bellotto paintings of the Königstein fortress in his notebook from 31 August 1866, titled the 'Earl of Derby's London pictures & some at Knowsley', observing in a pencil annotation that the two Bellottos were 'bought at Lord Palmerston's for £200'.[26] Scharf's completed catalogue was privately printed in 1875 and paid for by Edward Henry Stanley (1826–1893), the 15th Earl of Derby, who was twice foreign secretary, twice colonial secretary, and a long-time trustee of the National Portrait Gallery.[27]

Scharf described the two Königstein landscapes at Knowsley as being by Bernardo Canale, called 'Il Canalettino', or 'the little Canaletto', to distinguish him from his uncle. When the 17th Earl of Derby remodelled the Hall together with the architect W.H. Romaine-Walker and then rehung the paintings in 1908–13, he had gilt-wood label plaques affixed to the bottom rails of many of the paintings with simple inscriptions painted black, identifying either the artist or the sitter in the portraits. The two Bellottos were thus labelled as 'Il Canalettino'; the original plaques still survive on both the London and Knowsley views of the fortress, taken from the north and south-west respectively (cats 1, 3). Scharf's descriptions of the two paintings are vivid and informative. He concludes the account of the view from the north with a perceptive comparison of its brooding landscape to the mid-seventeenth-century Dutch landscapist Jacob van Ruisdael's famous composition *Bentheim Castle* (fig. 30), featuring a castle looming over forests, while taking the opportunity to rate Bellotto as a superior artist in painting greenery compared with his uncle Canaletto: 'The picture possesses many of the powerful effects of Canaletto ... with the great advantage of well-executed landscape foliage, in which his uncle ... was strikingly deficient.'[28]

Bellotto's two magisterial depictions of the fortress remained at Knowsley, where they were rehung occasionally in various staterooms, though usually displayed together as a pair. They ended up being put on show in the revamped Picture Gallery and Library at the Hall for most of the second half of the twentieth century, alongside some of the most important larger old masters in the Derby Collection. The view of Königstein from the south was loaned to the Walker Art Gallery, National Museums Liverpool, between 2000 and 2010. The view of the fortress from the north (cat. 1) was acquired for the nation by the National Gallery in 2017.

Remarkably, this in-focus exhibition at the National Gallery in London and Manchester Art Gallery, marking the tercentenary of Bellotto's birth, is only the second show ever devoted to Bellotto held in Britain. The first, an ambitious touring exhibition in 1957, was organised by curators Bryan Roberston and F.J.B. Watson and first shown at London's Whitechapel Art Gallery, before touring to Liverpool's Walker Art Gallery and to York City Art Gallery. The show comprised an astonishingly generous loan, a group of 30 paintings and 60 drawings created by the artist during his long stay as a court artist in Warsaw at the end of his life. The whole exhibition, which later travelled on to the Museum Boijmans Van Beuningen in Rotterdam, another city almost completely destroyed during the Second World War, was loaned from the collection of the National Museum of Warsaw in an outstanding act of cultural co-operation at the height of the Cold War.[29]

Despite the total devastation in early 1945 of the exceptionally beautiful eighteenth-century baroque cities of Dresden and Warsaw, both historic city centres were painstakingly rebuilt in the post-war period under their Communist governments. Bellotto's celebrated series of paintings depicting Dresden and Warsaw not only miraculously survived the war, but with the aid of the Venetian artist's extraordinary attention to detail and perspectival rigour, both city centres were reconstructed with almost forensic accuracy. The 1957 exhibition, which was shown in the East End of London and at the heart of the great port city of Liverpool, both of which were very badly damaged by aerial bombardment in the Second World War, can be seen as an inspiring act of cultural friendship between post-war Britain and Eastern Europe at a time of great economic austerity and political tension, thus showcasing the masterly northern vision of arguably the greatest of the Venetian eighteenth-century landscapists, Bernardo Bellotto.

1 For the most comprehensive recent illustrated account in German of the five Königstein fortress paintings, see Schmidt 2000, pp. 31–7, 43–56, 142–73. For the best short account in English of the series, see Bowron 1993.

2 For Bellotto in Saxony and the context of Italian artists working for the German courts in the eighteenth century, see Haskell 1980, pp. 293–8. For the history of the Königstein fortress, see Taube 2000, and Hagishima 2014, pp. 74–8. For Bellotto's 1762 inventory of the contents of his grand apartment, library and studio in Salzgasse, which was badly damaged during the Prussian bombardment of Dresden in 1760, see Manikowska 2012 and Manikowska 2017.

3 Venice 1986, pp. 97–9, nos 26–7, figs 96–7. For Bellotto's etchings after his paintings of Dresden and Pirna, see the British Museum's online catalogue. For further bibliography on these etchings, see Chiswell's essay in this volume (p. 39, n. 23).

4 Bernardo Bellotto had a younger brother, Pietro Bellotti (1725–about 1804/5), a view painter who spent spent most of his adult career in France, mainly based in Toulouse between 1747 and 1778, but working all over the country in cities such as Nantes and Lille. In France he was known as 'Pietro Bellotti di Canalletty'. See Venice 2014, and Treves' essay in this volume (p. 25, n. 5).

5 A notable astronomer and friend of William Herschel, Hans Moritz von Brühl was elected a Fellow of the Royal Society in 1765. He spent the rest of his life in London.

6 Kozakiewicz 1972, vol. 2, no. 98. It would seem that the prime pair of Verona paintings was originally commissioned by an English collector, probably one of the many 'milordi' or young noblemen travelling through northern Italy on the Grand Tour. According to an inscription by Bellotto on a drawing (now in a collection of the artist's drawings in Hessiches Landesmuseum, Darmstadt), copied from the Powis Castle composition (fig. 21), he stated that it was a 'copia del quadro dela Vista stando su il ponte novo verso il castelo di Verona a Verona di Bernard. Belotto de:tto il Canaletto per ingilterra' ('copy of picture of the View standing on the new bridge towards Verona Castle to Verona by Bernard. Belotto called Canaletto for England').

7 NACF 1981, pp. 53–4; London 1995, pp. 86–7, no. 30, and pp. 202–3; Venice and Houston 2001, pp. 142–3, no. 37. Another version of the composition by Bellotto is in the Gemäldegalerie, Dresden. Kozakiewicz 1972, vol. 2, no. 99.

8 Kozakiewicz 1972, vol. 2, no. 101.

9 This picture was sold at auction by Robinson and Fisher in 1895, and by Christie's in 1771 and 1971, where it was listed as fomerly owned by Sir George Burns, North Mymms Park, Hertfordshire; see Camesasca 1974, p. 95, no. 67. Another version of the painting by Bellotto is in the Gemäldegalerie, Dresden. Kozakiewicz 1972, vol. 2, no. 102.

10 Kozakiewicz 1972, vol. 2, nos 238 and 241.

11 NACF 1983, p. 140, and NACF 1984, pp. 139–40, entry J. Byam Shaw; Ingamells 1997, pp. 139–40.

12 Much of the family's portrait collection was also displayed at Londonderry House, Park Lane, London from the 1820s until the house was sold in 1962; see Hyde 1937. Wynyard Park was sold in 1987. Vane-Tempest-Stewart and Londonderry pictures, mostly family portraits and equestrian paintings, can be seen at Mount Stewart, County Down, Northern Ireland (National Trust); see Bailey and Rowell 2017.

13 Connell 1957; Broadlands 1980; Russell 1982; Coltman 2006, pp. 172–5; Guilding 2014, pp. 158–65.

14 Kozakiewicz 1972, vol. 2, nos. 233 and 235; the third painting, now in Washington, was not known by Kozakiewicz when he published his catalogue raisonné. See Chiswell's essay in this volume (p. 30).

15 Broadlands Archives BR 126/11, cited by kind permission of Special Collections, Hartley Library, University of Southampton. As a point of comparison with the valuation of other old master paintings listed as hanging at the house in Hanover Square, a 'View of Venice Cannaletti' in the Dressing Room was valued at £30. This could have been painted by either Bellotto or his uncle Canaletto, and was probably a small work. The two most expensive pictures listed were a 'Landscape with Figures Berghem', in the First Dressing Room, painted by the highly regarded seventeenth-century Dutch landscapist Nicolaes Berchem; and *The Infant Academy* by Sir Joshua Reynolds, hung in the Inner Drawing Room, with each picture valued at £500.

16 Broadlands Archives, BR 126/15, cited by kind permission of Special Collections, Hartley Library, University of Southampton; with many thanks to archivist Karen Robson for her kind assistance.

17 These frames are not dissimilar to others made in London during the 1780s and 1790s for some of George Romney's portraits. I am grateful to Jacob Simon for this information.

18 These two auction catalogues, annotated by the 3rd viscount with prices made at the sales, were in the Palmerston Papers at Broadlands House in Hampshire, but have not as yet been located in the Broadlands Archive in the Special Collections, Hartley Library, University of Southampton; see Connell 1957, p. 473. The Palmerston lots in the Christie's 1844 sale were nos 127–40, but the Bellotto paintings were not sold then. The Foster's 1850 auction of the major contents of Lord Palmerston's London house included paintings, furniture, books and porcelain, sold during a three-day-long sale. The 1850 auction catalogue's title page states: 'Great Stanhope Street. Catalogue of all the excellent Household Furniture [...] also the valuable Collection of Italian & Dutch Pictures [...] including those of A. Canaletti, B. Canaletti [...] the Property of a Nobleman [Lord Palmerston], which will be sold by Auction by Messrs Foster and Son on the Premises, 9, Great Stanhope Street, Park Lane, on Monday 4th November, & 2 following days at One precisely each Day'. The entry for the painting by 'B. Canaletti' (lot 290) on 5 November, which in the priced copies of the catalogue is marked as sold to 'Anderson' for '95 G[uineas]', states: 'A View of Konigstein on the Elbe, cattle and group of figures in the costume of the time in the foreground; the buildings and figures on this remarkable height are beautifully sketched in, and the environs and approaches painted with great truth and power. Canvas 7 ft 8[in] by 4 ft 4[in]'. See the Getty Provenance Index online database of British auction catalogues, Br-5804, Lot 0290. I am grateful to Lynda McLeod, associate director and archivist at Christie's, London, for this information.

19 Sotheby's 1991.

20 The painting is referred to in Scharf 1875, p. 10, no. 17: 'A fine picture, taken from the extreme end, and showing means of ascent, is at Madresfield in the Collection of Earl Beauchamp, painted by the same artist.' See also Beauchamp 1927, p. 26, no. 100, 'Castle of Koenigstein. Bernardo Canale (1724–1780). Formerly in the Collection of Viscount Palmerston, KG.' I am grateful to Charles Sebag-Montefiore for this reference.

21 See provenance on p. 56 in this volume. Bowron 1993; London and Washington 1994–5, pp. 361–76 and 429, no. 256; Bowron in De Grazia and Garberson 1996, pp. 14–18; Venice and Houston 2001, pp. 200–3. I am grateful to Mark Griffiths-Jones and Georgina Eliot of Sotheby's, London, for their assistance.

22 Fisher 2002; Lloyd 2016.

23 Knowsley Hall 1850.

24 I am grateful to Xanthe Brooke for her comments on the inserted note in the 1850 catalogue.

25 Knowsley Hall 1860.

26 George Scharf notebooks, Heinz Archive, National Portrait Gallery, London; also see De Grazia and Garberson 1996, p. 18, n. 16.

27 Scharf 1875, p. 10, no. 17 and pp. 14–15, no. 27.

28 Ruisdael painted this castle in Westphalia at least 14 times. A well-known version dated 1653, which was formerly in the Beit Collection, is in the National Gallery of Ireland, Dublin (fig. 30).

29 London, Liverpool and York 1957. Since the completion of the faithful reconstruction of the Royal Castle in Warsaw, after it was destroyed during the Second World War, the majority of Bellotto's Warsaw paintings have been reinstalled in the Canaletto Room at the castle, exactly where they were originally displayed in the 1770s; see Rizzi and Jursz-Salvadori 2006, and Treves' essay in this volume (p. 24, fig. 11). For this information I am grateful to Anna Zasadzińska, Head of the Heritage Interpretation Centre, Museum of Warsaw.

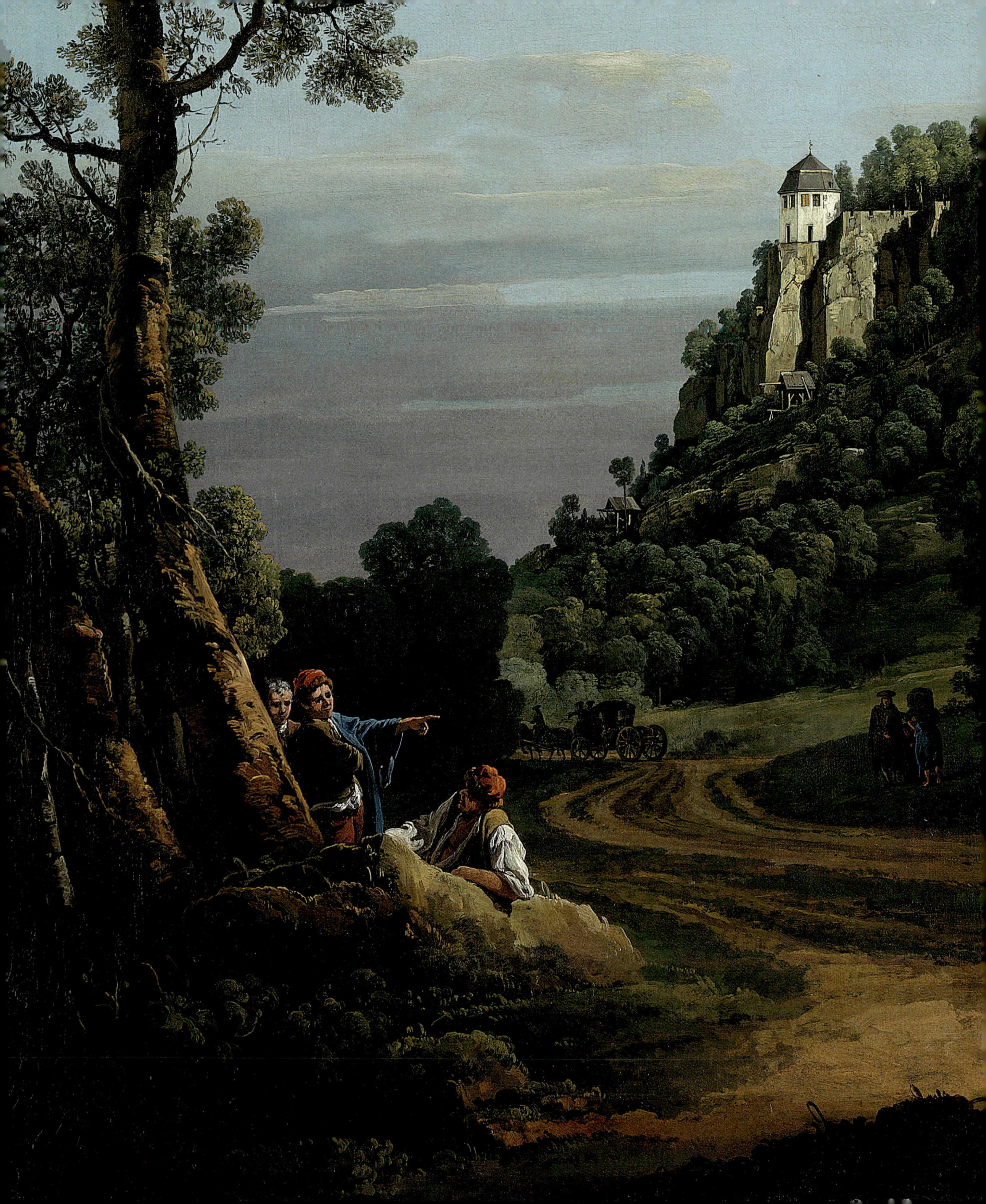

CATALOGUE ENTRIES

1 THE FORTRESS OF KÖNIGSTEIN FROM THE NORTH

1756–8
Oil on canvas, 132.1 x 236.2 cm
The National Gallery, London, NG6668

Bought with the support of the American Friends of the National Gallery, the National Gallery Trust, the Estate of Mrs Madeline Swallow, Art Fund (with a contribution from The Wolfson Foundation), Howard and Roberta Ahmanson, The Deborah Loeb Brice Foundation, Mrs Mollie W. Vickers, The Manny and Brigitta Davidson Charitable Foundation and The Sackler Trust with additional support from Mrs Charles Wrightsman, Jean-Luc Baroni, The Linbury Trust, The Monument Trust, Mr Fabrizio Moretti, Sir Hugh and Lady Stevenson, The John S. Cohen Foundation, Mr Jonathan Green, Christoph and Katrin Henkel, Ernst Nissl, Mr Peter Scott CBE QC, Mr and Mrs Ugo Pierucci, Sir Michael and Lady Heller, Mr Adrian Sassoon, Mr Mark Storey, Mr Neil Westreich, Nicholas and Judith Goodison, John and Flavia Ormond and other donors including those who wish to remain anonymous, 2017

Bellotto's view is taken from below the fortress, from the outer edge of a sandy track that winds through the Elbe Valley. Königstein rises above its surroundings like a bejewelled crown, the jagged profile of the fortress sharply silhouetted against the pale blue sky. Warm evening light illuminates the mottled facades of the battlements and buildings, dancing over the craggy exterior, casting shadows between the natural breaks in the rock and across the sharp, angular walls. A shepherd on the brow of the hill on the right leans wearily on a cow, perhaps resting at the end of a long day working in the sun. Above him, the light catches the clouds, which are loosely rendered in expressive strokes of creamy paint. A dense thicket of trees, painted in different shades of light and dark green, surrounds the base of the fortress, while small groups of figures and animals enliven the grassy glades below. Bellotto characteristically places the immediate foreground in shadow, applying loose flicks of the brush to silhouette the stretch of turf on which we sit. He places us within the composition, integrated into the peaceful, bucolic life that exists beyond the forbidding walls of the fortress.

The white building on the far left of the rocky outcrop, radiant in the sunshine, is the Friedrichsburg, or Frederick's Castle, recognisable by this date for its mansard roof. Formerly known as the Christiansburg, after Elector Christian I, it had been built in 1589 as a watchtower for the original fortress; its ground floor was used to store cannons and its upper storey was a venue for small courtly festivities. By the late 1750s, when Bellotto was drawing his Königstein views, it had come to be known as the Friedrichsburg, and had been converted into an octagonal baroque pavilion by the architect Matthäus Daniel Pöppelmann under the direction of Augustus the Strong. However, the newly renovated building was destroyed by a bolt of lightning in 1744; its redundant status is faithfully recorded by Bellotto, who paints the boarded-up window on the north side. Above and to the right is the Rösschen: a tall, narrow observation tower with a pitched roof that had originally formed part of the medieval complex. Sunken into the rock, its

PROVENANCE
Commissioned from the artist by Frederick Augustus II (1696–1763), Elector of Saxony and King of Poland (as Augustus III), in Dresden, by the spring of 1756; probably Henry Temple, 2nd Viscount Palmerston (1739–1802), London, and by descent to his son Henry John Temple, 3rd Viscount Palmerston (1784–1865), who served as prime minister 1855–8 and 1859–65, with two other pictures from the Königstein series (cats 2, 3); sold with its pendant (cat. 3) by 'Palmerston' for £200 to the Earls of Derby, probably to Edward Smith-Stanley, 13th Earl of Derby (1775–1851), first at Derby House, Grosvenor Square, London, and by 1850 at Knowsley Hall, Lancashire; thence by descent until 2016, when purchased by a private collector and stopped at export by the Reviewing Committee on the Export of Works of Art; acquired by the National Gallery in 2017.

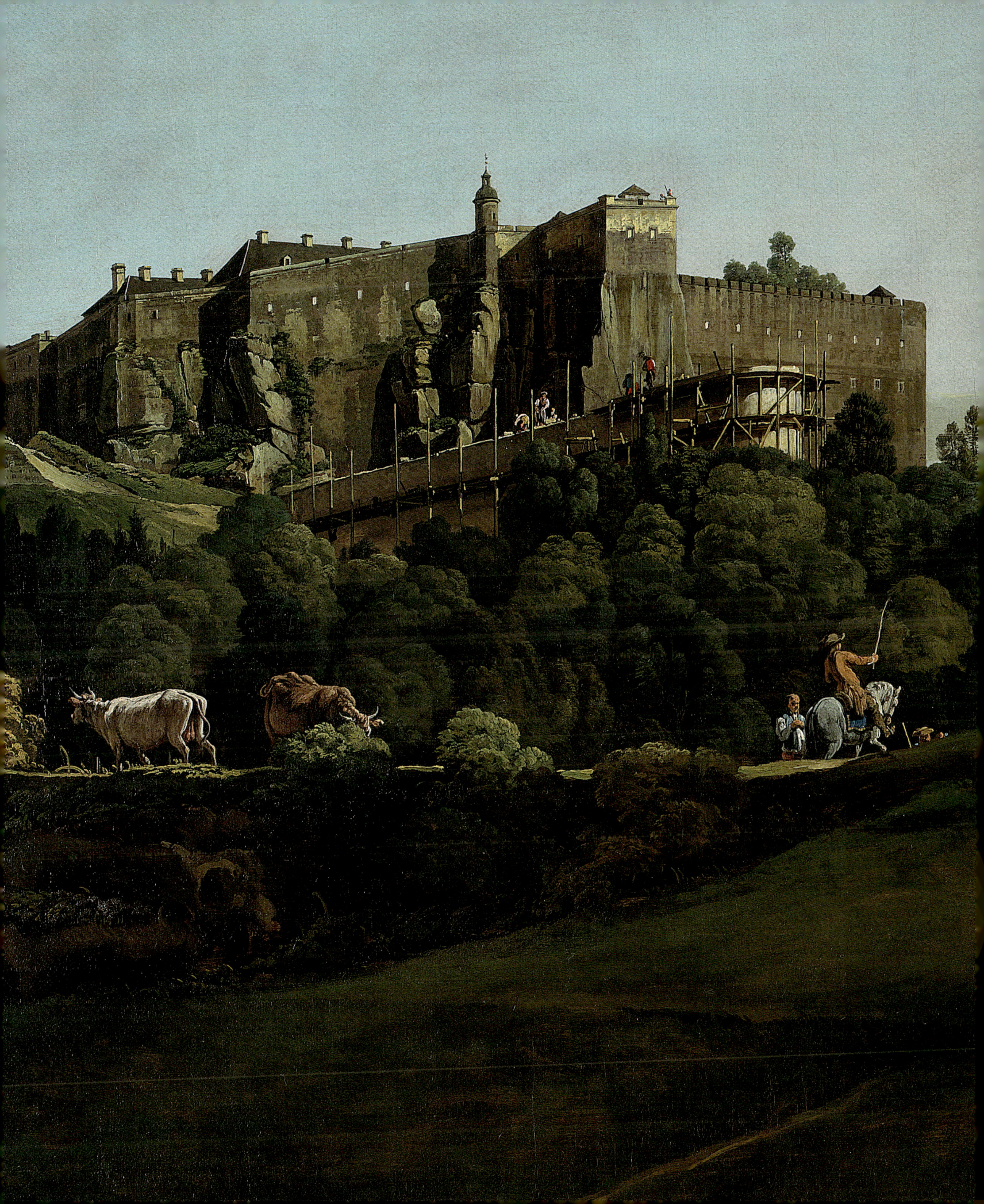

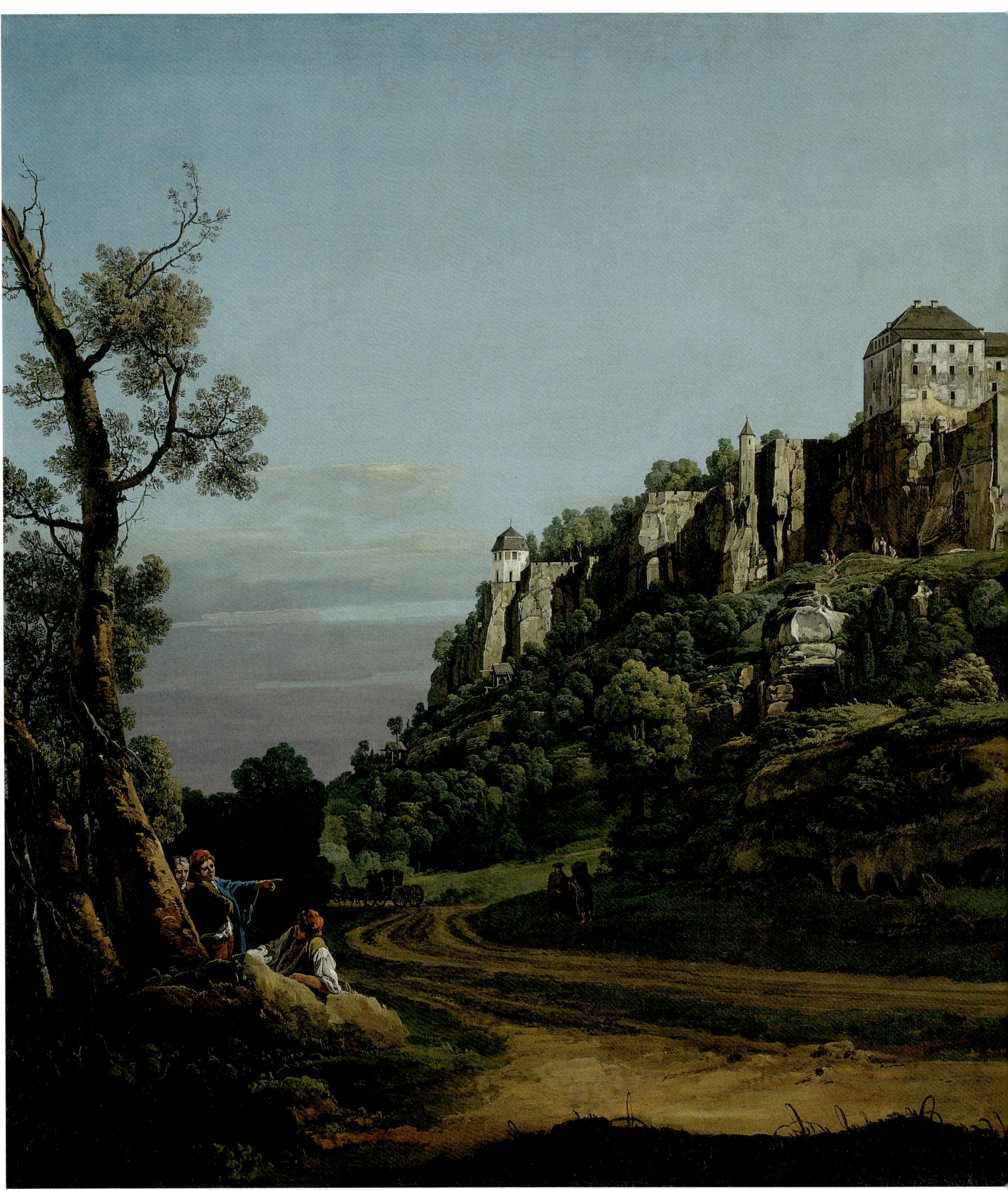

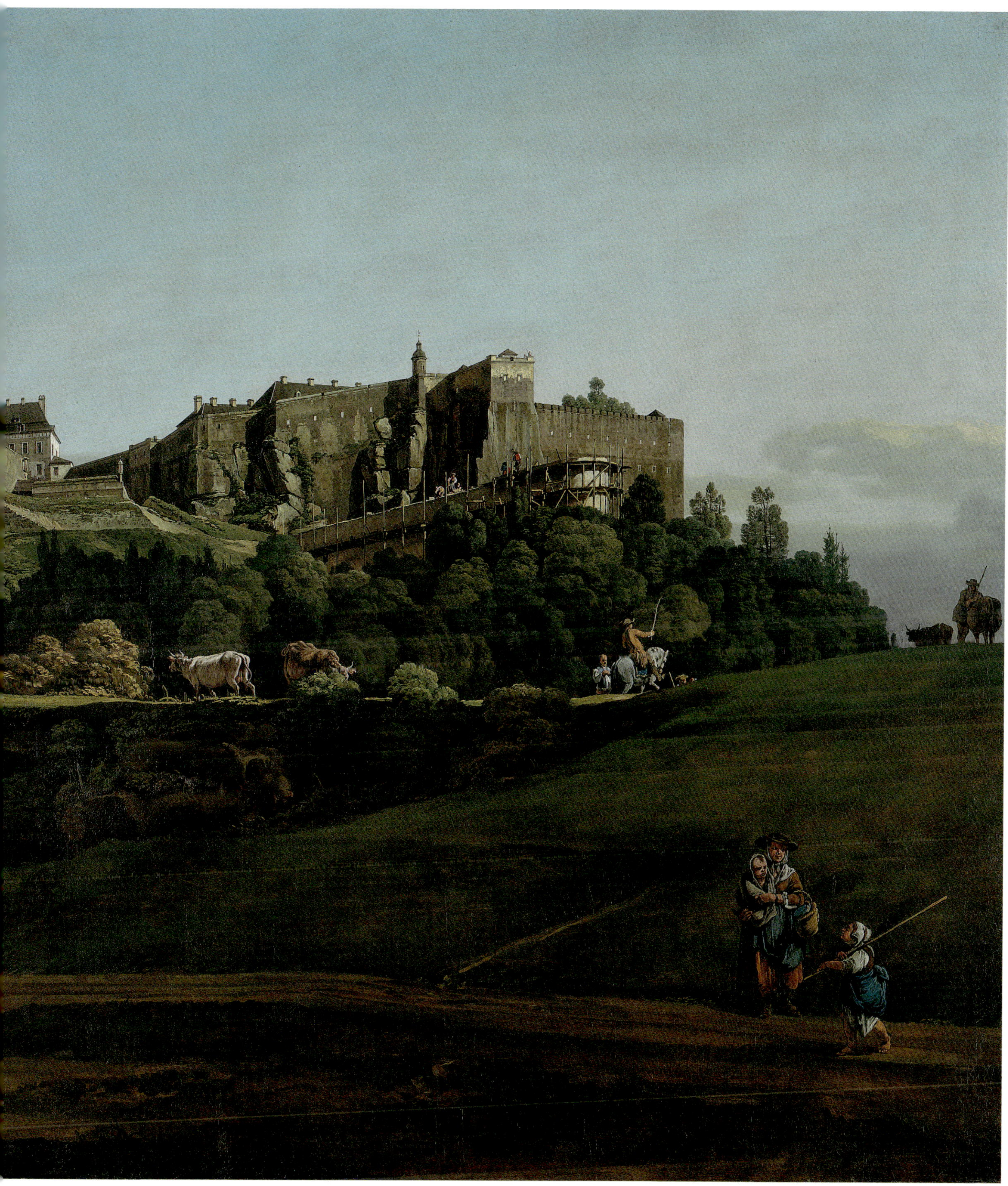

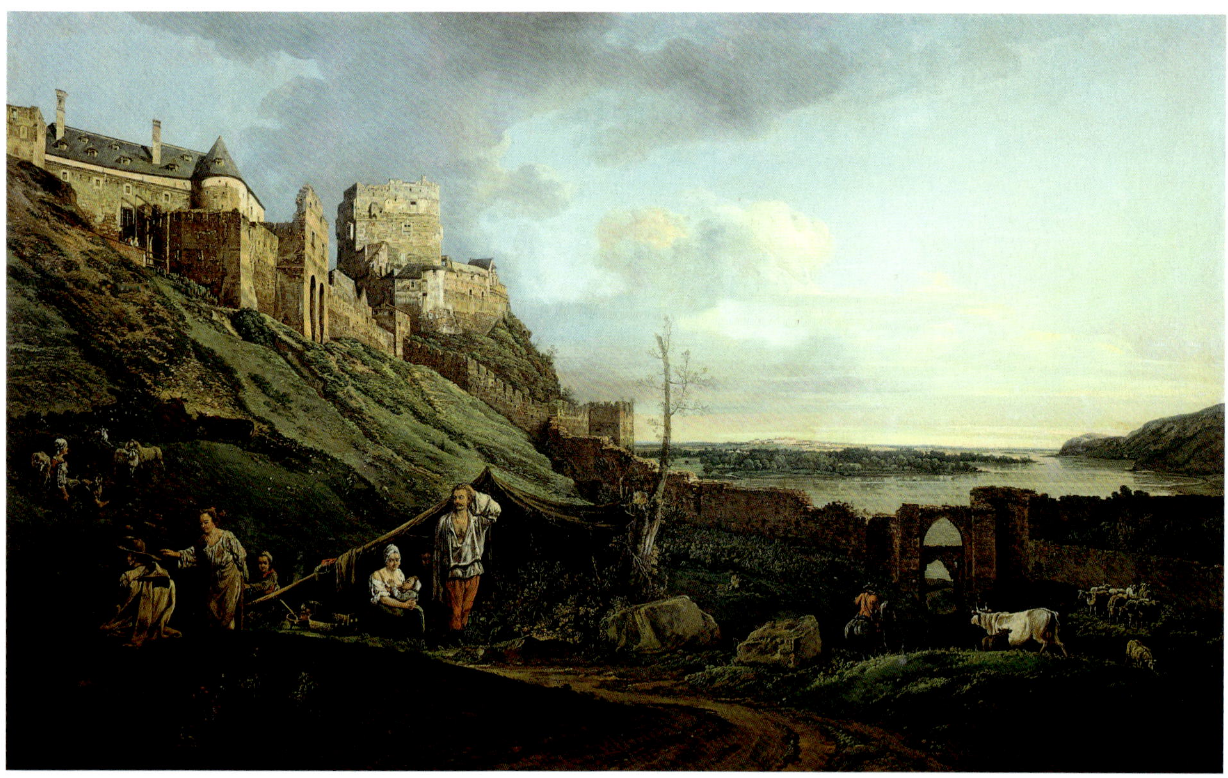

Fig. 25 Bernardo Bellotto, *The Ruined Castle of Theben*, 1759–60. Oil on canvas, 136 x 214 cm. Kunsthistorisches Museum, Vienna

distinct profile emerges from the impressionistic brushwork of the natural foundations below. The tower is set away from the edge of the plateau, connected only by a small bridge, whose shadow is defined in dark brown paint on the rocks beyond. Occupying the apex of this mound of rocks and trees is the Georgenburg, the medieval site that was transformed into a Renaissance-style hunting lodge by Elector John George I (1585–1656) in 1619. Standing proud and in three-quarter view, the building is rendered by Bellotto with geometric precision. The dark roofs of the Georgenburg and its adjoining buildings are sharply delineated, an effect Bellotto achieves by setting them against a pale blue sky. The Georg bastion, protruding like the prow of a ship from beneath the Georgenburg, provides a focal point to the composition. Bellotto blends the colours of its smooth facade to give the impression of a flat, stony surface. An abrupt transition of light to dark marks out its sharp corner, and a fine streak of paint illuminates the edge of rough rock on the adjacent side. Above and below, Bellotto demonstrates his skill in rendering different surface textures: the thick, blotchy brushstrokes of the stained facades above contrast with the smooth wall and, in turn, with the interlocking strokes of paint for the brick wall below. The far end of the Georgenburg complex, which housed the commander and his family, is illuminated in white paint; the very same facade is shown in Bellotto's courtyard view with the Brunnenhaus (cat. 5). The spiny roofs of the barracks are glimpsed above the fortress walls to the right, and the Seigerturm, a bell tower built in 1601, marks the easterly corner of the promontory, known as the Horn. Hempel's Corner, the furthest reaches of the fortress wall to the right, together with the Seigerturm and the Horn, are also

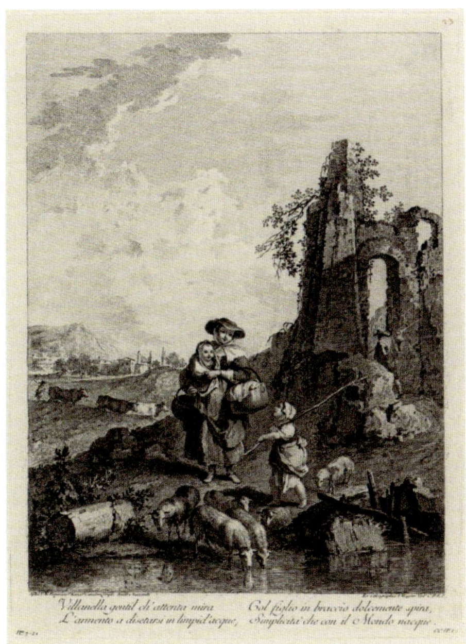

Fig. 26 Joseph Wagner (1706–1780) after Francesco Zuccarelli (1702–1788), *Villanella gentil ch' attenta mira [...]*, before 1774. Engraving, 59.3 x 42.9 cm. Herzog Anton Ulrich-Museum, Braunschweig, JWagner AB 2.129

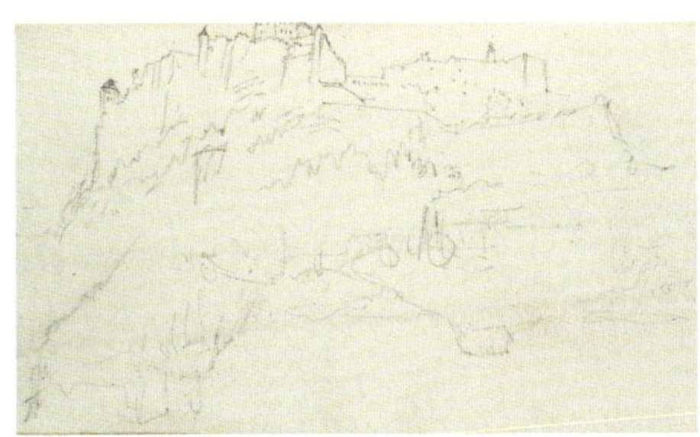

Fig. 27 Joseph Mallord William Turner (1775–1851), *Königstein Fortress, North Side*, from *Dresden and Saxon Switzerland Sketchbook*, 1835. Graphite on paper, 10.4 x 17 cm (sheet). Tate Britain, Turner Bequest, CCCVI 28a, D30939

visible on the extreme left of Bellotto's view from the south-west (cat. 3), creating a view of the fortress 'in the round' when viewed side by side. Beneath the ramparts, workmen build a defensive platform known as the Flèche, commissioned by Augustus III and constructed between 1755 and 1756, when Bellotto was making his drawings. The platform, which was used to fire arrows over the surrounding open area, is taller and longer than in the Washington painting (cat. 2), appearing closer here to the path that leads up to the entrance.

Figures and animals enliven the scene, a device Bellotto uses to guide our eye around the composition. The bodies and clothes of the workmen on the scaffold are just small dabs of coloured paint; their pink skin and white shirts are picked out by the evening light, and a man's waistcoat is highlighted with a dash of red. Bellotto expertly marks out the individual scaffold poles, using a fine brush to paint thin, controlled lines. Above the platform, two tiny soldiers, described with dots of colour, stand watch from the Horn. A sliver of sunlight breaks through the clouds and illuminates a grassy ridge below, whose tufts and undulations are roughly rendered with strokes of yellow paint. The light also falls on a rider, two men on foot and, further along, two cows grazing contentedly. One lifts its right hoof, poised as it looks towards a group of people who disturb the serenity of the moment. Bellotto's source for this cow is a composition by Francesco Zuccarelli, published as an engraving by Joseph Wagner (1706–1780) in which it appears in reverse.[1] Bellotto had used the same cow in an earlier view of Dresden from 1748 and had recourse to it again for his view of *The Ruined Castle of Theben*, painted several years later (fig. 25).[2] Bellotto has lifted the brown cow, grazing behind a nearby shrub, from a design by Nicolaes Berchem, reproduced in the same series of prints by Wagner.[3] Another of Zuccarelli's pastoral scenes has been identified as the source for the woman holding her baby encountering a young child in the foreground (figs 24, 26). The group, bathed in dusky light, is conceived with great attention to detail, probably a result of Bellotto directly copying Zuccarelli's design. Three male figures talk and relax at the base of a tree, which frames and balances the composition on the left side. The track pulls the viewer into the depths of the painting, drawing our attention to the woman dressed in blue who has stopped to talk to a man with a small child. A carriage, caught in a single moment, kicks up clouds of dust as it disappears into the forest in the distance.

A smaller replica of this view, with similar dimensions to those repeating the compositions of the other two external views, was on the art market in Munich in 1966.[4] When compared to the National Gallery painting, this replica has minor differences: the tree in the foreground is larger, the man and his two cows on the far right are omitted, there is no horse and carriage, and the clouds are given greater emphasis.

Also inspired by this viewpoint was J.M.W. Turner who, during a trip to Dresden and its environs in 1835, filled 18 sheets of a sketchbook with drawings of the fortress. In addition to two views of the west side, Turner drew one view from the north, taken from exactly the same position (fig. 27).[5] LC

2 THE FORTRESS OF KÖNIGSTEIN FROM THE NORTH-WEST

1756–8
Oil on canvas, 133 x 235.7 cm
National Gallery of Art, Washington, Patrons' Permanent Fund, 1993.8.1

LONDON ONLY

This is the only view of Königstein in which Bellotto locates the fortress in its wider context. The dramatic elevation occupies the right half of the canvas, while the left side opens up onto a patchwork of rolling green fields and the neighbouring mesa of Lilienstein on the opposite side of the Elbe Valley. At 415 metres, Lilienstein is among the highest of the many isolated sandstone mountains in this part of Saxony, which, since the eighteenth century, has come to be known as 'Saxon Switzerland' for its rocky topography and outstanding scenery. Yet Königstein remains the dominant force in Bellotto's composition, which takes its view from a small hillock nearby. The buildings and ramparts of the fortress sit perched atop the rugged foundation, their sheer facades distant and inaccessible. Bellotto's panoramic view is both theatrical, in its placement of groups of figures in the foreground, set against a magnificent backdrop, and cinematic, in its crystalline precision and 'wide-angle' format. The fortress exists in an expanse of lateral and vertical space; the composition 'hinges upon the equilibrium between the fortress on its rock massif and the towering expanse of sky on the left'.[1] The sky gives rhythm to the landscape, with clouds casting shadows onto patches of woodland and distant fields; sunlight sporadically breaks through them to spotlight figures below.

The two crumbling white facades on the far left of the fortress belong to the Georgenburg, the same building that stands proud in the London painting (cat. 1), viewed here from further to the west. Connected, to the right, is the Streichwehr (a defensive building used to protect the entrance to the fortress) and the Torhaus (gatehouse), the furthest reaches of which were home to the commandant and his family. Construction of these buildings started in 1589 under Elector Christian I, who was responsible for converting the medieval castle into a country fortress. The ascent to the fortress was lowered in 1729, and two casemated defensive structures were built in front of the Torhaus, known as the Tenaille and the Horn Ravelin. Bellotto depicts the angular wall of the Horn Ravelin and above, the upper reaches of a new baroque portal dedicated to Augustus the Strong are visible on the Torhaus entrance. On the far left, lower than the rest of the buildings and attached by a small stone bridge, is the Rösschen, an observation tower from the original medieval complex. To the other side, the Horn promontory is seen almost frontally, which, together with the small dome of the Seigerturm (bell tower), is set against the roofs of the barracks beyond. Bellotto expertly paints the jagged, elongated shadow of the Seigerturm – which had functioned as a watchtower and a clock since 1601 – on the smooth face of the ramparts below.

Bustling activity surrounds the fortress as two carts and several figures make their way along the track that winds its way up to the entrance. A short

PROVENANCE
Commissioned from the artist by Frederick Augustus II (1696–1763), Elector of Saxony and King of Poland (as Augustus III), in Dresden, by the spring of 1756; probably Henry Temple, 2nd Viscount Palmerston (1739–1802), London, and by descent to his son Henry John Temple, 3rd Viscount Palmerston (1784–1865), who served as prime minister 1855–8 and 1859–65, with two other pictures from the Königstein series (cats 1, 3); by whom sold, Foster's, London, 5 November 1850, lot 290, for £99 15s to 'Anderson', probably for Henry, 4th Earl Beauchamp (1784–1863), Madresfield Court, Worcestershire, and by descent to Else, Countess Beauchamp (1895–1989); sold at Sotheby's, London, 11 December 1991, lot 18, to Bernheimer Fine Arts Ltd and Meissner Fine Art Ltd, London, from whom acquired on 3 June 1993 by the National Gallery of Art, Washington.

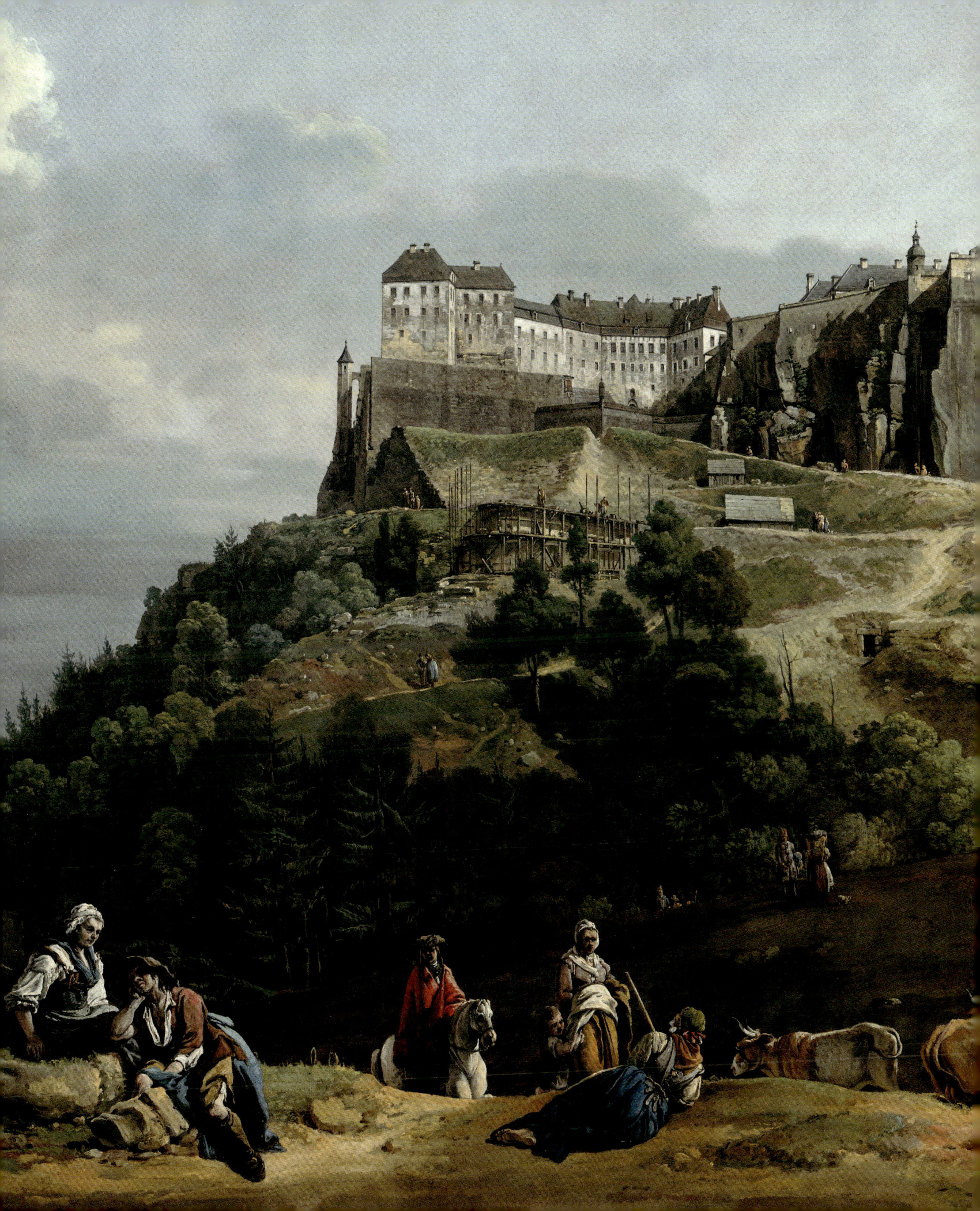

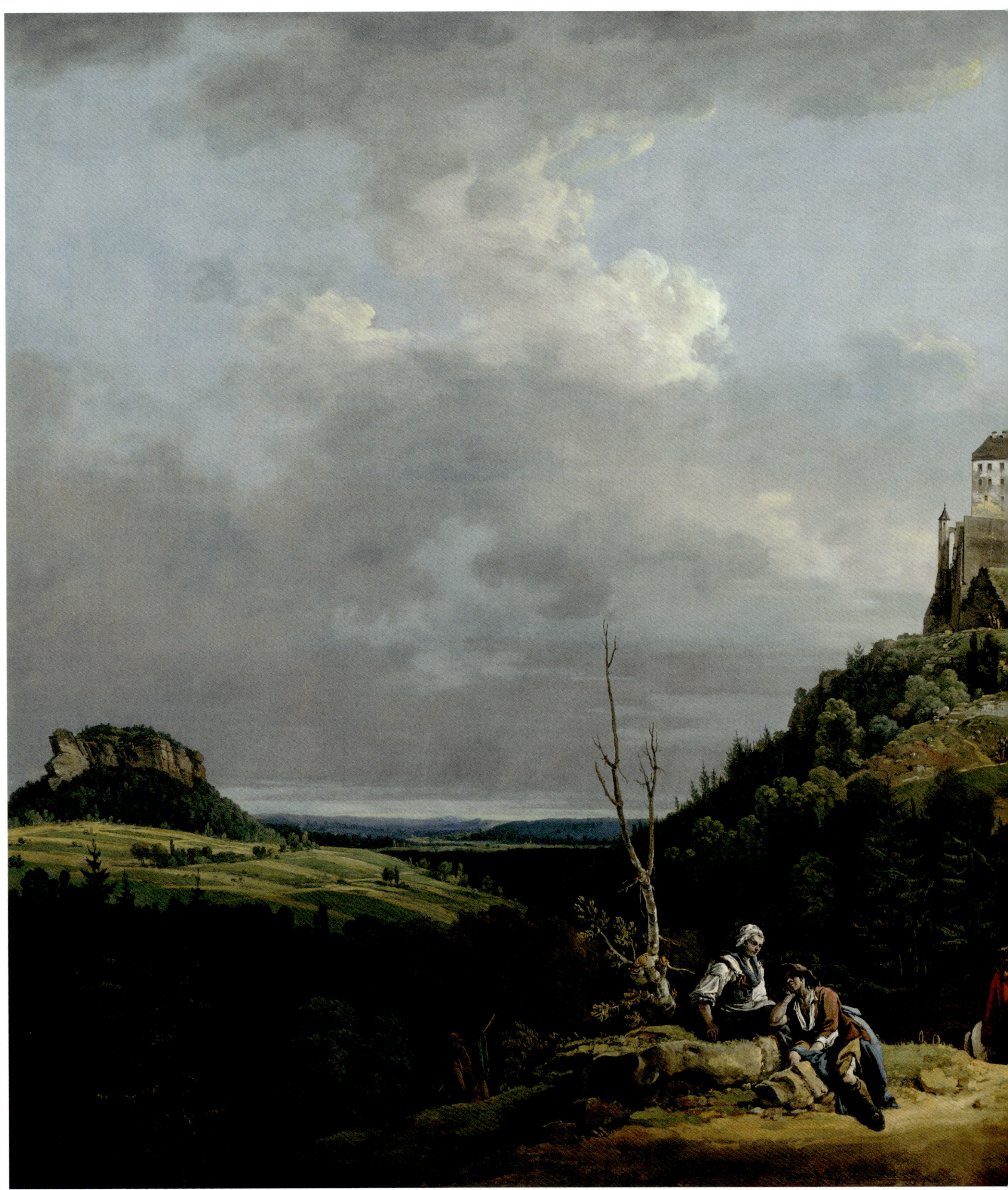

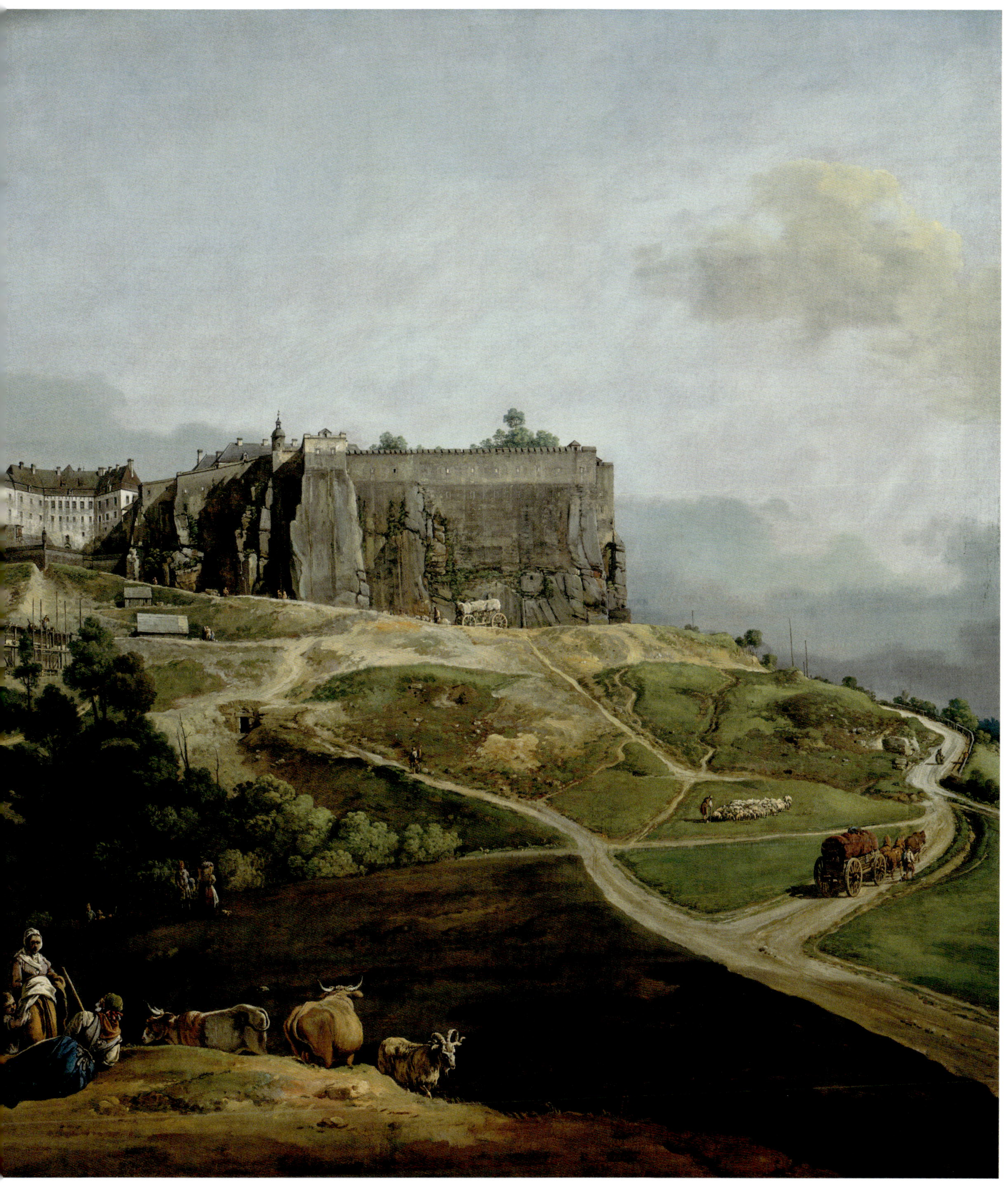

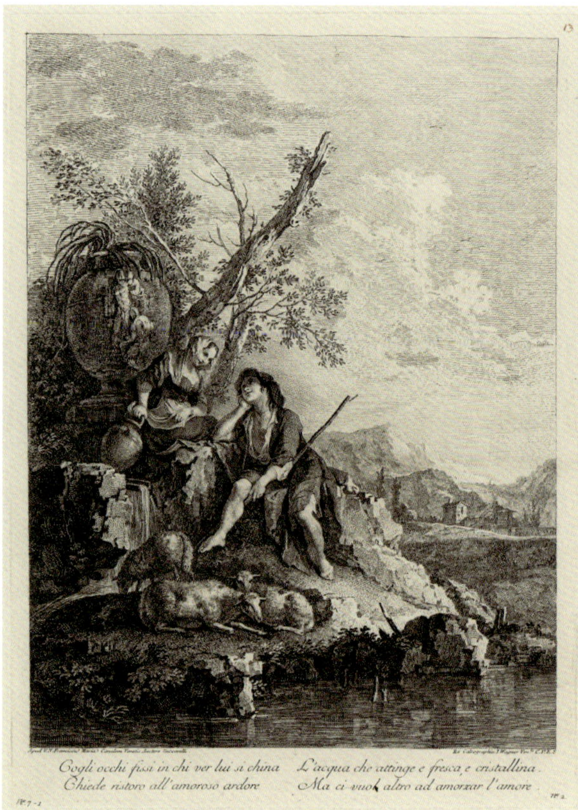

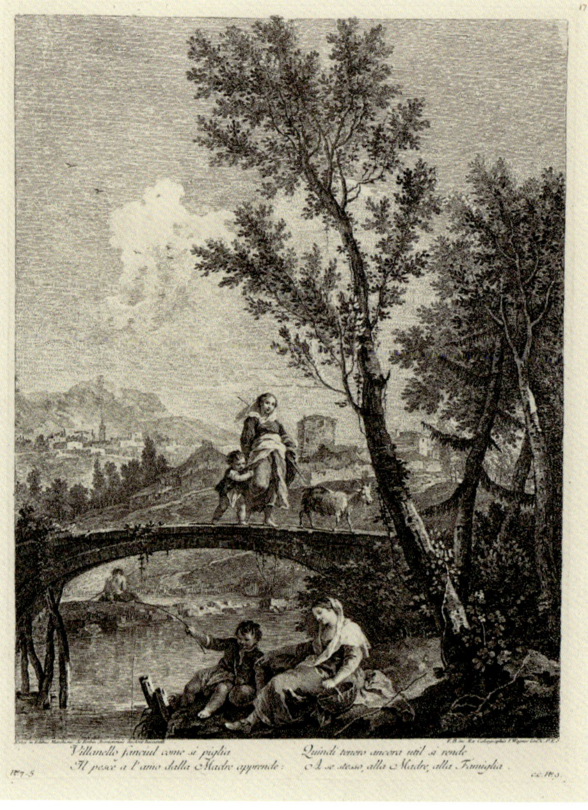

Fig. 28 Joseph Wagner (1706–1780) after Francesco Zuccarelli (1702–1788), *Cogli occhi fissi in chi ver lui si china […]*, before 1774. Engraving, 59.2 x 41.8 cm. Herzog Anton Ulrich-Museum, Braunschweig, JWagner AB 2.123

Fig. 29 Francesco Bartolozzi (1727–1815) after Francesco Zuccarelli (1702–1788), *Villanello fanciul come si piglia […]*, 1762. Engraving, 59.1 x 42.2 cm. Herzog Anton Ulrich-Museum, Braunschweig, FBartolozzi AB 2.83

shadow cast by the loaded cart in the foreground gives the impression of sunlight falling from high in the sky, suggesting it is the middle of the day. Gullies and small tracks run freely over abraded slopes, where trees have been cleared for military advantage. The green grass has eroded to expose sandy areas, painted in spirited strokes of white, grey and ochre. A shepherd tends to a flock of sheep, while another figure walks towards a gunpowder magazine, pierced deep into the side of the mountain and rendered with a single stroke of dark paint. Above, two shepherd huts are positioned on a zigzagging track leading up to the fortress. Bellotto shows the nearby Flèche under construction, the first part of the lower defensive outworks built between 1755 and 1756. Its vertical scaffold contributes to the upward force of the picture, and the structure is foreshortened more dramatically here than in the London view (cat. 1). The sharp red accent of a cloaked horseman, positioned directly beneath the Georgenburg, provides a central focus in the foreground. The austere presence of the fortress beyond is softened by the gentle interaction of women and children and the wistful gaze of the hatted man. Unlike the blotchy figures in the distance, those on the sandy plateau are detailed and characterised (see detail opposite). Bellotto drew inspiration for them from other artists: the cows and the ram are taken from pastoral scenes by Nicolaes Berchem, and the two figures by the tree and the woman with the small child are based on designs by Francesco Zuccarelli (figs 28, 29).[2]

The atmosphere in this painting is quite unlike that in the London and Knowsley views. Bellotto typically used a grey ground for his canvases, a colour that suited the cool tones of his palette, though he occasionally applied a red-grey layer in the sky. Here the reddish ground is visible through the clouds on the far left, giving them a pinkish hue. Bellotto's application of paint in diagonal brushstrokes adds further drama to the enormous sky.[3]

Bellotto produced an etching of this painting, perhaps the 'Vue de la Fortresse de Koenigstein' delivered to the Kupferstichkabinett in Dresden on 11 February 1765, an impression of which is in the British Museum, London (fig. 20).[4] Like the etching after the Knowsley painting (fig. 19), the plate is large. Its French inscription describes the view as being taken from the west, from the site of the Neuen Schänke inn, with the Lilienstein and the Lusatian mountains in the distance. The inscription attributes both the painting and engraving to Bellotto, 'Peintre Elec' (electoral painter), and states that it was published by Pierre Fouquet, an art dealer in Amsterdam. The coat of arms of the Elector of Saxony dates the engraving to after 1764, when Saxony broke off its ties with Poland following the death of Augustus III. The most notable difference from the painting is the tree in the foreground, which appears much larger and fuller in the etching. The rest of the woodland, including the tips of the trees visible within the fortress itself, remains as it appears in the painting. The scaffolding is also not recorded in the etching, probably because work to the defensive platform was complete by the time Bellotto was making his etching in the 1760s.

A reduced replica was thought to be the only surviving painted version of this view until the rediscovery of the present work in 1991.[5] This replica, whose dimensions roughly match those of the other replicas of the external views, was in the Galerie Liechtenstein in Vienna before entering a private collection in Zürich until at least 1965. It differs from the present painting in the absence of several figures – notably the reclining female in the foreground – and in the foremost tree, which is larger (though not as dominant as in the etching). A later copy of Bellotto's view from the north-west is in Hradec nad Moravicí Castle, near Opava, in the Czech Republic.[6] As was the case with the view from the north (cat. 1), J.M.W. Turner sketched this particular view (twice) in 1835.[7] LC

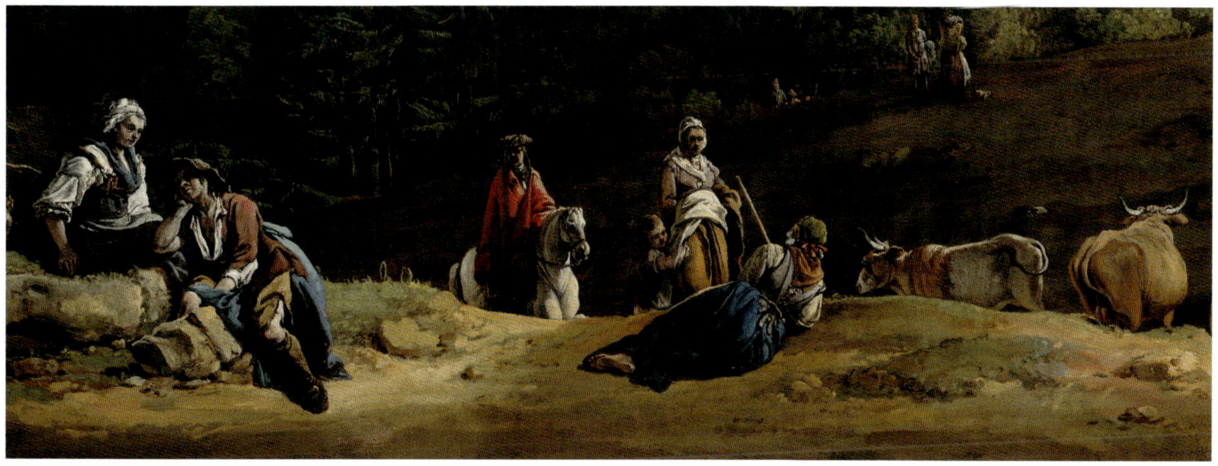

3 THE FORTRESS OF KÖNIGSTEIN FROM THE SOUTH-WEST

1756–8
Oil on canvas, 133.9 x 238 cm
Lent by The Earl of Derby

The view of Königstein from the south-west gives an entirely different perspective of the fortress, not least because very little can be seen of the buildings within. Rather, the focus lies on the impenetrable nature of the ramparts. Their smooth facades, interconnected at sharp angles, emerge from the sprawling natural sandstone formations on which the fortress was built in the late sixteenth century. Jean de Bodt (1670–1745), master builder under Augustus III, had the rock foundations cut away to steepen the fortress walls on the south side in the 1730s. Bellotto relishes the opportunity to paint different textures, juxtaposing the deep grooves and undulating surfaces of the rocks with the yellow and grey marbling on the fortress walls, and the slope of loose scree below. The fortifications are topped with crenels – indentations along the top edges allowing for protected fire – which Bellotto paints with regimented precision. Less frequent and less regular defensive embrasures are dispersed along the stained wall below. The sharp silhouette of the fortress cuts into the sky above, which is loosely blended with thick strokes of white and blue paint.

The Old Armoury with its peaked roof and its extension is one of the few buildings visible beyond the ramparts. Constructed in 1594 as a weapons store, this structure would have served the same purpose at the time Bellotto was painting.[1] Further towards the centre, just right of the two trees blocking the view of the fortress, the wall juts out beneath a small rounded dome with a spire, and two lengths of wooden scaffold protrude from a pointed arch. This 'crane' lift had been in use since 1589 to transport goods up into the fortress. On the ground below, a cart, partially hidden from view, a small shed with two guards standing nearby, and a stream of figures making their way back up the path to the left suggest that this area was a hub of activity on the otherwise barren south side. The same path, which runs beneath the Horn promontory and Hempel's Corner on the far left of the composition, is visible in the Washington painting (cat. 2), which shows it leading up to the entrance of the fortress.

We know Bellotto made drawings on site, as evidenced by the decree issued to him on 30 March 1756 (fig. 16). It is tempting to imagine him as he portrays himself in his first painting of Dresden (fig. 8), sitting on a stone with his legs elegantly crossed, sketching the fortress from the point where the hillside pastures meet the edge of the wooded valley. Bellotto must have made multiple preparatory drawings – a combination of freehand sketches and detailed perspectival drawings using the camera obscura – before working up the final composition in the studio. The trees that frame the composition on the far right were added at a late stage in the painting process; Bellotto's adjustments to the placement of the lower branches are visible against the pale blue sky.

PROVENANCE

Commissioned from the artist by Frederick Augustus II (1696–1763), Elector of Saxony and King of Poland (as Augustus III), in Dresden, by the spring of 1756; probably Henry Temple, 2nd Viscount Palmerston (1739–1802), London, and by descent to his son Henry John Temple, 3rd Viscount Palmerston (1784–1865), who served as prime minister 1855–8 and 1859–65, with two other pictures from the Königstein series (cats 1, 2); sold with its pendant (cat. 1) by 'Palmerston' for £200 to the Earls of Derby, probably to Edward Smith-Stanley, 13th Earl of Derby (1775–1851), first at Derby House, Grosvenor Square, London, and by 1850 at Knowsley Hall, Lancashire; thence by descent.

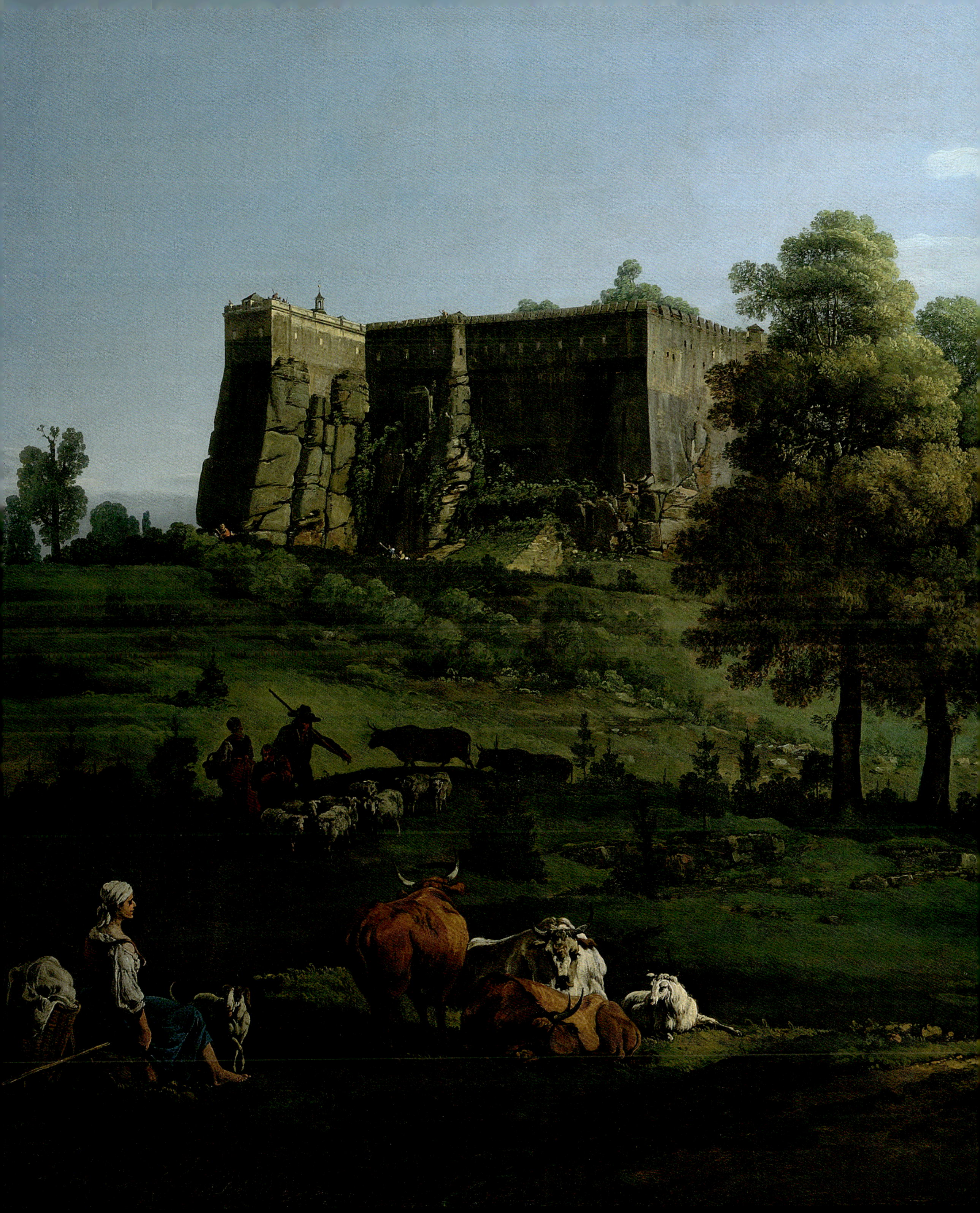

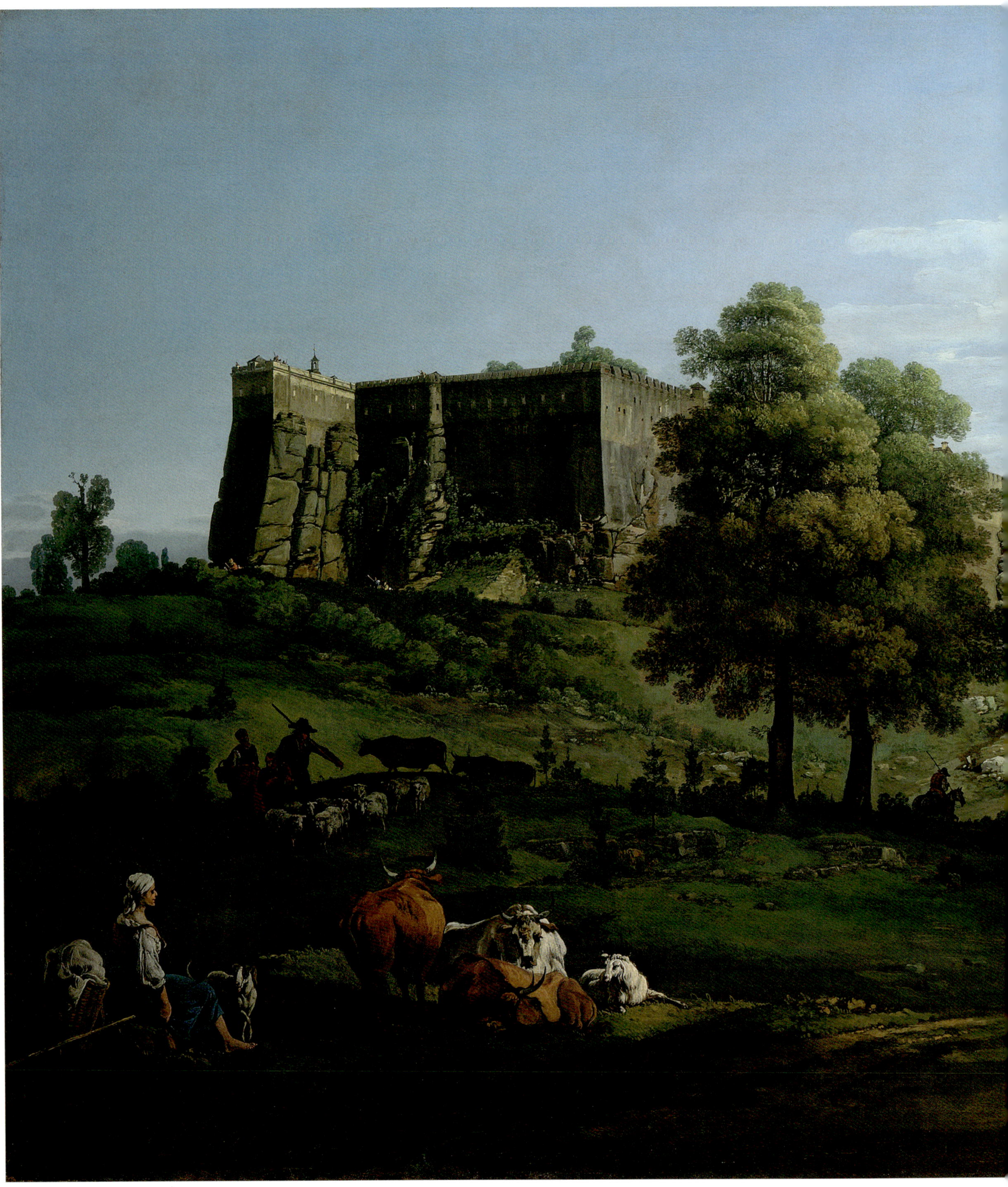

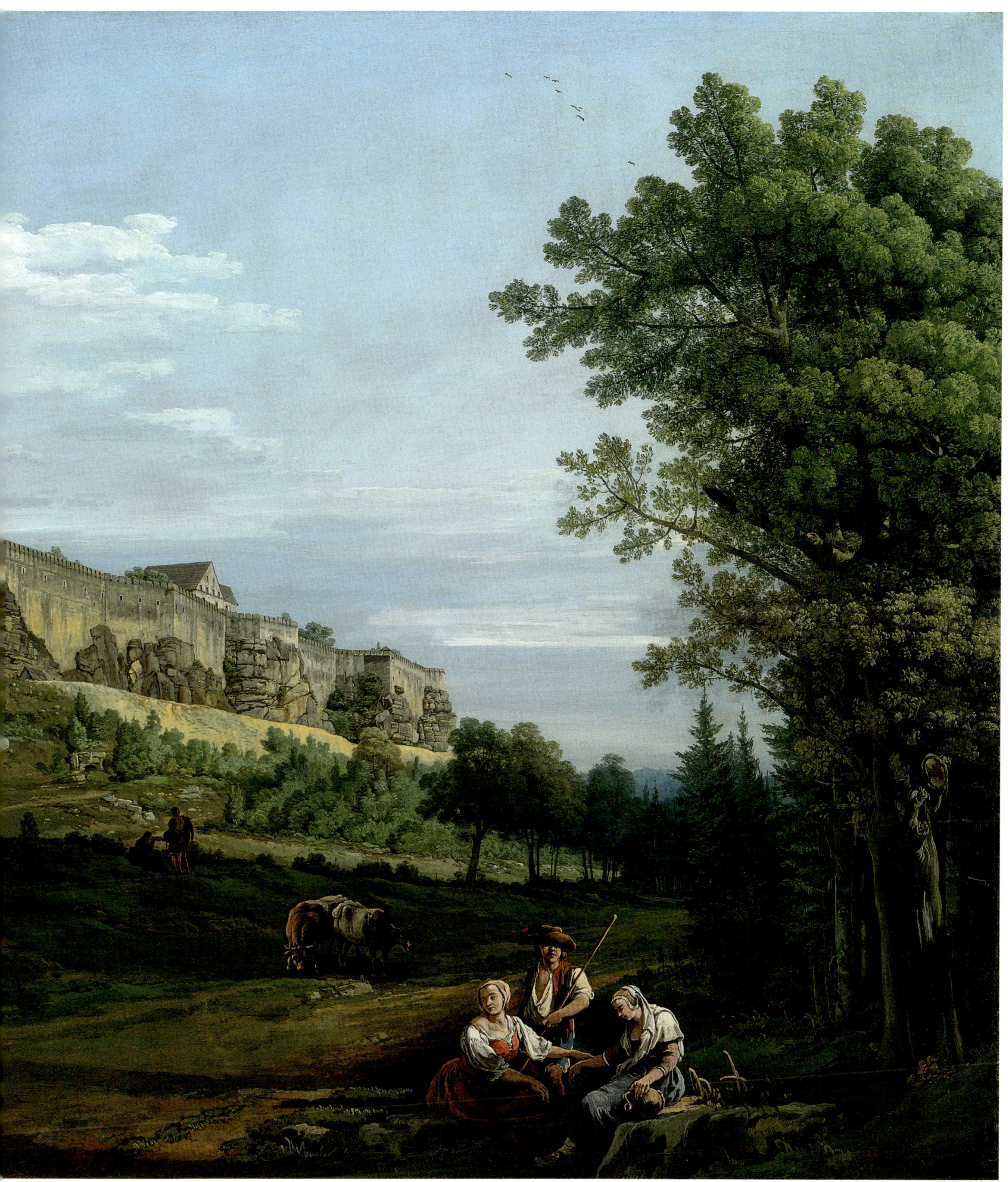

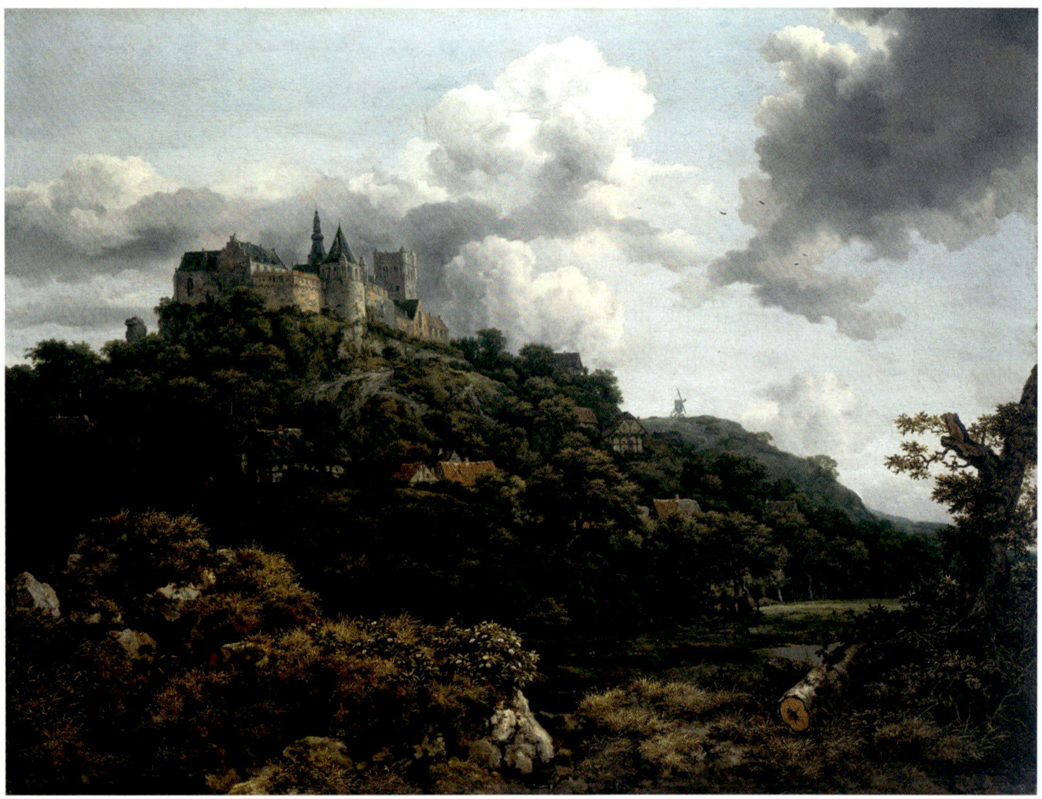

Fig. 30 Jacob van Ruisdael (1628/9–1682), *Bentheim Castle*, 1653. Oil on canvas, 110.5 x 144 cm. The National Gallery of Ireland, Dublin

His controlled application of paint for these passages contrasts with the lively brushstrokes he uses for the grass and rocks in the foreground.

Both the low vantage point and the golden morning sunshine washing over the fortress ensure that it is the dominant force in Bellotto's composition. Jacob van Ruisdael had adopted a similar position for his view of Bentheim Castle now at the National Gallery of Ireland, Dublin (fig. 30). Though Ruisdael's painting is significantly smaller than Bellotto's, his castle is depicted from an oblique angle and is shown perched atop a wooded mountain, towering over the grassy glades below.[2] Bellotto would later revisit this format for his painting *The Ruined Castle of Theben* (fig. 25).

Here, Bellotto's view is partially interrupted by two verdant trees, whose soft foliage contrasts starkly with the solid geometry of the ramparts. The dark shadow beneath the central group of trees, concentrated on a small brow in the middle distance, separates the activity in the foreground from what is beyond. A shepherd and a young boy herd a flock of sheep and a woman carries a basket. The silhouettes of two cows disappear behind a gentle undulation in the ground, a man on horseback makes his way off into the sunlight, and two figures converse nearby. It is for the figures and animals in this view that Bellotto relies most heavily on works by Francesco Zuccarelli and Nicolaes Berchem. An engraving published by Joseph Wagner, after Zuccarelli, shows Bellotto as having lifted the entire shepherd group – including two of the cows on the brow of the hill – and transposed it to the left of the two trees in his painting (fig. 31).[3] From the same print, he takes the seated woman in the lower left corner, replacing the child with a dog, lowering the woman's arm, covering her head and adjusting the basket behind her. Another of Zuccarelli's compositions provides the motif for the rider in the distance.[4] Many of the cows in Bellotto's paintings of Königstein and Pirna are taken from compositions by Nicolaes Berchem; the group of cows to the right of the seated woman are lifted directly from designs by Berchem in Wagner's same series of engravings.[5] Bellotto was not always content to copy figures without altering them to suit his requirements. For the three figures in the lower right corner, Bellotto lifts independent elements from different compositions by Zuccarelli, adjusting and combining them to create a single harmonious group.[6] The same is the case for the cows grazing in the middle distance, which originate from the same source by Berchem, but in a different configuration.[7]

An etching of this view by Bellotto (fig. 19) explains that it is taken from the south side, on the path leading to a paper mill, which still survives in the nearby village of Hütten, in the Biela Valley.[8] The path is called Der Eselsweg, and also leads to the Neuen Schänke, the site from which the Washington view is taken (cat. 2). The sizeable etching, measuring 42.2 x 64.1 cm, describes Bellotto as 'Member of the Electoral Academy of Fine Arts', of which he had been made teacher of perspective in 1764, the year it was founded. The etching was published in the *Bibliothek der Schönen Wissenschaften und der freyen Künste* (*Library of the Fine Sciences and the Free Arts*) in 1765, in an account of the first exhibition at the Dresden Academy.[9] It shows minor differences with respect to the painting, principally in the removal of a figure from the group on the right and the replacement of the two cows in the middle ground with a rider and his dog.

A reduced-size painted replica of this view also exists, similar in scale to the replicas of the two other external views. The replica is not a direct copy of either the present painting or the etching, its main difference being the lack of foliage on the tree framing the composition to the right. It was painted as a companion piece to Bellotto's *Pirna from the Vineyards at Posta*, and both have been at Schloss Fachsenfeld in Aalen since 1829.[10] LC

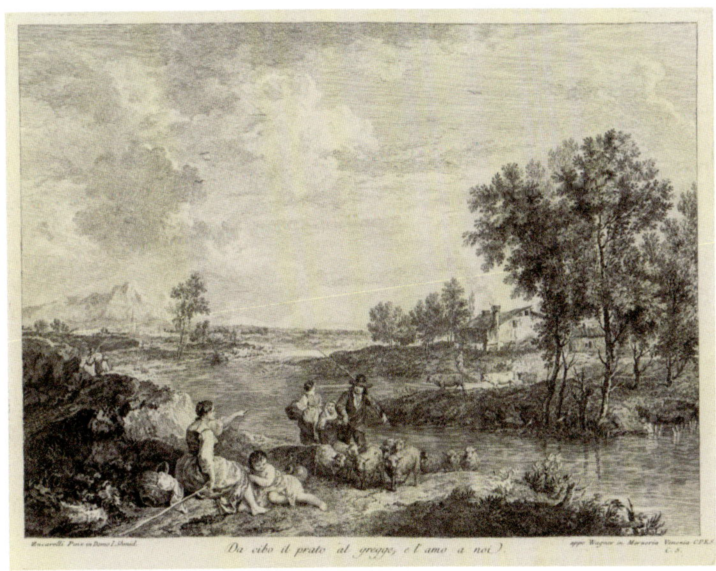

Fig. 31 Joseph Wagner (1706–1780) after Francesco Zuccarelli (1702–1788), *Da cibo il prato al gregge [...]*, before 1774. Engraving, 36.5 x 47.7 cm. Herzog Anton Ulrich-Museum, Braunschweig, JWagner AB 2.114

4 THE FORTRESS OF KÖNIGSTEIN: COURTYARD WITH THE MAGDALENENBURG

1756–8
Oil on canvas, 133.9 x 238.8 cm
Manchester Art Gallery, 1983.806

Purchased with the assistance of the Victoria & Albert Museum Purchase Grant Fund, the National Heritage Memorial Fund, Art Fund, the Manchester Art Gallery Art Fund, Patrons, Associates and Friends of Manchester Art Gallery

Here Bellotto shows the fortress courtyard on a summer morning, replete with quiet civilian life. The view is taken from in front of the Old Barracks, facing north-west, with the Magdalenenburg the most prominent building on the centre right. It is convincingly accurate in terms of what would have been visible when standing in a certain spot, although Bellotto has adjusted angles slightly to create his composition. From the far left in the distance, the first building is the end of a newer barracks block, labelled 'Front Barracks' in a plan of the fortress dating from after 1743 (fig. 14).[1] Beyond the Front Barracks, distant hills are visible over trees and a fence that surrounds the private garden reserved for the fortress's chief military officer, the commandant, and his family. Continuing to the right, the small stub of a white building is the commandant's house. At the centre left we are viewing the narrow side of the Brunnenhaus, or well-house. Protruding diagonally behind its right side is the New Armoury. Then a glimpse of the market square is seen just before the primary subject of the picture, the palace-cum-storehouse known as the Magdalenenburg. On the far right is the garrison church dedicated to St George (fig. 32).

The Magdalenenburg, a castle in the Northern Renaissance style, was built at the behest of Elector Johann Georg I in 1621–2. It was subsequently named after Magdalene Sibylle of Brandenburg-Bayreuth (1612–1687), the wife of his son, Elector Johann Georg II, who is said to have greatly enjoyed court life in the castle as Electress of Saxony.[2]

When Bellotto was at Königstein, between 1756 and 1758, the Saxon court still used the upper floors of the Magdalenenburg for making merry, while the basement held supplies. There is a clue to these functions in the form of the baroque stone sculpture above the door. Allegorical figures, possibly Hercules and Ceres, representing strength and plenty, flank a Bacchus figure on a barrel.[3] The Magdalenenburg cellar housed the 60,000-gallon wine cask that Augustus the Strong had had constructed by the renowned architect Matthäus Daniel Pöppelmann in 1722–5 (fig. 33). A platform above the cask afforded dancing room for 30 couples. Having won his wager to build the biggest wine cask in Europe, Augustus reportedly had it filled only once. Although it was beautifully ornamented, flaws in its construction meant that it had to be decommissioned in 1819, and it is likely that even by Bellotto's time at Königstein the wine was

PROVENANCE

Commissioned from the artist by Frederick Augustus II (1696-1763), Elector of Saxony and King of Poland (as Augustus III), in Dresden, by the spring of 1756; probably Sir Robert Brown, Bt (d. 1760) and his widow Lady Margaret Brown, née Cecil (1698-1782) by whom sold ('A Capital Collection of Italian, French, Flemish and Dutch Pictures'), Christie's, London, 7 March 1778, lot 79 ('A view of the fortress at Koningstein in Saxony painted for the King of Poland') or lot 80 ('Ditto, ditto, its companion'), bought for £79 16s by 'Tempest', probably John Tempest (1739-1794) of Wynyard Park, County Durham; by descent to his niece Frances Anne Vane-Tempest (1800-1865), who married Charles Stewart, later 3rd Marquess of Londonderry (1778-1854); by descent until sold by Alistair Vane-Tempest-Stewart, 9th Marquess of Londonderry (1937-2012); purchased through David Carritt Ltd, London, by Manchester Art Gallery in 1983.

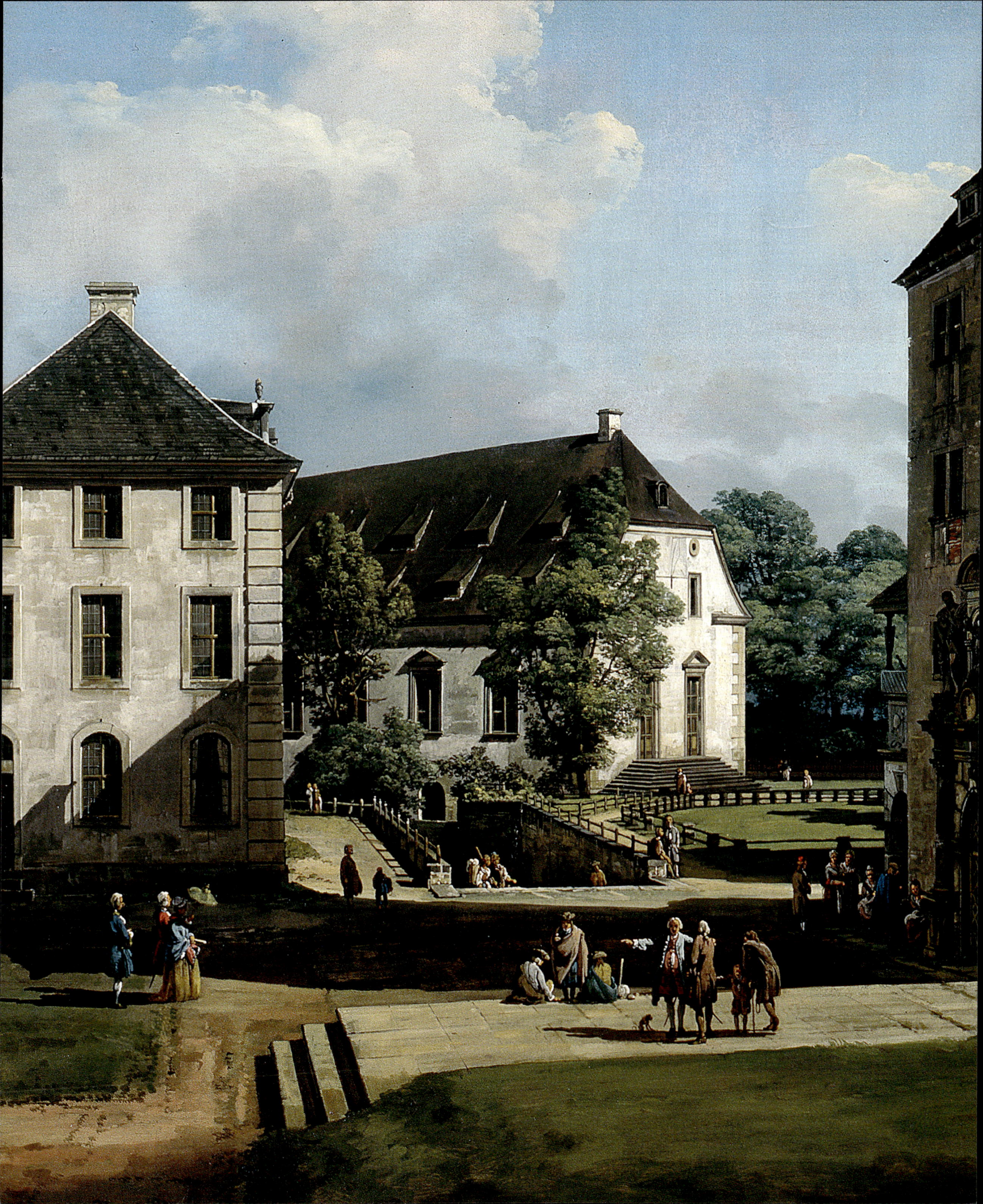

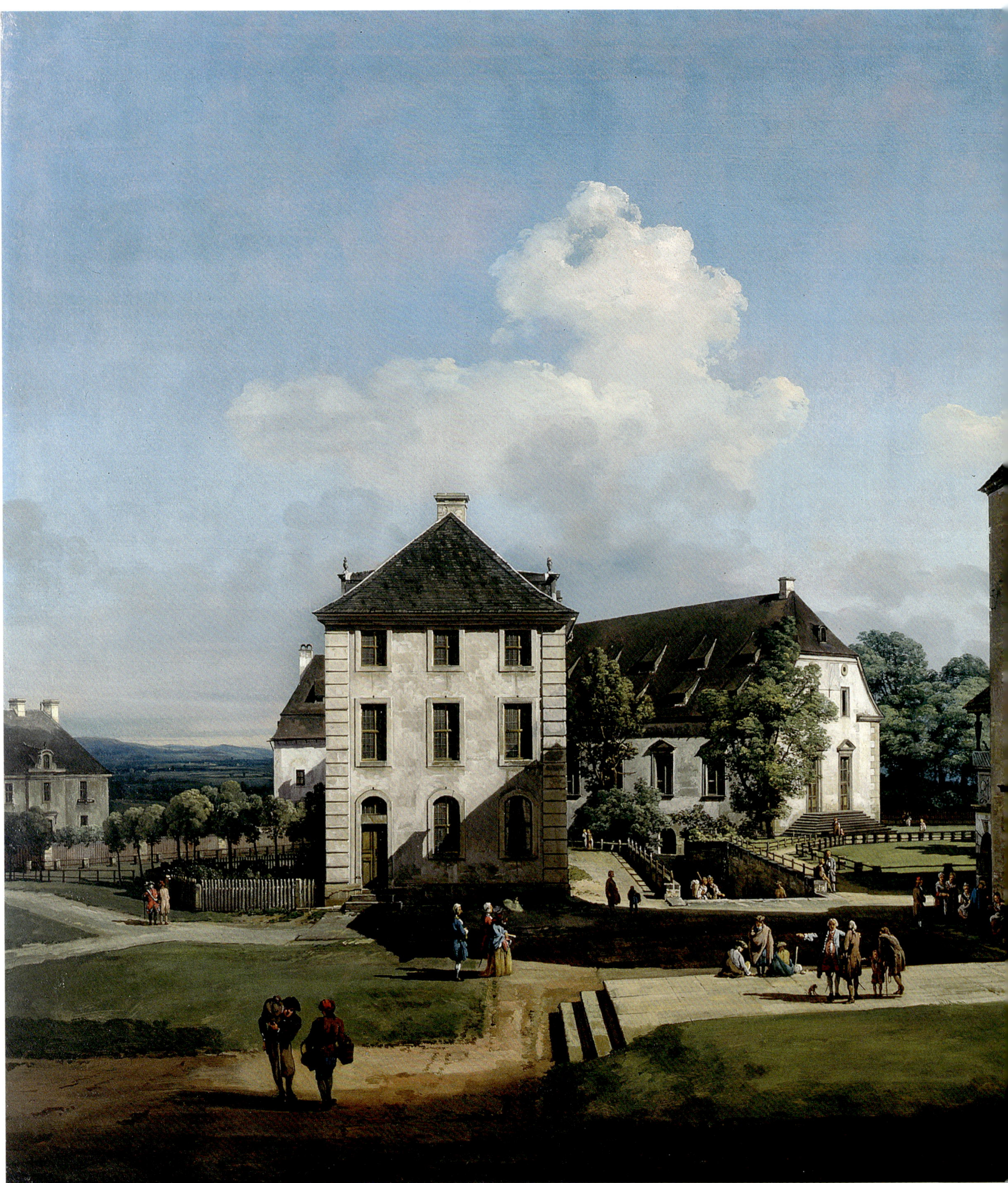

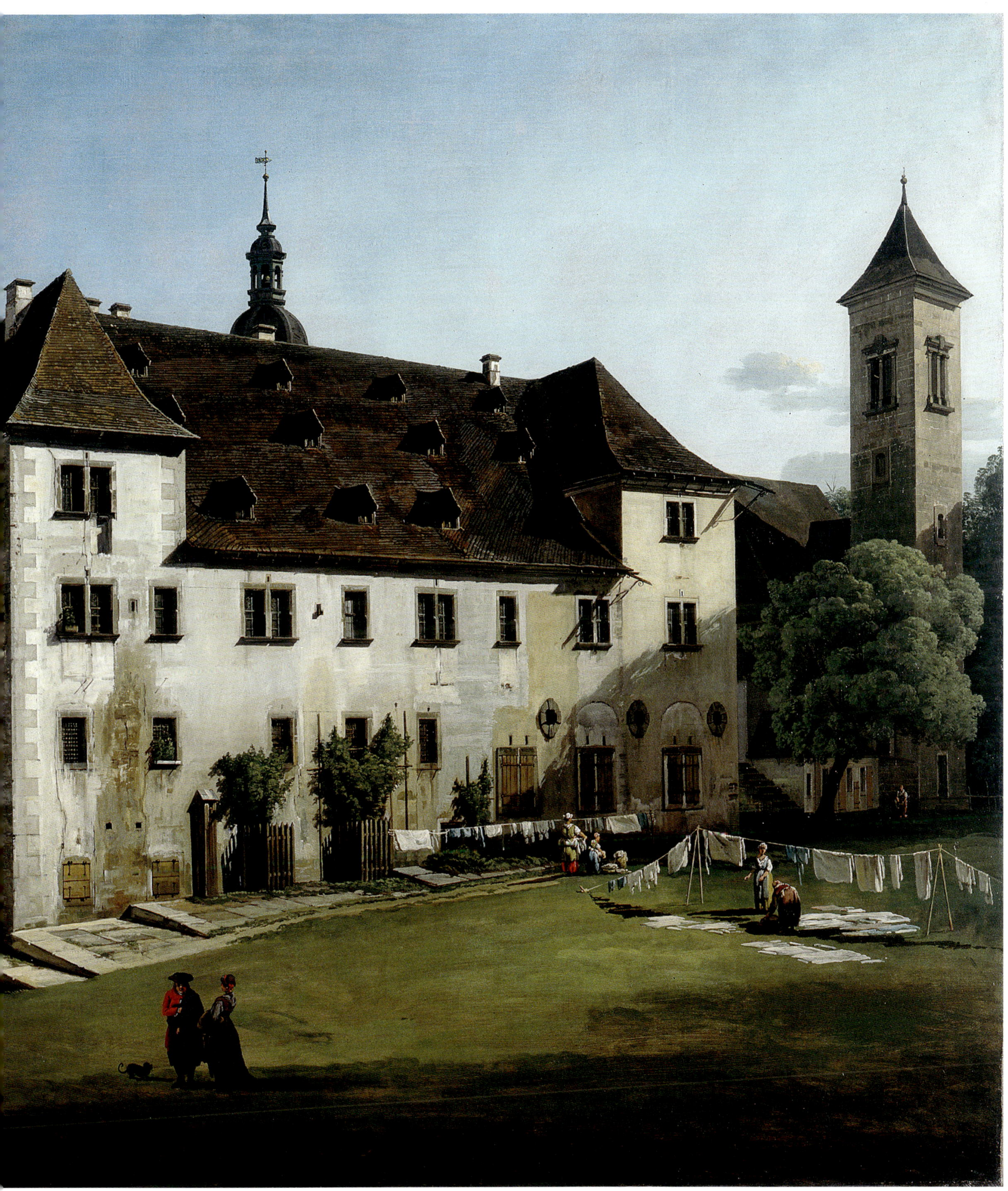

drawn from a small barrel hidden within the giant cask.[4] In this painting, the three shuttered windows and three round ventilation points on the wall indicate its location at the rear of the building.[5]

At the centre of our view there is a glimpse of a fenced lawn, overlooked by a canopied balcony and staircase to the rear of the Magdalenenburg. This area was known as the market square, although a 1762 plan of the fortress labels it as the parade ground.[6] Bellotto includes neither market nor military parade. He has caused a low-angled sunlight to strike the end of the New Armoury, illuminating a portion of the square. This is a classic Bellotto touch: sophisticated deployment of lighting and viewpoint combine to depict the principal buildings clearly, yet treat us to more than flat architectural fact. We are given a tantalising glance at a sunlit gathering point, just around the corner.

There are two pentimenti, or visible alterations made during the painting process, that can be seen with the naked eye. One appears to be the result of moving the glimpsed Magdalenenburg tower slightly to the left, leaving a very faint pale outline on the right. The other is harder to make sense of. To the left of the Magdalenenburg, level with the top-floor window, is a scroll-like shape in the sky with a diagonal at its right corner. On the whole, however, Bellotto remained true to what would have been a meticulously prepared composition, incising lines in the layer of red ground, or underpainting, to fix the position of the buildings before beginning to paint in detail.[7]

The figures that populate the painting are from different walks of life. The group of two bewigged gentlemen and a woman with a parasol who stand contemplating the Magdalenenburg seem to be visitors. Their upright figures are contrasted with other, hunched bodies: we see shoulders rounded to bear burdens or to shift weight onto a crutch. Few among the figures can be identified as garrison personnel – for a painter a useful way of incorporating touches of bright red and blue. To the left we can identify a soldier and his companion as they walk together. The figure on the lawn in the foreground wearing a military-red jacket, however, is a ruminative older man, who chats to a woman as a small dog capers at their feet. This latter group is notorious among Manchester's regular visitors for their contrariwise shadows – the explanation for which cannot be simple error, as the same shadows are present in two smaller replicas (made by Bellotto himself) of the painting.[8] The sheer variety of figures conveys the community nature of fortress

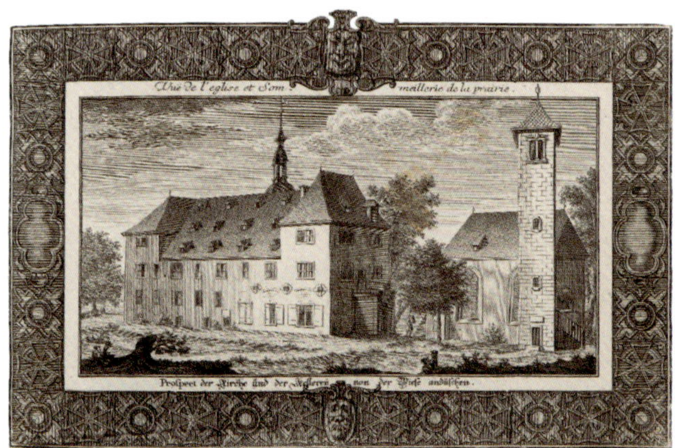

Fig. 32 Johann Georg Pintz (1697–1767), *The Magdalenenburg and the Garrison Church*, about 1735. From the album *Various Prospects Drawn from Nature of the World-famous Königstein Fortress*, published by Martin Engelbrecht, Augsburg. Königstein Fortress Collection, G 3353

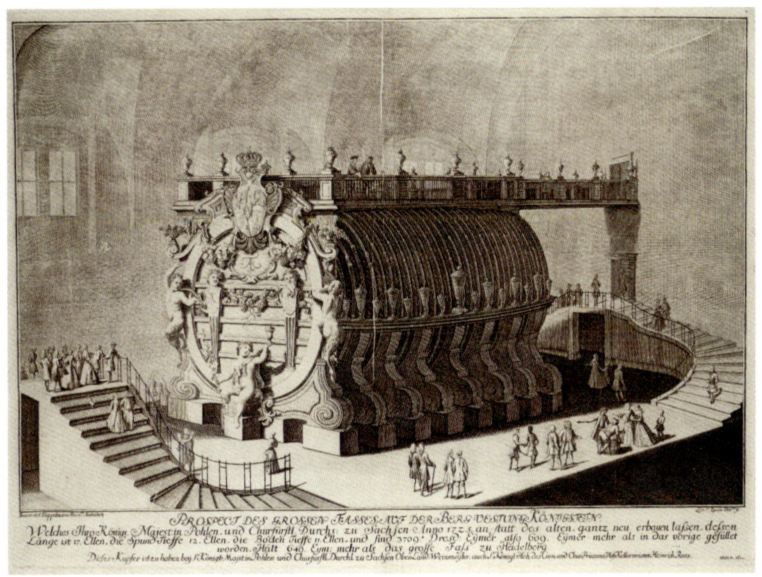

Fig. 33 Lorenzo Zucchi (1704–1779) after Matthäus Daniel Pöppelmann (1662–1736), *The Large Barrel in the Magdalenenburg on the Königstein Fortress*, 1729. Etching, 47.3 x 61.5 cm. Königstein Fortress Collection, G 1386

life. Bellotto also skilfully uses his staffage, or human figures, to aid spatial understanding: to the left of the market square, the way the two figures emerge from the darkness into the sunlight on the subterranean stairway helps us to see that this descent is both substantially built and in regular civilian use.[9] It leads under the New Armoury to the gatehouse and main defensive buildings of the fortress.

One of the most appealing details in *Courtyard with the Magdalenenburg* is the scene of the washing being hung out to dry: to the right, smocks and aprons, shirts and stockings are being draped over the line and spread upon the grass by women, with children lending assistance. These are real clothes, not generic shapes but sleeves that have not quite unfurled properly, and apron strings that need looping crossways on the line. The satisfaction of laying out a clean wash in an orderly way is conveyed, while at the same time Bellotto does not gloss over the hard work of bending and lifting.

Perhaps it was Bellotto's straightforward approach to the depiction of labour that spurred the then director of Manchester City Art Gallery, Timothy Clifford, to make such heroic efforts to acquire the two paintings for Manchester in 1982–3.[10] Clifford's determined stance that the two Bellottos should belong to Manchester rested on this firm foundation of their being simultaneously 'quite the most delicious pictures I have seen on the London art market for years' while also showing ordinary household chores taking place against sharply delineated architecture.[11]

The frame, with its distinctive classical rosette decoration, is of the same design as that of the other fortress courtyard view in the collection of Manchester Art Gallery (cat. 5). It appears that the frames were made especially for these works, but is not clear when, although they appear to date from the mid-nineteenth century or earlier.[12]

Smaller painted replicas of the Magdalenenburg view, with minor differences in the foreground figures, are in the Gräflich Schönborn-Buchheimschen Galerie in Vienna and in the Cooley Collection in West Hartford, Connecticut.[13] HW

5 THE FORTRESS OF KÖNIGSTEIN: COURTYARD WITH THE BRUNNENHAUS

1756–8
Oil on canvas, 133.9 x 238 cm
Manchester Art Gallery, 1982.712

Purchased with the assistance of the Victoria & Albert Museum Purchase Grant Fund, the National Heritage Memorial Fund, Art Fund, the Manchester Art Gallery Art Fund, Patrons, Associates and Friends of Manchester Art Gallery

This is a view of the fortress courtyard facing north-east, taken from a position near to the promontory known as the Horn. Obtruding on the left is the commandant's house. Next to it, a stand of trees on the square partly obscures St George's Church, but its square tower can clearly be seen, alongside the octagonal tower of the Magdalenenburg (fig. 32). The white facade of the Brunnenhaus is brightly illuminated in the painting's centre. Along the right runs the Kasemattengebäude, or Old Barracks, home to soldiers and their families garrisoned at the fortress. The commandant's walled garden occupies the middle ground, with its dilapidated plastered wall offering a humble textural contrast at the fore. The building on the far right is the Central Barracks.[1]

The Brunnenhaus was perhaps placed centrally here by Bellotto to reflect its vital importance to Königstein. The French Baroque facade, designed by Jean de Bodt and erected in 1735, hides the fortress's most precious asset: access to fresh water. De Bodt's building was designed to be bomb-proof, and it would be hard to guess from its elegant exterior that it contained, essentially, a functional four-man hamster wheel. Behind the palatial facade, soldiers manned this treadwheel on a rota, marching 28,800 steps in a day to bring up the 33-gallon tanks 36 times (fig. 34).

To understand this view in relation to the other painting of the fortress's courtyard (cat. 4), it is helpful to focus on the Magdalenenburg. Its tower, visible in full here, revealed only its lanterned cupola in the other painting. The three circular ventilation holes, which would have allowed air to circulate around the giant wine cask, are matched by three on the opposite side, visible in this view in the deep shadow to the left of the tower.

Taken together, the two views of the fortress's courtyard provide an elegant sense of well-regulated community life. Bellotto's use of light in the Magdalenenburg view indicates, through the judicious illumination of certain surfaces, that gathering, storage, drinking and labour all have their place. Here it is the commandant's house, the chapel and the well-house that receive the emphatic beams, suggesting the importance of earthly and heavenly authority, and of the water of life. An orderly balance between the various functions of the fortress is woven in a breathtaking demonstration of Bellotto's particular talent in the meaningful deployment of light and shade.

PROVENANCE
Commissioned from the artist by Frederick Augustus II (1696–1763), Elector of Saxony and King of Poland (as Augustus III), in Dresden, by the spring of 1756; probably Sir Robert Brown, Bt (d. 1760) and his widow Lady Margaret Brown, née Cecil (1698–1782) by whom sold ('A Capital Collection of Italian, French, Flemish and Dutch Pictures'), Christie's, London, 7 March 1778, lot 79 ('A view of the fortress at Koningstein in Saxony painted for the King of Poland') or lot 80 ('Ditto, ditto, its companion'), bought for £79 16s by 'Tempest', probably John Tempest (1739–1794) of Wynyard Park, County Durham; by descent to his niece Frances Anne Vane-Tempest (1800–1865), who married Charles Stewart, later 3rd Marquess of Londonderry (1778–1854); by descent until sold by Alistair Vane-Tempest-Stewart, 9th Marquess of Londonderry (1937–2012); purchased through David Carritt Ltd, London, by Manchester Art Gallery in 1982.

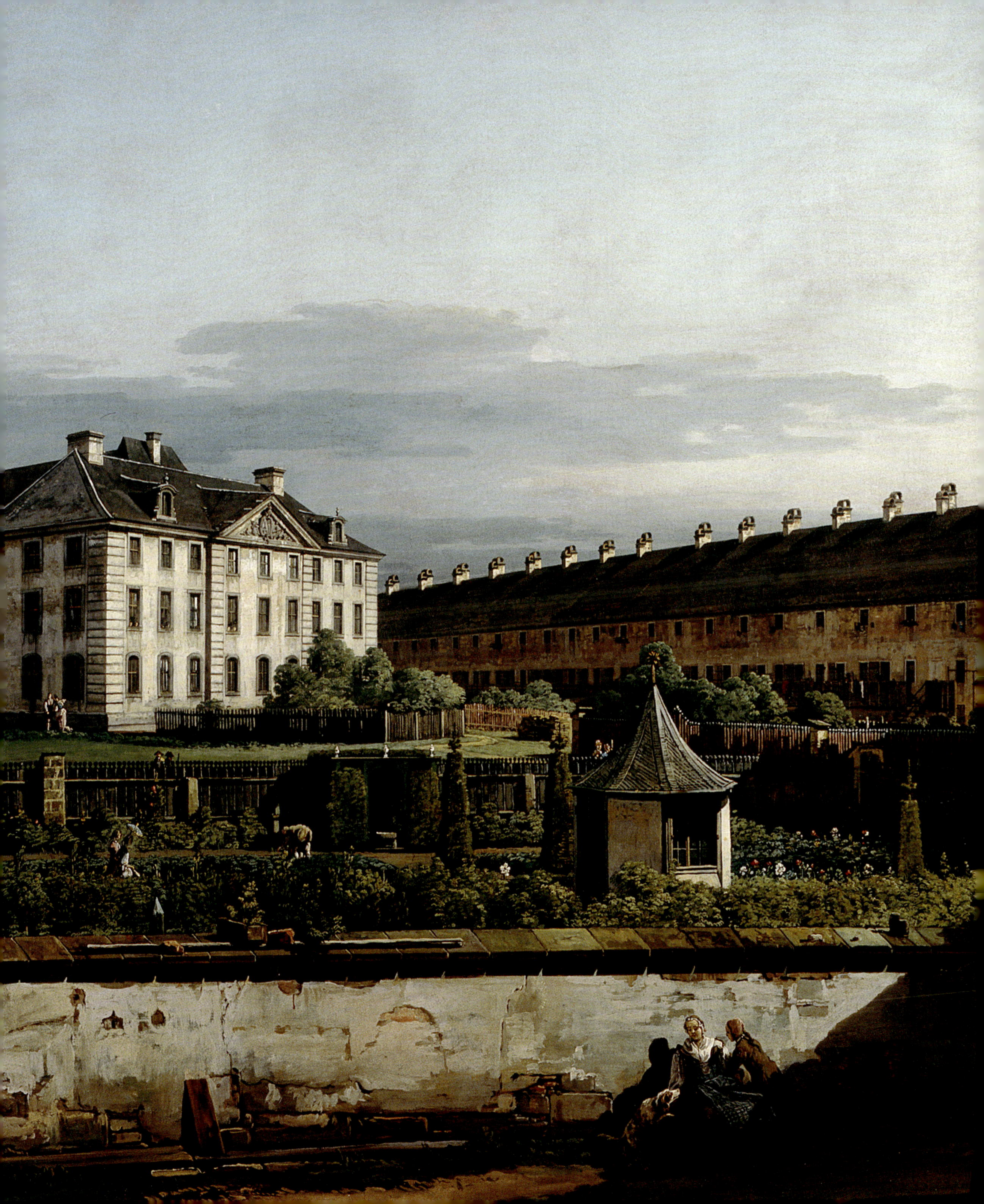

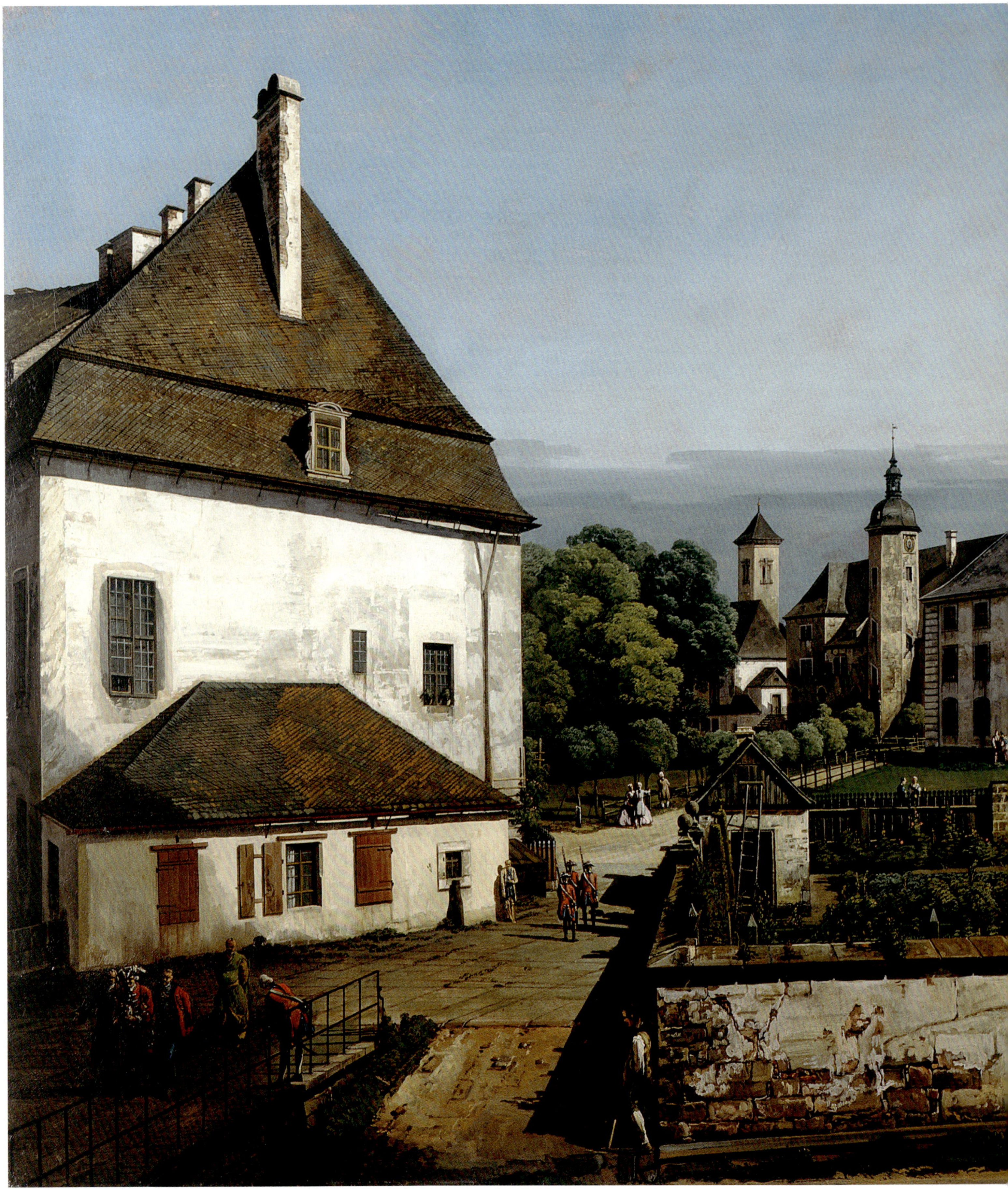

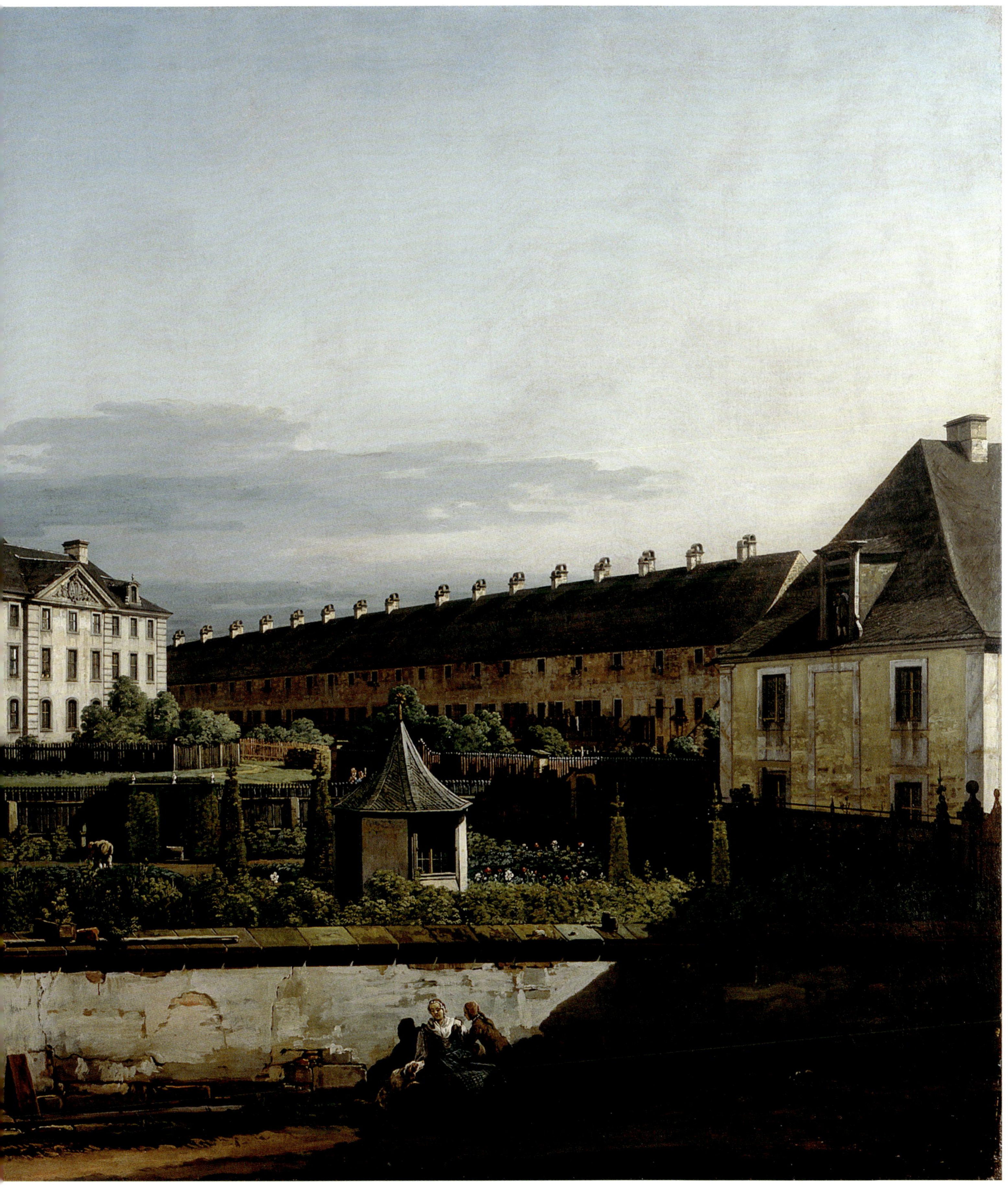

Just as Bellotto intersperses light and shadow across the painting, so he alternates verdant growth with neat fencing. A particularly intricate fence finished with a double-oval silhouette to each slat makes up the far side of the garden boundary (the fence can just be seen from the other side below the distant prospect in the Magdalenenburg view), while the garden borders themselves are shaggily luxuriant. However, it is the remarkably dilapidated wall that dominates the foreground. Werner Schmidt light-heartedly mentions anticipatory echoes of *tachisme*, the mid-twentieth-century European abstract expressionist movement, in his description of this wall, and it is admittedly almost impossible not to try to read some expressive significance into the wall's prominence.[2] Perhaps in the context of the Seven Years' War the obvious interpretation is one of solidity underlying the ephemeral: the blocks of stone revealed by the failing plaster are massive. In this reading, without having to resort to depicting military strength, Bellotto conveys a metaphorical stability beneath what he must have hoped was only temporary disarray.

Particularly contrasting with this '*tachiste*' wall is the roof of the commandant's house on the left. Bellotto has achieved an effect of geometrical precision and structural integrity through the cross-hatching of parallel strokes. The long straight lines intersect to create diamond shapes, but each diamond cannot represent a roof tile. While it is a standard way to convey a planar surface in an etching, use of this technique on such a large scale is bold: Bellotto is confident in his abilities.

The figures that populate the picture are various: in what Stefan Kozakiewicz describes elsewhere as Bellotto's tendency to 'human capriccio', different social

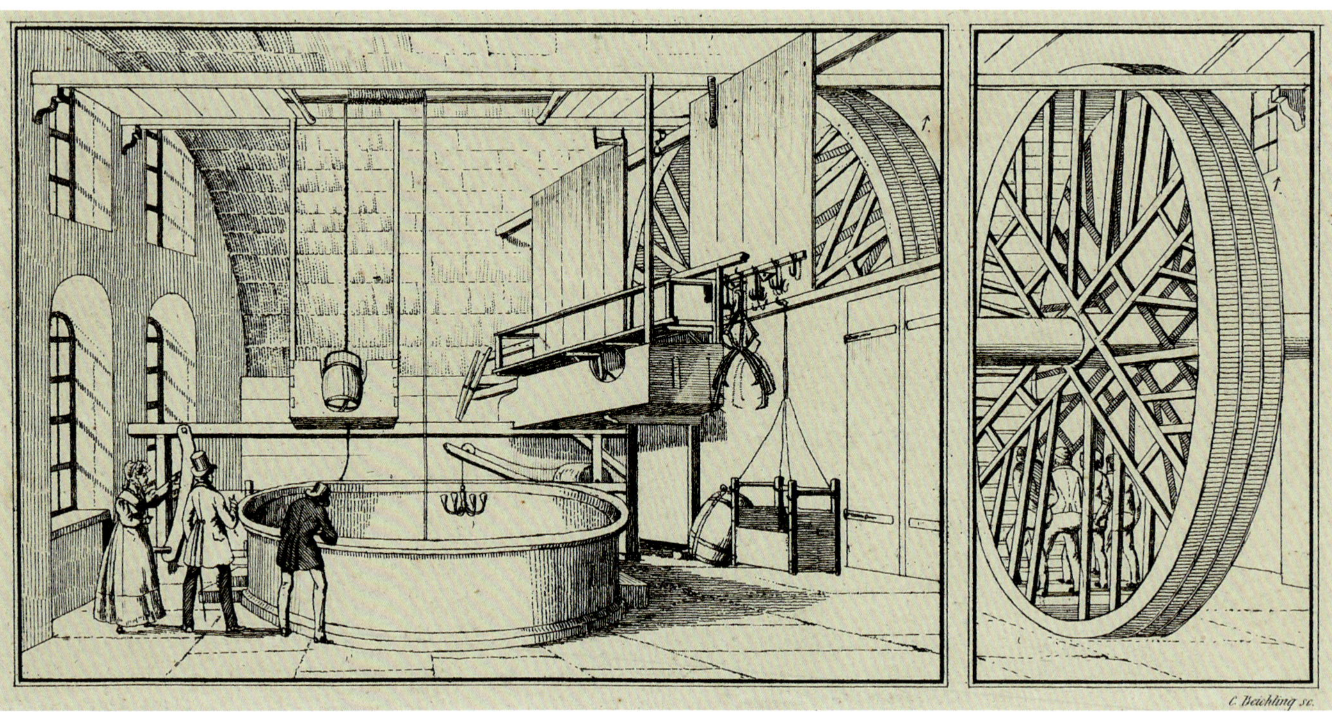

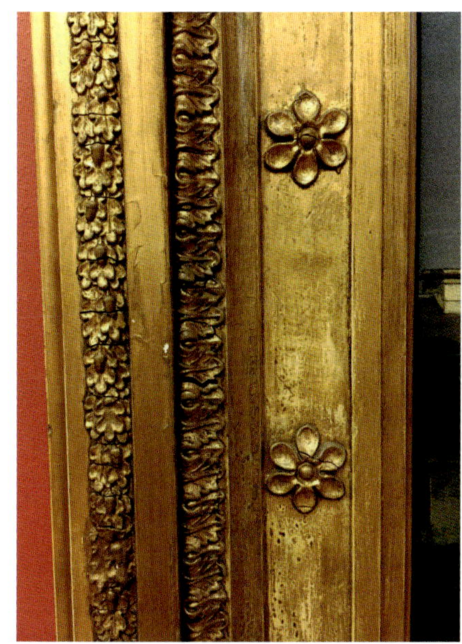

Fig. 35 Frame detail of *The Fortress of Königstein: Courtyard with the Magdalenenburg* (cat. 4)

types are juxtaposed, for example the genteel couple promenading close to a stooping gardener.[3] Visitors and civilian labourers or tradespeople amble in the middle distance, a couple of injured or retired soldiers rest against walls, and at the front a seated woman with a boy and dog form a decorative pyramid. The dramatic shadow to the right of this group leads the eye diagonally up to a curious sight – a precarious labourer with a sack over his shoulder, placed high up in the first floor opening on the Central Barracks. To the left of the garden a military patrol has crossed paths with an important group: a senior military man, perhaps the commandant of the fortress, being assisted to walk by a civilian and a high-ranking Polish officer (see detail on p. 81). Behind them, following at a respectful distance, is a subordinate, a shaven-headed man in Polish national costume, wearing a green *kontusz* or tunic. Throughout this period, Poland had a personal connection to Saxony in the form of Augustus III and so, as Edgar Peters Bowron notes, it cannot have been too unusual to see Polish national dress at the Saxon court.[4] Bellotto is indicating with these Polish figures the range and sophistication of military personnel at the fortress.[5]

There is a smaller painted replica of the Brunnenhaus view in the Pushkin Museum, Moscow, dated 1764, which Kozakiewicz judged to be entirely by Bellotto's own hand, due to its 'high and consistent technical standard.'[6] No preparatory drawings have come to light for either of the fortress courtyard views, and it is presumed that they were destroyed with the contents of Bellotto's Dresden residence in the Prussian bombardment of 1760 (see p. 8 and p. 25, n. 1).

The frames of the two courtyard paintings are worth noting. They were with the works when they were purchased by Manchester Art Gallery from the Marquess of Londonderry in 1982, and seem to have been made expressly for them. There was some controversy on acquisition as an unwanted coat of paint had been applied to the frames by the dealer's agents in a misguided attempt to smarten them up.[7] To rectify this, a harsh stripping back was undertaken, followed by re-gilding on a lemon-yellow ground.[8] Despite such brutal intervention, the classical rosette decoration, leaf-and-tongue moulding and oak-leaf-and-acorn outer moulding are relatively intact (fig. 35). Further research is needed to ascertain at what date the frames were commissioned, and if whether they were part of a wider decorative scheme at Wynyard Park.[9] HW

Fig. 34 Karl Heinrich Beichling (1803–1876), *Well with Water-conveyance System (Tread Wheel)*, mid-nineteenth century. Engraving, 22.5 x 26.5 cm. Königstein Fortress Collection, G 24

NOTES TO THE CATALOGUE ENTRIES

1 THE FORTRESS OF KÖNIGSTEIN FROM THE NORTH

1 Joseph Wagner after Francesco Zuccarelli, *Stança siede la Madre e il figlio abbraccia [...]* (Herzog Anton Ulrich-Museum, Braunschweig, JWagner AB 2.119); see Weber 2005, p. 42, fig. 4. This is the same source Bellotto uses for the rider in the Knowsley painting (cat. 3). Weber has done extensive work on the staffage in Bellotto's Dresden paintings: see Weber 1998, 2001, 2005.
2 For the Dresden view, see Kozakiewicz 1972, vol. 2, no. 154.
3 Joseph Wagner after Nicolaes Berchem, *Senza pensier sol della Mandra ho cura* (Kupferstichkabinett, Staatliche Kunstsammlungen, Dresden, A 29179). Bellotto repeatedly returned to this print for his Dresden and Pirna views; see Weber 2005, p. 45, fig. 9.
4 The dimensions for the replica of this painting are 47.6 x 78.7 cm. Kozakiewicz, who knew it only from photographs, considered it to be 'a studio work, probably with the collaboration of Lorenzo, the artist's son' (Kozakiewicz 1972, vol. 2, no. 234). Kozakiewicz lists a third version whose 'attribution to Bellotto is without foundation; the picture appears to be the work of a later imitator, perhaps of the early nineteenth century' (Kozakiewicz 1972, vol. 2, no. Z-507).
5 Turner's drawing includes improvements made to the defensive outworks beneath the Horn salient, which were completed by 1802.

2 THE FORTRESS OF KÖNIGSTEIN FROM THE NORTH-WEST

1 Bowron in De Grazia and Garberson 1996, pp. 14–18; see also Bowron in Venice and Houston 2001, cat. 65.
2 For the ram, see Joseph Wagner after Nicolaes Berchem, *Rozzo è il mio suon, ma pur alletta, e piace* (Kupferstichkabinett, Staatliche Kunstsammlungen, Dresden, A 29178); for the cows, see Joseph Wagner after Nicolaes Berchem, *Senza pensier sol della Mandra ho cura* (Kupferstichkabinett, Staatliche Kunstsammlungen, Dresden, A 29179). Both are reproduced in Weber 2005, p. 45, figs 8 and 9.
3 The ageing of the paint, abrasion and past restoration treatments have increased the amount of red ground that shows through; Bowron in De Grazia and Garberson 1996, p. 14. For more about Bellotto's ground layers, see Bendfeldt 2019, pp. 89–90.
4 Kozakiewicz 1972, vol. 2, no. 232 (according to Kozakiewicz, it exists in its first and second state). For the etchings delivered to the Kupferstichkabinett, see Metze 2011, and Kowalczyk in Milan 2016–17, cat. 91.
5 Sotheby's 1991, pp. 35–7. For the replica see Kozakiewicz 1972, vol. 2, no. 231 (dimensions: 49 x 80 cm).
6 Kozakiewicz 1972, vol. 2, no. Z-506 (dimensions: 91.5 x 138 cm). Fritzsche and Lippold believed the Hradec nad Moravicí Castle painting to be Bellotto's primary version of this subject: see Fritzsche 1936, VG 121; Lippold 1963, p. 31, pl. 42. Kozakiewicz states that the colouring and handling are not typical of Bellotto and believes it is likely to have been painted later, perhaps at the beginning of the nineteenth century.
7 J.M.W. Turner, *Königstein Fortress: West Side* and *Königstein Fortress: West Side, from the Hillside*, both from *Dresden and Saxon Switzerland Sketchbook*, 1835. Tate Britain, Turner Bequest.

3 THE FORTRESS OF KÖNIGSTEIN FROM THE SOUTH-WEST

1 It was not until 1871 that cells were built on the upper floor to house civil prisoners.
2 It is possible that Bellotto may have known this painting through copies or engravings (no related engravings are listed by Slive 2001, cat. 15); in 1835, John Smith stated that Ruisdael painted the picture 'expressly for the Count of Bentheim, in whose family it is said to have remained until the entrance of the French into Germany about which time [about 1792–4] it was taken to Paris' (cited in Slive 2001, cat. 15).
3 Bellotto takes only two of the cows from Zuccarelli's composition, repositioning them so that they are closer together. He also adjusts the group of sheep, removing one of the three from the right side of the flock.
4 See n. 1, under cat. 1. This is the same work Bellotto uses for the white cow in the London view (cat. 1).
5 Joseph Wagner after Nicolaes Berchem, *Nella mia Gregge il parco Cibo io trovo* (Kupferstichkabinett, Staatliche Kunstsammlungen, Dresden, A 29176); see Weber 2005, p. 44, fig. 7. The posterior view of the brown cow, as well as the seated lady, her basket and the dog, are motifs Bellotto later repurposed for his view of *The Ruined Castle of Theben* (fig. 25).
6 Joseph Wagner after Francesco Zuccarelli, *Alla fonte costei bagna le piante [...]*, and Francesco Bartolozzi after Francesco Zuccarelli, *Villanello fanciul come si piglia [...]* (both Herzog Anton Ulrich-Museum, Braunschweig, JWagner AB 2.122 and FBartolozzi AB 2.83 respectively); reproduced in Weber 2005, p. 47, figs 12 and 13, and in this volume (fig. 29).
7 See n. 3, under cat. 1.
8 Kozakiewicz 1972, vol. 2, no. 237.
9 *Bibliothek der Schönen Wissenschaften und der freyen Künste*, Leipzig 1765, p. 369, where it appears under the heading *Vermischte Nachrichten* ('Miscellaneous News'); cited by Kozakiewicz 1972, vol. 2, no. 237.
10 For the replica, see Kozakiewicz 1972, vol. 2, no. 236 (dimensions: 49 x 80 cm); Kozakiewicz describes it as 'a studio piece, perhaps by Lorenzo Bellotto, showing no trace of Bellotto's own hand'. For the Pirna view, see Kozakiewicz 1972, vol. 2, no. 191.

4 THE FORTRESS OF KÖNIGSTEIN: COURTYARD WITH THE MAGDALENENBURG

1 See plan in Schmidt 2000, p. 30 (fig. 14).
2 Taube 2000, p. 34.
3 With thanks to Stephen Lloyd for his advice on this sculptural group.
4 Taube 2000, p. 44.
5 Schmidt 2000, p. 160.
6 Schmidt 2000, p. 156.
7 As noted in the conservation report, May/July 2001, Elizabeth Holford Associates, Manchester Art Gallery archives.
8 Both of the secondary versions of the painting are illustrated in Kozakiewicz 1972, p. 187.
9 Schmidt 2000, p. 158.
10 The acquisition fulfilled two criteria for the gallery: firstly, rarity. The paintings increased the sophistication of a 'provincial' gallery through the perception of Bellotto as a lesser-known Canaletto. He was at that time thought to be unrepresented in any public gallery in the country. Secondly, the painting style has a straightforward clarity and realism traditionally considered to have a wide appeal, perhaps an easier sell to the art-indifferent taxpayer, the often silent presence in the acquisition of any work by a local authority.
11 T. Clifford to Brian Lang, secretary of National Heritage Memorial Fund, 24 June 1982, Bellotto artist file, Manchester Art Gallery archives. The paintings were acquired through the London art dealer David Carritt. With Manchester's art acquisition budget having been slashed in half in 1982, to purchase both of the paintings was a huge undertaking, even allowing for a substantial tax discount. The gallery's press releases in connection with the acquisition stressed value for money, with the second release proudly entitled, 'Half a million pound masterpiece costs city £52,000'. Manchester Art Gallery press release, 15 November 1982, Bellotto artist file, Manchester Art Gallery archives.
12 With thanks to Jacob Simon for assistance in examining photographs of the frames.
13 Kozakiewicz 1972, vol. 2, nos 239, 240. The latter remains in the Cooley Collection, but it was offered for sale at Christie's, London, 8 December 2016, lot 35 (unsold).

5 THE FORTRESS OF KÖNIGSTEIN: COURTYARD WITH THE BRUNNENHAUS

1 Labelled *'Mittel Caserne'* on the plan of the fortress in Schmidt 2000, p. 30 (fig. 14).
2 Schmidt 2000, p. 162.
3 Kozakiewicz 1972, vol. 1, p. 119.
4 Venice and Houston 2001, p. 228.
5 With thanks to Stephen Lloyd for assistance in interpreting this group of figures.
6 Kozakiewicz 1972, vol. 2, no. 242.
7 Letter from T.S. Bathurst at David Carritt to T. Clifford, 30 April 1982, Bellotto artist file, Manchester Art Gallery archives.
8 As noted in the conservation report, May/July 2001, Elizabeth Holford Associates, Manchester Art Gallery archives.
9 With thanks to Jacob Simon for assistance in examining photographs of the frames.

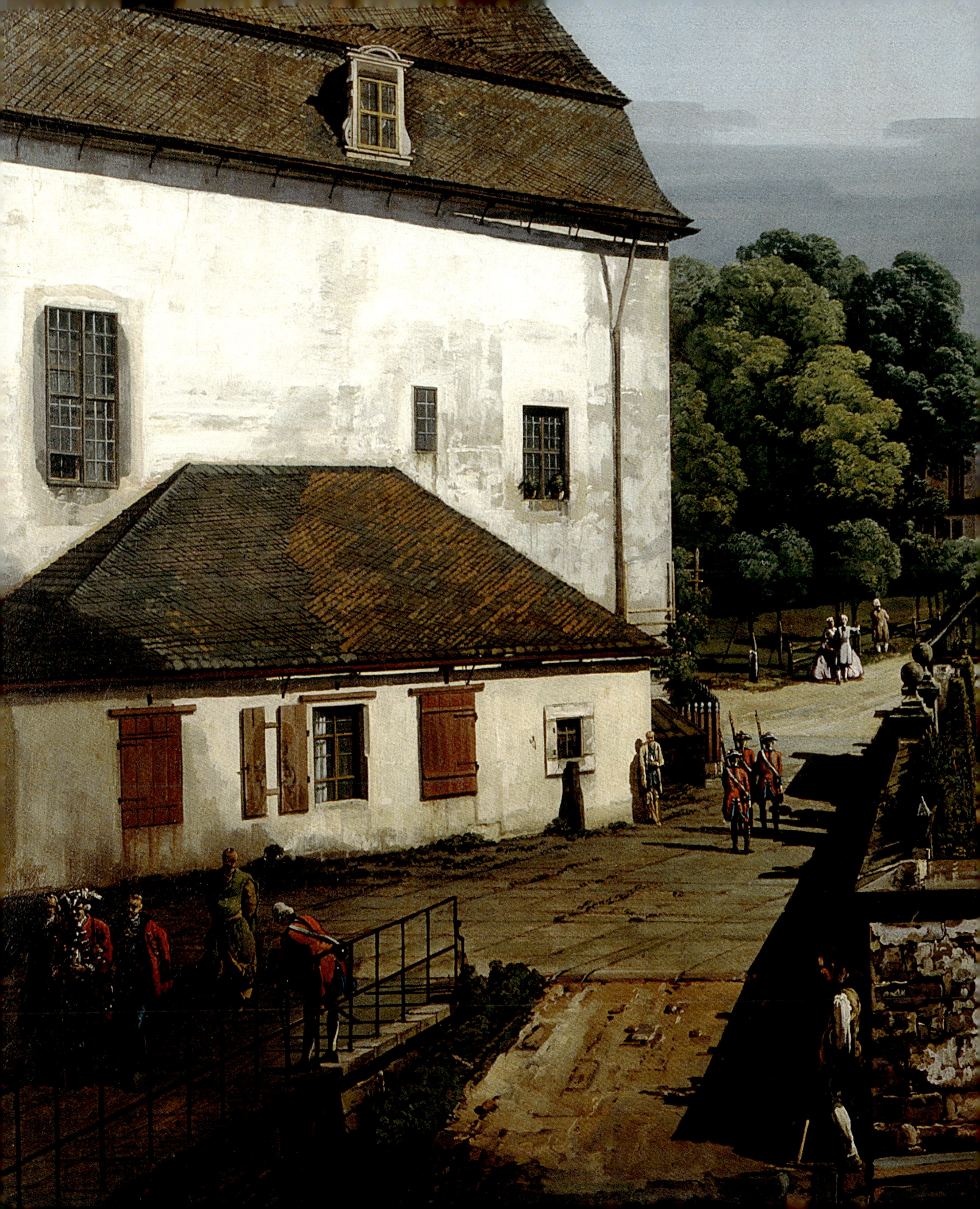

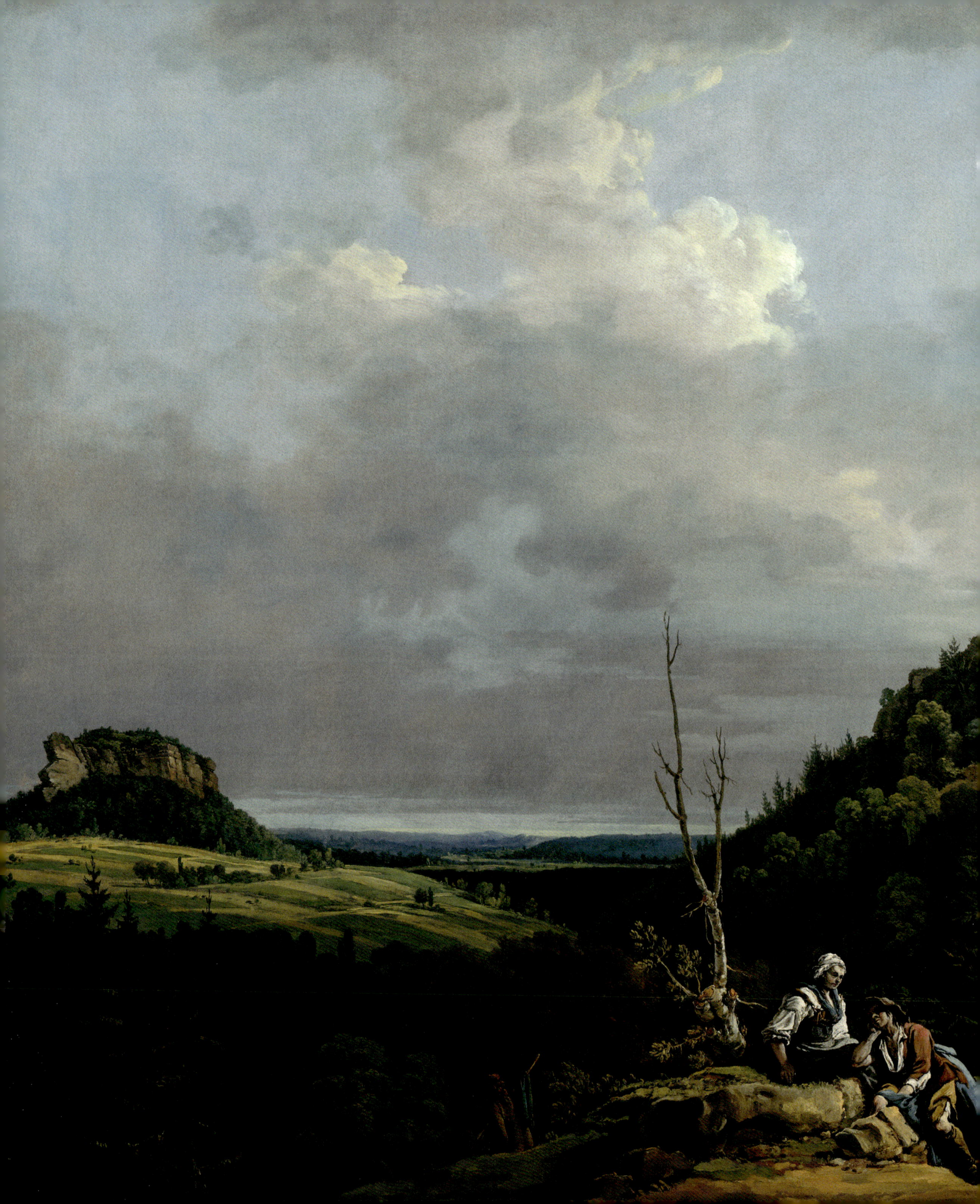

BIBLIOGRAPHY

BAILEY AND ROWELL 2017
F. Bailey and C. Rowell, *Mount Stewart: National Trust Historic Houses & Collections Annual 2017*, London 2017

BEAUCHAMP 1927
H. Lygon, 7th Earl Beauchamp, *A Catalogue of the Pictures, Chiefly Historical Portraits, at Madresfield Court*, privately printed, Worcester 1927

BEDDINGTON 2004
C. Beddington, 'Bernardo Bellotto and His Circle in Italy. Part I: Not Canaletto but Bellotto', *The Burlington Magazine*, vol. 146 (2004), pp. 665–74

BEDDINGTON 2010–11
C. Beddington, 'Venetian View Painting in the Eighteenth Century', in London and Washington 2010–11, pp. 10–53

BENDFELDT 2019
S. Bendfeldt, 'Observations on Bellotto's Painting Technique', in Fort Worth 2019, pp. 85–93

BOWRON 1993
E.P. Bowron, *Bernardo Bellotto: The Fortress of Königstein*, Washington DC 1993

BOWRON 2011
E.P. Bowron, *Bernardo Bellotto (Venice 1722–1780): Architectural Capriccio with a Self-Portrait in the Costume of a Venetian Nobleman*, Otto Naumann Ltd, New York 2011

BROADLANDS 1980
Broadlands: The Home of Lord Mountbatten, St Ives 1980

CAMESASCA 1974
E. Camesasca, *L'opera completa del Bellotto*, Milan 1974

CLAYTON 2005
M. Clayton, *Canaletto in Venice*, London 2005

COLTMAN 2006
V. Coltman, *Fabricating the Antique: Neoclassicism in Britain, 1760–1800*, Chicago and London 2006

CONEGLIANO 2011
Bernardo Bellotto. Il Canaletto delle corti europee, ed. D. Succi, exh. cat., Palazzo Sarcinelli, Conegliano 2011

CONNELL 1957
B. Connell, *Portrait of a Whig Peer: Compiled from the Papers of the Second Viscount Palmerston, 1739–1802*, London 1957

CONSTABLE 1976
W.G. Constable, *Canaletto: Giovanni Antonio Canal 1697–1768*, ed. J.G. Links, Oxford 1976

DE GRAZIA AND GARBERSON 1996
Italian Paintings of the Seventeenth and Eighteenth Centuries: The Collections of the National Gallery of Art. A Systematic Catalogue, eds D. De Grazia and E. Garberson, Washington DC 1996

DRESDEN 2011
Bernardo Bellotto: Der Canaletto-Blick, eds A. Henning, S. Oesinghaus and S. Bendfeldt, exh. cat., Gemäldegalerie Alte Meister, Dresden 2011

FINBERG 1920–1
H.F. Finberg, 'Canaletto in England', *The Walpole Society*, vol. 9 (1920–1), pp. 21–76

FISHER 2002
A Passion for Natural History: The Life and Legacy of the 13th Earl of Derby, ed. C. Fisher, Liverpool 2002

FORT WORTH 2019
The Lure of Dresden: Bellotto at the Court of Saxony, eds S. Koja and I.Y. Wagner, exh. cat., Kimbell Art Museum, Fort Worth 2019

FRANK 2001
M. Frank, 'Bellotto in Vienna and Munich', in Venice and Houston 2001, pp. 27–32

FRITZSCHE 1936
H.A. Fritzsche, *Bernardo Bellotto genannt Canaletto*, Burg bei Magdeburg 1936

GOTTDANG 2014–15
A. Gottdang, 'The Seduction of the Gaze: Architectural Fantasies of the 1760s', in Munich 2014–15, pp. 96–113

GREVEMBROCH 1981
G. Grevembroch, *Gli abiti de veneziani di quasi ogni età con diligenza raccolti e dipinti nel secolo XVIII*, 4 vols, Venice 1981

GUILDING 2014
R. Guilding, *Owning the Past: Why the English Collected Antique Sculpture, 1640–1840*, New Haven and London 2014

HAGISHIMA 2014
S. Hagishima, *Bernardo Bellotto: Paintings from the Viewpoint of Urban Landscape Design Theory*, Fukuoka 2014

HASKELL 1980
F. Haskell, *Patrons and Painters: A Study in the Relations between Italian Art and Society in the Age of the Baroque*, New Haven and London 1980 (revised edn)

HENNING 2011
A. Henning, 'Bernardo Bellotto und der Blick auf Dresden', in Dresden 2011, pp. 13–21

HYDE 1937
H.M. Hyde, *Londonderry House and its Pictures*, London 1937

INGAMELLS 1997
A Dictionary of British and Irish Travellers in Italy, 1701–1800, ed. J. Ingamells, New Haven and London 1997

KERBER 2017–18A
P.B. Kerber, 'The View Painter as Eyewitness', in Los Angeles, Minneapolis and Cleveland 2017–18, pp. 1–17

KERBER 2017–18B
P.B. Kerber, 'Ambassadorial Patrons Make their Entrance', in Los Angeles, Minneapolis and Cleveland 2017–18, pp. 19–60

KNOWSLEY HALL 1846
A Catalogue of Most of the Pictures in the Principal Rooms at Knowsley Hall; The Seat of the Right Honourable Edward Smith Stanley, XIIIth Earl Of Derby KG. Taken in September MDCCCXLVI, manuscript, Knowsley Hall Library, 1846

KNOWSLEY HALL 1850
Catalogue of the Pictures at Knowsley Hall, 1850, privately printed, Knowsley Hall Library, 1850

KNOWSLEY HALL 1860
List of the Pictures. Knowsley Hall, manuscript, Knowsley Hall Library, 1860

KOJA 2019
S. Koja, '"My Astonishment Surpassed Every Conception": Art Collecting in Baroque Dresden', in Fort Worth 2019, pp. 101–21

KOWALCZYK 1995
B.A. Kowalczyk, 'Il Bellotto veneziano nei documenti', *Arte Veneta*, vol. 47 (1995), pp. 68–77

KOWALCZYK 1998
B.A. Kowalczyk, 'I Canaletto della National Gallery di Londra', *Arte Veneta*, vol. 53 (1998), pp. 73–99

KOWALCZYK 1999
B.A. Kowalczyk, 'I primi sostenitori veneziani di Bernardo Bellotto', *Saggi e Memorie di Storia dell'Arte*, vol. 23 (1999), pp. 198–218

KOWALCZYK 2001
B.A. Kowalczyk, 'Bernardo Bellotto: The Formation of an Original Style', in Venice and Houston 2001, pp. 3–13

KOWALCZYK 2008
B.A. Kowalczyk, 'Canaletto e Bellotto: l'arte della veduta', in Turin 2008, pp. 13–21

KOWALCZYK 2012
B.A. Kowalczyk, 'Bellotto and Zanetti in Florence', *The Burlington Magazine*, vol. 154 (2012), pp. 24–31

KOWALCZYK 2016–17
B.A. Kowalczyk, 'Bellotto e Canaletto: Il successo di una separazione', in Milan 2016–17, pp. 15–37

KOZAKIEWICZ 1972
S. Kozakiewicz, *Bernardo Bellotto*, 2 vols, London and New York 1972

LEVEY 1986
M. Levey, *National Gallery Catalogues: The Seventeenth and Eighteenth Century Italian Schools*, London 1986

LIEBSCH 2019
T. Liebsch, 'Canal, Bellotto, and the Camera Obscura: "Dolci cose a vedere e dolci inganni"', in Fort Worth 2019, pp. 95–9

LIPPOLD 1963
G. Lippold, *Bernardo Bellotto genannt Canaletto*, Leipzig 1963

LLOYD 2016
Art, Animals and Politics: Knowsley and the Earls of Derby, ed. S. Lloyd, London 2016

LONDON 1995
In Trust for the Nation: Paintings from National Trust Houses, ed. A. Laing, exh. cat., National Gallery, London 1995

LONDON, LIVERPOOL AND YORK 1957
Bernardo Bellotto 1720–1780: An Exhibition of Paintings and Drawings from the National Museum of Warsaw, eds S. Lorentz and F.J.B. Watson, exh. cat., Whitechapel Art Gallery, London, Walker Art Gallery, Liverpool, and York City Art Gallery 1957

LONDON AND WASHINGTON 1994–5
The Glory of Venice: Art in the Eighteenth Century, eds J. Martineau and A. Robinson, exh. cat., Royal Academy of Arts, London and National Gallery of Art, Washington DC 1994–5

LONDON AND WASHINGTON 2010–11
Venice: Canaletto and His Rivals, ed. C. Beddington, exh. cat., National Gallery, London, and National Gallery of Art, Washington DC 2010–11

LOS ANGELES, MINNEAPOLIS AND CLEVELAND 2017–18
Eyewitness Views: Making History in Eighteenth-Century Europe, ed. P.B. Kerber, exh. cat., J. Paul Getty Museum, Los Angeles, Minneapolis Institute of Art and Cleveland Museum of Art 2017–18

MANIKOWSKA 2012
E. Manikowska, 'The Rediscovery of Bernardo Bellotto's Inventory', *The Burlington Magazine*, vol. 154 (2012), pp. 32–6

MANIKOWSKA 2014
E. Manikowska, *Bernardo Bellotto I jego drezdeński apartament: O tożsamości społecznej I artystycznej weneckiego wedutysty*, Warsaw 2014

MANIKOWSKA 2017
E. Manikowska, 'Tra Venezia e Dresda: Il gabinetto di quadri di Bernardo Bellotto nella Salzgasse', in *Heinrich Graf von Brühl: Ein sächsischer Mäzen in Europa*, eds U.C. Koch and C. Ruggero, Dresden 2017, pp. 212–20

MAŃKOWSKI 1932
T. Mańkowski, *Galeria Stanislawa Augusta*, 3 vols, Lvov 1932

MARIETTE 1851–3
Abcedario de P. J. Mariette et autres notes inédites de cet amateur sur les arts et les artistes, eds P. de Chennevières and A. de Montaiglon, vol. 2, Paris 1851–3

MARINELLI 2016–17
S. Marinelli, 'I lumi neri dell'illuminista', in Milan 2016–17, pp. 39–49

METZE 2011
G. Metze, 'Die Schauseiten von Dresden Bellottos radierte Veduten', in Dresden 2011, pp. 37–41

MILAN 2016–17
Bellotto e Canaletto: Lo stupore e la luce, ed. B.A. Kowalczyk, exh. cat., Gallerie d'Italia, Milan 2016–17

MUNICH 2014–15
Canaletto: Bernardo Bellotto Paints Europe, ed. A. Schumacher, exh. cat., Alte Pinakothek, Munich 2014–15

NACF 1981
National Art Collections Fund: Annual Report 1981, London 1981

NACF 1983
National Art Collections Fund: Annual Report 1983, London 1983

NACF 1984
National Art Collections Fund: Annual Report 1984, London 1984

NEW YORK 1978
The Splendor of Dresden: Five Centuries of Art Collecting, exh. cat., National Gallery of Art, Washington, Metropolitan Museum of Art, New York, and Fine Arts Museums of San Francisco 1978, pp. 15–30

QUAEITZSCH 2014–15
C. Quaeitzsch, 'City and Palace – Duty and Leisure: Bellotto's Works for the Munich Residenz in the Context of Ceremonial and Flattery', in Munich 2014–15, pp. 286–93

RIZZI 1991
A. Rizzi, *Bernardo Bellotto: Warschauer Veduten*, Munich 1991

RIZZI AND JURSZ-SALVADORI 2006
A. Rizzi and K. Jursz-Salvadori, *Canaletto w Warszawie: Dziela Bernarda Bellotta, zwanego Canalettem w stolicy Stanislawa Augusta*, Warsaw 2006

ROTTERMUND 2001
A. Rottermund, 'Bernardo Bellotto in Warsaw', in Venice and Houston 2001, pp. 33–9

ROTTERMUND 2005A
A. Rottermund, 'Von Venedig nach Warschau', in Vienna 2005, pp. 11–37

ROTTERMUND 2005B
A. Rottermund, 'Der Canaletto-Saal im Königlichen Schloß: Bellottos Tätigkeit in Warschau (1767–1780)', in Vienna 2005, pp. 157–63

RUSSELL 1982
F. Russell, 'A Connoisseur's Taste: Paintings at Broadlands – I', *Country Life*, vol. 171 (January 1982), pp. 224–6

SCHARF 1875
G. Scharf, *A Descriptive and Historical Catalogue of the Collection of Pictures at Knowsley Hall*, privately printed, London, 1875

SCHMIDT 2000
W. Schmidt, *Bernardo Bellotto genannt Canaletto in Pirna und auf der Festung Königstein*, Pirna 2000

SCHUTZ 2005
K. Schütz, 'Bernardo Bellottos Wirklichkeit: Die Korrektur der Realität zum Kunstwerk', in Vienna 2005, pp. 51–8

SLIVE 2001
S. Slive, *Jacob van Ruisdael: A Complete Catalogue of his Paintings, Drawings, and Etchings*, New Haven 2001

SOTHEBY'S 1991
Sotheby's, London, *Old Master Paintings*, 11 December 1991

STUBEL 1911
M. Stübel, 'Der jüngere Canaletto und seine Radierungen', *Monatshefte für Kunstwissenschaft*, vol. 4, no. 11 (1911), pp. 471–501

SUCCI 2011
D. Succi, 'Bellotto in Italia, da Venezia a Verona (1738–1747)', in Conegliano 2011, pp. 18–51

TAUBE 2000
A. Taube, *Königstein Fortress*, trans. A. Puschnerus and D., V. and N. Mayper, Berlin 2000

THOMA 2014–15
J. Thoma, 'Made for the Dining Room, the Antechamber, and the Gallery: Commissioners and Functions of Bellotto's Vedute', in Munich 2014–15, pp. 46–71

TURIN 2008
Canaletto e Bellotto: L'arte della veduta, ed. B.A. Kowalczyk, exh. cat., Palazzo Bricherasio, Turin 2008

VENICE 1986
Le Vedute di Dresda di Bernardo Bellotto: Dipinti e incisioni dai musei di Dresda, ed. A. Bettagno, exh. cat., Fondazione Giorgio Cini, Venice 1986

VENICE 2001
Canaletto prima maniera, ed. B.A. Kowalczyk, exh. cat., Fondazione Giorgio Cini, Venice 2001

VENICE 2014
Pietro Bellotti: Un altro Canaletto, eds C. Beddington and D. Crivellari, exh. cat., Ca' Rezzonico, Venice 2014

VENICE AND HOUSTON 2001
Bernardo Bellotto and the Capitals of Europe, ed. E.P. Bowron, exh. cat., Museo Correr, Venice, and Museum of Fine Arts, Houston 2001

VERTUE 1933–4
'Vertue – III. Note-books', eds L. Cust and A.M. Hind, *The Walpole Society*, vol. 22 (1933–4)

VESME 1906
A. de Vesme, *Le Peintre-Graveur italien*, Milan 1906

VIENNA 2005
Bernardo Bellotto genannt Canaletto: Europäische Veduten, ed. W. Seipel, exh. cat., Kunsthistorisches Museum, Vienna 2005

WAGENER 2014–15
T. Wagener, 'Bernardo Bellotto, Called Canaletto: A Venetian Look at Central Europe', in Munich 2014–15, pp. 114–43

WEBER 1998
G.J.M. Weber, 'Bernardo Bellotto, Nicolaes Berchem und das pastorale Pirna', *Dresdener Kunstblätter*, vol. 42 (1998), pp. 46–53

WEBER 2001
G.J.M. Weber, 'The Freedom of a *Veduta* Painter: Bernardo Bellotto in Dresden', in Venice and Houston 2001, pp. 15–25

WEBER 2005
G.J.M. Weber, 'Zwischen Kunst und Natur: Anmerkungen zur Staffage auf Gemälden Bernardo Bellottos', in Vienna 2005, pp. 39–49

ZANETTI 1771
A.M. Zanetti, *Della pittura veneziana e delle opere pubbliche de' veneziani maestri*, 5 vols, Venice 1771

ACKNOWLEDGEMENTS

In 2017 the National Gallery was able to purchase Bernardo Bellotto's magnificent view of *The Fortress of Königstein from the North* with the support of the American Friends of the National Gallery, The National Gallery Trust, the Estate of Mrs Madeline Swallow, Art Fund (with a contribution from The Wolfson Foundation), Howard and Roberta Ahmanson, The Deborah Loeb Brice Foundation, Mrs Mollie W. Vickers, The Manny and Brigitta Davidson Charitable Foundation and The Sackler Trust, with additional support from Mrs Charles Wrightsman, Jean-Luc Baroni, The Linbury Trust, The Monument Trust, Mr Fabrizio Moretti, Sir Hugh and Lady Stevenson, The John S. Cohen Foundation, Mr Jonathan Green, Christoph and Katrin Henkel, Ernst Nissl, Mr Peter Scott CBE QC, Mr and Mrs Ugo Pierucci, Sir Michael and Lady Heller, Mr Adrian Sassoon, Mr Mark Storey, Mr Neil Westreich, Nicholas and Judith Goodison, John and Flavia Ormond, and other donors including those who wish to remain anonymous.

The acquisition resulted in the National Gallery finally possessing a work whose sheer scale, ambition and visual impact uphold Bellotto's reputation as one of the most innovative view painters of the eighteenth century, bringing him out definitely from the shadow of his uncle, Canaletto. From the moment the acquisition was under consideration, I longed to reunite Bellotto's five spectacular views of the fortress of Königstein. Now this is finally taking place, more than 250 years since the paintings were last together.

On behalf of the National Gallery and Manchester Art Gallery, the two partner venues for this exhibition, I would like to express our heartfelt thanks to the Earl and Countess of Derby, and to Kaywin Feldman, National Gallery of Art, Washington, for agreeing to lend their respective views of Königstein: without their generosity this project would never have got off the ground. It has been a pleasure to work with colleagues at Manchester Art Gallery – Alistair Hudson, Natasha Howes, Philippa Milner, Siân Stephenson and, above all, Hannah Williamson. At the National Gallery I wish to especially thank Gracie Divall and Joanna Weston who, ably assisted by Olivia Threlkeld, have organised the exhibition in London.

The catalogue has benefited enormously from the invaluable insights and observations of Edgar Peters Bowron, whose unfailing generosity, enthusiasm and expertise in the field of eighteenth-century view painting have improved the book considerably. For their important contributions to the catalogue, I would like to thank Lucy Chiswell, Stephen Lloyd and Hannah Williamson. This book is the product of many hands (and eyes) and I am grateful to those who have shown exceptional care in creating such a beautiful publication: especially Diana Adell, the project editor, along with Suzanne Bosman, Robert Davies, Sarah Derry (in the early stages), Jane Hyne, Kathrin Jacobsen, Laura Lappin and Rebecca Thornton.

The exhibition organisers in London and Manchester would like to extend their gratitude to the following individuals for their assistance in matters relating to the exhibition and its accompanying publication: Julia Armstrong-Totten, Maria Balshaw, Paula Binari, David Alan Brown, Jonathan Chenevix-Trench, Judy Cline, Georgina Eliot, Mark Griffith-Jones, Gretchen Hirschauer, Jane Knowles, Tom Legh, Lynda McLeod, Harriet Owen Hughes, Nicholas Penny, Karen Robson, Francis Russell, Charles Sebag-Montefiore, Shannon Schuler, Jacob Simon, Eve Straussman-Pflanzer, Lucy Trench, Edward Whitley, Francesca Whitlum-Cooper, Marjorie E. Wieseman, Matt Yates and Anna Zasadzińska.

As always, I am incredibly grateful to the countless colleagues at the National Gallery who contribute to the realisation of every exhibition we put on, whether large or small.

Letizia Treves

LIST OF LENDERS

The Derby Collection
LIVERPOOL

The National Gallery
LONDON

Manchester Art Gallery
MANCHESTER

National Gallery of Art
WASHINGTON

PHOTOGRAPHIC CREDITS

BRAUNSCHWEIG
Herzog Anton Ulrich Museum, Braunschweig © Photo: Museum: figs 26, 28, 29, 31.

CAMBRIDGE
The Fitzwilliam Museum, Cambridge © Bridgeman Images: fig. 4.

DRESDEN
Gemäldegalerie Alte Meister, Staatliche Kunstsammlungen Dresden © Photo Scala, Florence/bpk, Bildagentur für Kunst, Kultur und Geschichte, Berlin: figs 2, 9, 15; photo: Hans-Peter Klut: figs 1, 7, 8.

Kupferstichkabinett, Staatliche Kunstsammlungen Dresden © Kupferstichkabinett, Staatliche Kunstsammlungen Dresden: fig. 19.

© Landesamt für Denkmalpflege Sachsen (Sven Köhler) (State Office for Monument Preservation Saxony): fig. 14.

Sächsisches Staatsarchiv, Hauptstaatsarchiv Dresden, 10024 Geheimer Rat (Geheimes Archiv) © Reproduction: Saxon State Archives: fig. 16.

Saxon State Library. State and University Library Dresden © SLUB Dresden/Deutsche Fotothek: fig. 17.

DUBLIN
National Gallery of Ireland Collection. Photo © National Gallery of Ireland: fig. 30.

EDINBURGH
Private collection (on long-term loan to the National Galleries of Scotland, Edinburgh). Photo © National Galleries of Scotland. Photography Antonia Reeve: fig. 22.

KÖNIGSTEIN
akg-images © akg-images/euroluftbild.de. Photo: Harald Anders: fig. 13.

Königstein Fortress Collection. Grafic Collection Fortress Königstein gGmbH: figs 32, 33, 34.

KNOWSLEY
The Derby Collection, Knowsley Hall. Reproduced courtesy of the Rt Hon. The Earl of Derby/Photo: © Christie's Images Limited: cat. 3; photography by Clare Bates: fig. 23.

LONDON
The British Museum, London © The Trustees of the British Museum: fig. 20.

The National Gallery, London © The National Gallery, London: cat. 1, figs 3, 24.

Tate, London © Tate: fig. 27.

MANCHESTER
Manchester Art Gallery © Manchester Art Gallery/Bridgeman Images: cats 4, 5.

POWIS CASTLE
Powis Castle, National Trust © National Trust Images/John Hammond: fig. 21.

SCHWERIN
Staatliches Museum Schwerin © Photo Scala, Florence/bpk, Bildagentur für Kunst, Kultur und Geschichte/Photo: Elke Walford, Berlin: fig. 18.

TURIN
Galleria Sabauda, Turin © Photo Scala, Florence – courtesy of the Ministero Beni e Att. Culturali e del Turismo: fig. 6.

VIENNA
Kunsthistorisches Museum, Vienna © De Agostini Picture Library/Scala, Florence: fig. 25.

WARSAW
Collection of National Museum, Warsaw © National Museum, Warsaw: fig. 5.

Royal Castle, Warsaw. Photo © Wilczyński Krzysztof/Muzeum Narodowe w Warszawie: fig. 10; photo Andrzej Ring, Małgorzata Niewiadomska: fig. 11; photo Andrzej Ring, Lech Sandzewicz: fig. 12.

WASHINGTON, DC
National Gallery of Art, Washington, DC. Courtesy National Gallery of Art, Washington: cat. 2.

Published to accompany
the exhibition

BELLOTTO:
THE KÖNIGSTEIN
VIEWS REUNITED

The National Gallery, London
22 July – 31 October 2021

BELLOTTO:
VIEWS ON
A FORTRESS

Manchester Art Gallery
20 November 2021 –
27 February 2022

The H J Hyams Exhibition Programme at the National Gallery is supported by The Capricorn Foundation

Art Fund_

This exhibition has been made possible by the provision of insurance through the Government Indemnity Scheme. The National Gallery would like to thank HM Government for providing Government Indemnity and the Department for Digital, Culture, Media and Sport and Arts Council England for arranging the indemnity.

All measurements give height before width.

First published in 2021 by
National Gallery Company Limited
St Vincent House
30 Orange Street
London WC2H 7HH
www.nationalgallery.co.uk

ISBN 978 1 85709 674 3
Product code 1050724

British Library Cataloguing-in-Publication Data
A catalogue record is available from the British Library
Library of Congress Control Number 2021934170

Publisher: Laura Lappin
Project Editor: Diana Adell
Editor: Robert Davies
Designer: Kathrin Jacobsen
Picture Researchers: Suzanne Bosman and Rebecca Thornton
Production: Jane Hyne

Colour origination by DL Imaging
Printed in Belgium by Graphius

FRONT COVER *The Fortress of Königstein from the North* (detail from cat. 1)
BACK COVER *The Fortress of Königstein: Courtyard with the Magdalenenburg* (detail from cat. 4)
PAGE 2 *The Fortress of Königstein from the North-West* (detail from cat. 2)
PAGE 4 *The Fortress of Königstein from the South-West* (detail from cat. 3)
PAGE 6 *The Fortress of Königstein from the North* (detail from cat. 1)
PAGE 48 *The Fortress of Königstein from the North* (detail from cat. 1)
PAGE 81 *The Fortress of Königstein: Courtyard with the Brunnenhaus* (detail from cat. 5)
PAGE 82 *The Fortress of Königstein from the North-West* (detail from cat. 2)

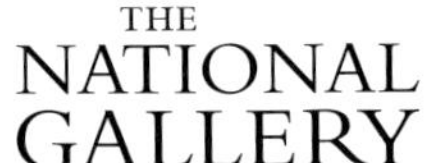